£15
TRAVEL

Australian Aboriginal Mythology

W E H STANNER

Australian Aboriginal Mythology

Editor L R Hiatt

Essays in honour of W E H Stanner

Social Anthropology Series No 9
Australian Aboriginal Studies No 50
Australian Institute of Aboriginal Studies   Canberra 1975

The views expressed in this publication are those of the authors and are not necessarily those of the Australian Institute of Aboriginal Studies.

National Library of Australia card number and ISBN 0 85575 044 8

Printed in Australia by
Excelsis Press Pty Ltd, 76 Planthurst Road, Carlton, N.S.W. 2218
6.75.2000

Contents

Preface

I first met Professor Stanner in 1934 when he was writing economico-political speeches for the Premier of New South Wales, Mr B.S.B. Stevens, later Sir Bertram Stevens, in his continuing controversy with the Federal Government. This he did with the skill and eloquence which have marked his work in all the fields where I have since encountered him. Subsequently he performed similar tasks for the Minister for the Army, this time with the background of knowledge and understanding of military strategy and tactics which impressed me despite the fact that I was convinced that his interest in these matters was evidence of intellectual perversion. He was subsequently involved, with competence and distinction both as a staff and field soldier, in the conduct of some aspects of Australia's war effort. In this performance I have always felt he was assisted by the fact that, despite his intelligence and profound wide-ranging knowledge, he managed to look like a traditional army colonel.

In the magic post-war reconstruction days, we conferred from time to time on matters as diverse as the economics of primitive communities, the basis of economic development for under-developed communities, and the inadequacies of imperial-built colonial bureaucracies.

In 1950 he joined the new Australian National University as Reader in Comparative Institutions where, as a member of the Council, I became aware of the high level of respect in which he was held by the best of his peers.

However, all these contacts, from my point of view, were merely a lead-up to our association over the last six years as members of the Council for Aboriginal Affairs. Here Bill and I have been involved with an attempt to change the attitudes of the Australian Government and Australian community towards the Aboriginal inhabitants of this continent and their successors — the tradition-oriented, the fringe dwelling, and the urban Aborigines. For me it has been a profound experience intellectually and emotionally. It is because Bill opened my eyes to many aspects of their life that I have come to hold Aboriginal Australians in deep respect and affection and to wonder at the subtlety and complexity of their way of life. It was by Bill that I was warned not to sentimentalise these people (historically, he said, sentimentality has been a precursor to the destruction of such peoples) and to understand how difficult it is to avoid putting into their mouths or minds words or values which are basically our own.

Working with Bill has opened for me new horizons and has made me aware of the infinite diversity and complexities of human cultures. We have, and I hope will continue to have, many differences, but at all times I will be a grateful learner in his company.

I am honoured therefore to be invited to write the preface to this book and to have the opportunity thereby to add my tribute to those of his professional colleagues.

H.C. COOMBS
Chairman
Council for Aboriginal Affairs
Canberra 1974

Introduction

L.R. Hiatt

In 1971 I circulated a request inviting contributions to the Social Anthropology section of the Biennial General Meeting of the Australian Institute of Aboriginal Studies, May 1972. In response, a number of people volunteered papers on mythology and so it was decided to hold a symposium on the topic. This book is the outcome.

To discover a current interest in myth analysis among students of Aboriginal culture is not surprising. By a lucky conjunction of circumstances, this season's fashion in Paris is practically all there is left to wear in Australia. Lévi-Strauss's influence, as will be apparent from the essays, is firmly established. And although modernisation leaves no aspect of traditional life untouched, opportunities for field research in the realm of concept, symbol and imagination remain on the whole better than in the domain of organisation, interaction and process (in so far as the two can be separated). It would be a mistake, however, to suppose that mythology has been a neglected field in Aboriginal studies: the amount of ethnographic and interpretative material is daunting. To introduce the present papers, I shall try to give an idea of the directions taken and ground covered by our predecessors.[1]

Terminology

With the notable exception of R. and C. Berndt, writers on Aboriginal mythology have not paid much attention to problems of definition and have often used terms such as myth, legend and tale interchangeably and without specification. A full list would include folktale, legendary tale, mythological tale and saga as well as the blanket terms story and narrative. I shall review what the Berndts have had to say on the matter and then mention some other opinions.

In *The Australian Encyclopaedia*, the Berndts (1958:53–5) divided Aboriginal verbal literature into myths and legends; then myths into sacred and secular; and finally secular myths (folk tales) into those concerned with unreal events, universal themes (jealousy, sweethearts, marriage, feuds, etc.) and spirits. For ease of reference, I have represented this classification in Diagram 1. By legends, the authors meant narratives that, although often distorted in transmission, are largely about actual events in the past. Myths were not defined but, in so far as these were counterposed against legends, I suppose they are basically imaginary or fictional. Sacred myths are of religious importance and are typically expressed in ritual; secular myths have no bearing on ritual and religious belief and only passing relevance to real life.

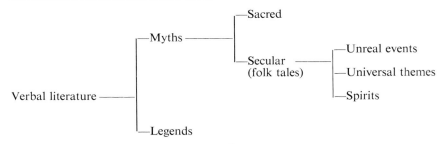

DIAGRAM 1   Classification of Aboriginal verbal literature by R. and C. Berndt, 1958.

In *The World of the First Australians* (1964), however, the Berndts changed their classification by dividing stories into sacred and ordinary and discussing them respectively under the headings of mythology (pp.198–216) and oral literature (pp.326–47). They made a further distinction between those ordinary stories based on contemporary experiences (including dreams) and those handed down through the generations. I summarise the modified classification in Diagram 2.

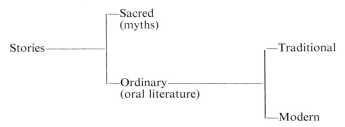

DIAGRAM 2   Classification of Aboriginal stories by R. and C. Berndt, 1964.

It is not easy to reconcile these two classifications. If verbal literature and stories are different terms for the same subject matter, and if verbal literature and oral literature are equivalent, then the occurrence of verbal literature as a genus in Diagram 1 and oral literature as a species in Diagram 2 seems to require explanation.[2] Furthermore, in the 1958 classification myths are both sacred and secular, whereas in the 1964 classification the term is reserved for sacred stories. A recent statement by the Berndts (1971:85–6) suggests that they regard flexibility in applying the term as a desirable convenience. This is fair enough. But the relationship between their 1958 and 1964 definitions is one of contradiction: some myths are not sacred (1958), all myths are sacred (1964).

Kirk (1970:26–8) raised the question whether the distinction between sacred and secular can be usefully, or even consistently, applied. He criticised the Berndts' 1964 classification on the grounds (a) that in ordinary usage the term myth is not confined to sacred stories, and (b) that some of the stories they presented in the section on oral literature possess as much 'significance' as those classed as sacred and discussed under the heading of mythology.

2

The sacred/secular distinction, which divides stories according to social context or role, reflects the influence of anthropological functionalism.[3] No doubt insistence on context in the study of Aboriginal oral literature was, in particular, a reaction against the earlier folk-loristic practice of publishing the stories as isolated entities, often without even an indication of the tribal sources.[4] Elkin criticised the trivialising effect of this procedure in *The Australian Aborigines* (1938:192): 'Now what is Aboriginal mythology? It is not a mere collection of stories concerned with the sun, moon and stars and various natural features, though these do figure in myths. We are apt to get a wrong idea of mythology from books, large or small, which give us lists of such stories quite unrelated to the social, economic and religious life of the tribe. The natives do possess make-believe and "just-so" stories, but mythology is a very important institution'.

It is one thing, however, to insist that mythology is an integral part of Aboriginal culture and another to make its external relationships crucial for the purposes of definition. To define myths as sacred stories is, typically, to use a certain relationship between the stories and something else (for example, ritual) as a differentia. There is nothing logically improper about such a procedure; the trouble, rather, is that the relationship may differ from one time or place to another while the story remains more or less constant.[5] In consequence, variants of the same story may be myths at time t_1 or place p_1 but not myths at time t_2 or place p_2.[6] For instance, during fieldwork on the north coast of New South Wales in 1929 Radcliffe-Brown (1929:403) collected a variant form of a story recorded earlier by Langloh Parker some 300 miles inland (1896:15–8). As the coastal version acted as a charter for an increase ceremony, the Berndts would presumably class it as a myth. But they describe the book containing the inland version as an early work on Aboriginal oral literature, that is, non-myth (1964:327).[7]

Given the current theoretical interest among anthropologists in the properties of the stories themselves and their relationships to each other, there is an obvious disadvantage in defining the subject matter in such a way as to exclude integral parts of it. For the moment, then, it seems advisable to use myth broadly to mean a traditional narrative which *in part* describes things that do not occur.[8] Whether the task of interpretation can be facilitated by making finer discriminations, either by applying European categories[9] or by invoking some other criteria,[10] is a matter for doubt.

Interpretation

The interpretation of Australian myths has been guided in the main by four separate though not necessarily incompatible ideas about the nature and purpose of the subject matter. They are that myth is, or may be at least in part, a kind of (a) history, (b) charter, (c) dream, or (d) ontology.[11] I shall illustrate the approaches in turn.

Myth as history

While not sharing the native view of myth as history, nor for that matter forming a school of thought among themselves, scholars from time to time have speculated that certain Australian myths may allude to real events in the past. The alleged occurrences seem to fall into three main categories: migration, social organisation and happenings in nature. I shall give some examples of each.

The main thesis of Mathew's *Eaglehawk and Crow* (1899) was that, at some point in the prehistory of Australia, the original inhabitants — people of Melanesian stock — were over-run by invaders of Dravidian stock. As well as evidence from physical anthropology, linguistics and archaeology, the author appealed to a class of myths in south-east Australia whose recurrent theme is conflict between two beings named Eaglehawk and Crow. Mathew asked: 'Now what is to be made out of these myths? Are they tales "told by an idiot and signifying nothing"? or are they confused evanescent echoes of a real past history? I take them to be the latter' (p.16). After noting that the eagle has regularly symbolised supremacy while the crow is widely despised, he concluded rhetorically: '. . . is there any better explanation of the facts possible than that the eaglehawk and the crow represent two distinct races of men which once contested for the possession of Australia, the taller, more powerful and more fierce "eaglehawk" race overcoming and in places exterminating the weaker, more scantily equipped sable "crows"?' (p.19).

Mathew's theory gained a limited acceptance.[12] Ehrlich (1922) recapitulated and expanded it under the heading 'The Myth, a Record of Tribal History' in his book *Origin of Australian Beliefs*; and, more recently, Tindale (1946) also supported the notion that 'ethnic clash between successive waves of Australoids' is preserved in the oral literature. But Radcliffe-Brown (1952) dismissed the hypothesis as 'imaginary history' and, instead, interpreted the opposition between Eaglehawk and Crow as an apt metaphor for moiety systems (many tribes of south-east Australia are divided into two halves, one named Eaglehawk and the other Crow). This interpretation, subsequently assigned by Lévi-Strauss (1964:82–91) to a place of special importance in the study of totemism, is re-examined in the present volume.[13]

In *The Native Tribes of Central Australia*, Spencer and Gillen (1899) drew attention to a class of myths that 'cannot be regarded as having been invented simply to account for certain customs now practised, for the simple reason that they reveal to us a state of organisation and a series of customs quite different from, and in important respects at variance with, the organisation and customs of the present time' (p.207). In particular, the authors were struck by a discrepancy between, on the one hand, contemporary prohibitions on killing and eating the totem animal and, on the other, traditions in which the ancestors are explicitly described as doing both. They concluded that such myths 'can only be understood on the hypothesis that they refer to a former time in which the relationship of the human beings to their totemic animals or plants was of a different nature from that which now obtains' (p.209).[14]

Frazer (1910:238) found himself 'entirely at one' with this conclusion. Durkheim (1915:129–30), on the other hand, regarded the inference as simple-minded and argued instead from the general position that the object of myths is to interpret existing rites rather than to commemorate past events. In the case in question, the myths sanction the occasional ritual killing and eating of the totem animal by the old men: mythical ancestors eat the sacred animal regularly, living men of ritual importance occasionally, the uninitiated or profane not at all.[15]

Róheim's main purpose in *Australian Totemism* (1925) was to confirm Freud's conjectures (1919) about the beginnings of human history. In order to do this, Róheim assumed that myths are phylogenetic records; and he found in the Australian data traces of the original Cyclopean form of social organisation, the primal revolt of the Brother Horde against the Jealous Sire, patricide, patriphagy and subsequent remorse. For instance. Eaglehawk and Crow myths are to be understood as symbolic statements about a clash not between two races, but between 'Father and Son at the dawn of humanity' (p.39). In his later writings, Róheim played down the phylogenetic interpretation of myth and emphasised rather its ontogenetic elements (which he had already recognised in *Australian Totemism*). I shall deal with this aspect of his analysis under 'Myth as dream'.

According to Tindale (1946:76), Aboriginal myths may occasionally refer to 'some half remembered cataclysm of nature, or an eclipse, or a meteoric shower . . .' (for an example, see Tindale 1938). Campbell (1967) has recently argued that certain Aboriginal legends record the change of sea level at the end of the last Ice Age, climatic conditions in southern and central Australia during the Pleistocene, the presence of crocodiles in southern Australia[16] and the existence of extinct animals like the Diprotodon.

Myth as charter

Anthropology in Australia during the second quarter of the present century saw the rise of professionalism, intensive fieldwork of the highest quality and widespread reliance on the doctrine of functionalism as a source of illumination. The functionalist position on myth is that the narratives constitute a conservative, socialising force whose function is to sanctify existing institutions and to foster the values of sociality. They invest the social order with necessity by linking it causally to an apocryphal past.

Undoubtedly the two most influential functionalists of the period were Radcliffe-Brown and Malinowski. Although this is not the place to discuss their similarities and differences, it is perhaps worth noting that, whereas Radcliffe-Brown dwelt upon the diffuse function of myths in cultivating sentiments essential to orderly social life and discouraging sentiments inimical to it (see *The Andaman Islanders*, esp. pp.397–402), Malinowski additionally emphasised their special role as charters for social interests and warrants for particular institutions (see *Myth in Primitive Psychology*; also Cohen 1969:344). Functionalist writings on Australian myth sometimes reflect Radcliffe-Brown's pre-occupation with sentiment (see, for example, McConnel 1957:163), while elsewhere they bear the imprint of Malinowski's pragmatism (see, for example, Kaberry 1939:162, 193, 197–203). But, on a broad view, such differences in emphasis and formulation are to be regarded as complementary orientations within a shared analytical framework (for a paradigm, see Elkin 1938:191–200).

Most functionalists have stressed the importance of Aboriginal myth as a charter for rite. Thus Warner began his account of Murngin totemism by

5

saying (1937:245): 'It should be stated explicitly that the thesis of this chapter is that, in meaning, the Wawilak myth is fundamental to, and organically related to, a certain group of rituals found in Murngin religious thought. The dramatic rituals express the oral rites.' Piddington (1950:374, in a section entitled 'The Charter of Mythology') spoke of the role of myths in validating ceremonies and exemplified the point with data from the Karadjeri (*ibid*:82–105). And, in numerous works, R. and C. Berndt have re-iterated the same theme: for instance in *The World of the First Australians* (1964:198) they wrote: 'Ritual is an acting out of events or instructions incorporated in myth, and mythology substantiates or justifies a whole range of rituals'. It is not always clear whether such statements are meant to imply merely that myth and ritual form a self-contained, mutually-reinforcing circle or that as a combined force they impinge on and validate behaviour in other spheres of social life.

The Berndts are undoubtedly the foremost exponents of functionalism in the field of study under review. Not only have they held consistently to the viewpoint for some thirty years,[17] but they have also wrestled with one of its main difficulties — what we may call 'the problem of the bad example'. If an indispensable function of myth is to safeguard and enforce morality (Malinowski 1926:23; 1931:640), how does one deal with the frequent occurrence of mythical immorality? Thus, speaking of northern Aranda myths, Strehlow (1947:38) said: 'The lives of the totemic ancestors are deeply stained with deeds of treachery and violence and lust and cruelty: their "morals" are definitely inferior to those of the natives of today' (see also I.M. White's paper later in the present volume.

The Berndts later expressed their disagreement with Strehlow on this point (1951:178). And, in general, they have used three main strategies to deal with the problem. First, they have argued that the bad behaviour is frequently punished or condemned in the myth itself (R. and C. Berndt 1970:28–9, 151–4; 1971:100–2; R. Berndt 1970:220,243). Second, they have described cases in which condemnation, though not part of the myth, is nevertheless provided by the storyteller or his audience in the form of a running moral commentary (R. and C. Berndt 1970:152–3; 1971:101; R. Berndt 1970:219–20). Third, they have implied that, in reflecting social reality, myth thereby sanctions it (R. and C. Berndt 1951:178; 1964:347; R. Berndt 1970:233–5, 243–4).

The last two arguments would not, I think, constitute a strong defence of the functionalist position. If a myth merely describes the good and evil that people do, then either it is a charter for both good and evil or not a charter at all. And to say that the telling of a myth occasions the expression of conventional moral sentiments by the narrator or his audience is not to say that the myth itself is a ratification of those sentiments. The resolution of the latter issue in favour of the doctrine of myth as moral charter must depend, therefore, on the first argument.

There are without question numerous Australian myths in which conventionally reprehensible behaviour is punished. To choose one among many, the Berndts (1951:165–6) recount a Goulburn Island story in which White Crane abducted Eagle's wife, Black Shag. Eagle finally caught up with them and speared White Crane in the leg. All the birds watching cheered. In other instances, however, it is not so clear that the moral purpose of the story is to punish the wicked or reward the good. Thus the Goulburn Islanders (*ibid*:153–4) tell of a man who died while trying to satisfy his wife's request for crocodile meat. Barely had the last bubbles risen to the surface when the younger brother arrived on the scene and treated the widow to a sexual extravaganza. The story ends as they walk happily back to the camp. One might add in passing that the main content of some of the myths reported by the Berndts in *Sexual Behaviour in Western Arnhem Land* (1951) is so fantastic that, in the absence of associated rituals, it would be inappropriate to regard them as charters for or against anything.[18]

The difficulty of reconciling the 'bad example' in myth with the view of myth as charter is well-illustrated by a case in Kaberry's *Aboriginal Woman* (1939:199). According to people of the Lunga tribe of north-west Australia, the Moon brought death into the world in the following circumstances. Moon, a married man, tried to seduce Snake, his classificatory mother-in-law (with whom sexual relations would be incestuous). She and the other women attacked him in a fury and cut off his sexual organs which turned to stone. Moon declared angrily: 'When I die, I shall come back in five days; when you die you will not come back; you will stop dead' (p.199).

Kaberry (*ibid*) remarked that the 'breaking of one of the most important kinship laws had disastrous consequences'. That is undoubtedly so, but the difficulty for a functionalist viewpoint is surely that the disastrous consequences were suffered not only by the wrongdoer but also by those who punished him. In another part of the book, dealing with the laws of marriage, Kaberry reported that people guilty of infringements justified their wrongdoing by appealing to the Moon myth (*ibid*:128). The latter's status as a charter, therefore, is clearly ambiguous: it can be (and apparently is) used to undermine morality as much as to safeguard it.

Myth as dream

In *The Interpretation of Dreams*[19] Freud suggested that certain myths and folktales are attempts to rationalise the wish-fulfilment content of 'typical' dreams. Thus the fairy tale, *The Emperor's New Clothes*, has its origin in the common dream of being naked which really expresses an infantile desire to exhibit. Likewise, the Oedipus myth is the reaction of the imagination to typical dreams of sexual intercourse with the mother[20] and death of the father: the story repudiates the latent wishes with expressions of horror and self-punishment and further rationalises the underlying dream material by translating it into metaphysical abstractions like Fate. In later works Freud[21] and his followers[22] formalised and developed this seminal idea by regarding myths as shared fantasies and interpreting them according to the principles already established for dream analysis.

After the publication of Freud's *Totem and Taboo* (1919), the task of applying psychoanalytic theory to the culture of the Australian Aborigines was carried out for the most part by Róheim. Although his interpretations were consistently inspired by psychoanalysis, they nevertheless reflected changes in the movement and in his own thinking. With regard to myth, we can distinguish three phases, each characterised by a different, though related, guiding notion. Thus in *Australian Totemism* (1925), as noted earlier, he approached myths primarily as memories of hypothetical events in the early history of mankind, in particular those supposed by Freud to have taken place within the 'primal horde'. In *The Riddle of the Sphinx* (1934) Róheim interpreted the data as reflecting the early history of the individual, in particular the experience of witnessing the 'primal scene' (parental coitus). Finally, the mature verdict of *The Eternal Ones of the Dream* (1945) was that the myths are attempts to deal with 'separation anxiety' (separation of the offspring from its mother). Although Róheim never entirely abandoned the first theory (see 1934:192; 1945:16, 254), the second and third stand independently of it and are properly considered under the present heading.

Róheim wrote *The Riddle of the Sphinx* not long after a period of fieldwork in central Australia during 1929. He began by asserting that the riddle of the sphinx is concerned with the primal scene,[23] and then proceeded to argue that the same preoccupation underlies various aspects of the culture of the Aborigines. Thus dreams, folktales and beliefs about demons may reflect infantile excitement aroused by witnessing the parents in coitus, desires to separate them and take the father's place or fears of reprisal for harbouring such wishes. Again, an important sacred object called *waninga* symbolises the parents locked together in sexual union. And myths about the Milky Way are projections of the primal scene into the heavens. Róheim's disjointed analytic procedure is often difficult to follow, but I shall try to trace the threads which link these phenomena together and enable them to be subsumed under a single explanation.

In the section on demons in central Australia (pp.23–41), Róheim discusses 'double devils', creatures believed to be capable of cutting a victim in two with a single bite. They look like two dogs joined in coitus and are referred to by an expression meaning 'stuck together'. The male partner is called 'like the father', the female partner 'like the mother'. Róheim interprets the belief as a projective denial of wishes aroused by the primal scene: 'The parents do not cohabit; I have seen nothing; it is the demons who do such things. Woe to him who sees them. He will be bitten in two' as punishment for wishing to separate the parents (p.31).

Later, in a section on central Australian magic, Róheim records (pp.57–82) the dream of a celebrated sorcerer in which the dreamer flies up to the Milky Way. In order to elucidate the episode, he recounts two versions of a circumcision myth in which a she-devil draws a boy's penis into her vagina, clamps it firmly with her labia and flies into the sky with him. There they turn into the Milky Way which is referred to by the same word as for double-devils ('stuck together'). Given the common terminology, together with dream and myth material linking demons with the Milky Way, Róheim concludes that the 'Milky Way is precisely the same as the diabolic vision of the copulating dogs' (p.71), that is to say, a projection of the primal scene.

But how do we account for the fact that the partners are a boy and a she-devil, particularly when we learn shortly afterwards (p.72) that another name for the Milky Way is 'Mother with Son'? The full answer is reserved for the next chapter ('Central Australian Totemism') and follows a description of a cult object named *waninga* and the presentation of a circumcision myth from South Australia. The *waninga* consists of two pieces of wood bound at right angles, around which hair-string is wound to form a quadrilateral (a *Fadenkreuz*). Various legends associate it with the Milky Way to the extent that the latter may be regarded as a celestial *waninga*. The South Australian myth describes how two brothers discover circumcision by accident and then perform the operation on their sleeping father. On waking, the latter copulates with his wife and dies from inflammation and loss of blood. The two brothers wander about showing people how to circumcise and eventually go up forever to the Milky Way.

Róheim now states his conclusion. The Milky Way and the *waninga* represent the same thing: the primal scene. The South Australian myth explicitly describes this scene and expresses the son's desire to castrate the father. The central Australian she-devil myth contains the idea of punishment: the son must die (be transported into the sky) because he wished to separate his parents and kill his father. But death is combined with satisfaction of the related wish: the youth is up above in eternal coitus with the demon-mother.

There is little in this to support the assertion that 'the Milky Way is a primal scene transported to the sky' (p.132). The only chain of evidence worth considering is linguistic: the Milky Way and double-devils are both referred to as 'stuck together', and the double-devil is said to consist of a 'father-like' and 'mother-like' component. A more significant consideration, I think, is that the boy and the she-devil are also stuck together and that the Milky Way is explicitly referred to as 'Mother with Son'. And, indeed, Róheim afterwards allowed the primal scene to fade from view, stating in *The Eternal Ones of the Dream* that 'the Milky Way is really a mother and her son, stuck together forever in the act of copulation' (1945:193).

The central theme of *The Eternal Ones of the Dream* is that Australian religion acts both to widen the gap created naturally by parturition and to compensate the offspring for the loss of his mother. Within this general scheme, myths play three important functions. First, by celebrating phallic heroes and libidinising the countryside that they created and wandered over, myths counteract the deprivation felt by maturing youths as they become increasingly isolated from the bosom of the family. Through absorption in the myth fantasies, the boy is able in effect to say to his mother: 'I do not need you (i.e. the nipple). I can get pleasure from my own penis' (p.66). Second, myths help to effect an eventual transfer of libido from the mother to the father (or, in social terms, the removal of the boy from the domestic group into the all-male cult group) by offering a heroic and supernaturally-conceived dual unity of Father and Son in place of the natural dual unity of mother and son. Finally, myths keep alive the dream of an eternal reunion with the mother.

Róheim's writings on Australian myth have not made much impact outside psychoanalytic circles. Although he claimed (1945:17) that T.G.H. Strehlow (1933:193) had accepted his interpretation of certain central

Australian traditions, Strehlow did not in fact mention him. Nevertheless, Strehlow did use the expression 'the great primal sire' (*ibid*), and, in a later publication (1947:35), 'the great sire and his horde of sons'. On these and other grounds (see 1947:7–14), it is reasonable to assume that psycho-analytic theory had made an impression on him.[24] Other Australianists have acknowledged a wish-fulfilment element in myths (Calley 1958:208), or at least sympathetically considered it as a possibility (R. and C. Berndt 1946:68); and, more recently, Meggitt and I have found some of Róheim's ideas persuasive in our investigations of secret male cults (Meggitt 1967:88; Hiatt 1971*a*; see also my essay later in the present volume).

Bettelheim discussed some aspects of Australian myth in *Symbolic Wounds* (1955:199–200), a book dedicated to Freud and based on psycho-analytic assumptions though breaking with tradition on important issues. His thesis was that puberty rites and associated myths express an envy of attributes and functions of the opposite sex. Following Spencer and Gillen, he also appeared to believe that myths describing women as originally dominant in religious life must have an historical basis (Bettelheim 1955:171, 190; Spencer and Gillen 1899:457–8).[25]

Myth as ontology

The view that comparative religion should be studied at the level of ontology is associated chiefly with the name of Eliade. In a series of publications since 1949 he has maintained that, while people in archaic and non-literate societies generally lacked words for abstract metaphysical concepts, they nevertheless expressed their ideas on the nature of reality through myth, rite and symbol. The foremost task of an anthropological study of religion is therefore to comprehend these forms of expression as ontological systems (an enterprise that seems to consist partly at least of translating the native idiom of thought into the technical language of metaphysics and theology). Such apprehensions of the ultimate reality of things cannot be explained away in terms of Freudian psychology, Durkheimian sociology and Marxist economics. They constitute the common and irreducible element of religious experience and must be studied and understood on their own level.[26]

The ontological dimension of Australian religion was, as a matter of fact, mapped in broad contour by Elkin during the 1930s.[27] Eliade's contribution, in the course of extensive writings on the Aborigines (1955, 1958*a*, 1958*b*, 1960, 1964, 1969, 1973), has been to recapitulate and review the ethnographic material in world perspective. An example of his speculations on myth is considered later in this volume.[28]

Stanner, although sharing Eliade's working assumptions, has limited himself by and large to Australia; indeed, in most of his writings, to an area of the Northern Territory he knows at first hand.[29] Nevertheless, there would be wide agreement among Australianists that his *Oceania* monograph *On Aboriginal Religion* (1959–63)[30] is the most sensitive analysis of the subject yet to have appeared.[31] Here I shall be concerned only with those aspects that seem relevant to the study of myth.

Stanner's aim was to show that the religion of the Murinbata (Port Keats region, N.T.), as expressed in particular through myth and rite, can best be comprehended in terms of an 'underlying ontology of life' (p.25). Put briefly, reality as conceived by the Murinbata is 'a joyous thing with maggots at the centre' (p.37)[32]; their religion is 'the celebration of a dependent life which is conceived as having taken a wrongful turn at the beginning, a turn such that the good life is now inseparably connected with suffering' (p.39). This conception is both the structure of the main Murinbata myths and rites and the message transmitted by them.

Stanner's demonstration begins with a morphological comparison of a rite and its validating myth. Later, however, he extends the analysis to myths lacking any direct association with extant rites and to rites lacking a mythical charter. I shall try to convey a notion of his method by summarising two myths and a rite, and then integrating the homomorphic congruities as set out in his Table 1 (p.101)[33] with the subsequent analysis (esp. p. 104). The rite, called Punj, inducts youths into a secret male cult (see pp. 6–9); one of the myths, about Mutjingga (the Old Woman, or Mother of All), is the myth associated with the rite (see pp. 40–2); and the other myth, about Kunmanggur (the Rainbow Serpent), has no direct ritual connections (see pp. 88–94). For convenience of exposition I shall present them in reverse order.

The myth of Kunmanggur (M1) begins when his two daughters announce that they intend to go in search of food. Tjinimin, his son, says he is off to visit the Flying Fox people but really he intends to follow his sisters. Subsequently he overtakes, deceives, threatens and ravishes them. Next day the sisters escape by a trick; and later they entice Tjinimin to climb a cliff by a rope which they cut as he nears the top. The fall injures him badly but he mends his broken bones and returns home. There he arranges a dance during which, without disclosing a motive, he spears his father in the back. The Old Man dies slowly, performing various marvels before disappearing into the sea. Tjinimin wonders what will happen but no one takes revenge upon him.

In the opening scene of the myth of Mutjingga (M2), the people decide to seek honey. They ask the Old Woman to look after the children and then depart. The Old Woman gathers the children around her and, on the pretext of looking for lice in their hair, swallows them one by one. She flees the camp but is eventually tracked down and killed by two men, Right Hand and Left Hand, who open her belly and find the children still alive.

The rite (R) begins when youths, having been asked to submit to the disciplines of Punj and to learn its secrets, are taken to the secret ground. Soon after arriving, they are told that food is needed and are led away, ostensibly on a hunting expedition, by one of the initiated men. The latter, however, takes them to a certain spot where they are told to remove all personal ornaments and to stay until instructed otherwise. After a build-up of tension over several days, the boys are led back to the ceremonial ground where they believe they will shortly be swallowed by Mutjingga, the Old Woman. Men, in hiding, swing bullroarers while others cry that the Old Woman is approaching. Then the hidden men leap into view and the true source of the Old Woman's supposed voice is revealed. Each youth is

11

presented with a newly-made bullroarer. From this point the men begin to treat the novices more as equals, though particular disciplines imposed at the beginning are not relaxed.

Stanner draws attention to the following common elements. The three dramas open with the statement of a need and an implied dependence (M1, M2: need for food, dependence on nature; R: need for understanding, dependence on men with knowledge of the supernatural). Initial trust, however, turns out to be flawed by duplicity (M1: trusting father and sisters deceived by libidinous son and brother; M2: trusting parents deceived by cannibal baby-minder; R: youths deceived by guardian, who subjects them to ritual discipline instead of taking them hunting). Duplicity leads to disaster (M1: sisters ravished by brother; M2: children swallowed by guardian; R: youths swallowed, in token, by Mutjingga). But the disaster is consummated by a good outcome (M1: incestuous brother punished; M2: children saved; R: youths given symbol of understanding). The good, however, is in its turn seen to be ambiguous, qualified adversely by its antecedents or consequences (M1: punishment of incestuous brother followed by death of the Father; M2: young life conserved only by death of the Mother; R: understanding attained only by fear and suffering under authority).

A comparison of the preceding exposition with the original will show that I have not only summarised drastically but also that I have taken certain liberties with the analysis. My intention has been to select the minimum necessary for a demonstration of the central thesis: that, through myth and rite, the Murinbata express symbolically a complex sense of dependence upon a ground and source beyond themselves, a sense that Stanner construes as one of perennial 'good-with-suffering', of 'order-with-tragedy' (p.70).

The originality of Stanner's approach consists in his attempt to demonstrate a homomorphic structure in rite and associated myth, mythless rite and riteless myth. He believes that the essential problem is to analyse, not 'myth sole', or 'rite sole', but 'myth in a situation of rite'; and he doubts (at least as far as Australia is concerned) whether there is much prospect of a 'theory of myth' except through a 'theory of myth plus rite' (personal communication, 25/5/73). In passing we may note that Lévi-Strauss sees Stanner's mode of analysis as being, at least in part, similar to his own. He says: 'Certainly Australia possesses complex myths which lend themselves to a semantic analysis inspired by that which we have applied to myths in other regions' (1966:228, first published in French in May, 1962). Lévi-Strauss refers here to Stanner's fourth article in the *Oceania* series, 'The Design Plan of a Riteless Myth', published in June 1961. This article, which cannot be understood properly in isolation from the rest of the series which Stanner began to publish in December 1959, does not in fact mention Lévi-Strauss. The only reference in the series to Lévi-Strauss comes in the sixth article, published in June 1963, where Stanner remarks that while writing the second article of the series in early 1960, his attention was drawn to the fact that Lévi-Strauss had already published 'a brilliant paper on the morphological analysis of myth' (presumably 'The Structural

Study of Myth' published in 1955). Stanner continues: 'I had been unaware of that fact. Rather than consciously straddle two approaches which, though obviously convergent, depended on distinct sets of concepts, I thought it the proper course to continue with the approach stated in [the first article in the series] which I had believed peculiar to myself' (1959–63:171). A comparison of the approaches developed by Stanner and Lévi-Strauss, though outside the scope of the present review, would be worth scholarly attention.

Discussion

I said at the beginning of the previous section that the four viewpoints (myth as history, charter, dream and ontology) were not necessarily incompatible. I shall now try to speak more positively about their inter-relationships and, in the process, to evaluate the kind of understanding they offer.

Róheim, as noted earlier, interpreted myth both as history and as dream. In *Australian Totemism* he saw no conflict between the two views, since in that work he shared the early psychoanalyst's sympathy for the biological notion that ontogeny recapitulates phylogeny and hence that, behaviourally, the early history of the child is analogous to the 'infancy of the race'. Later, however, he gave primacy to ontogeny in his interpretations of culture and even suggested that myths apparently describing the 'primal horde' might be projections of the oedipus complex into the distant past (1941:148).[34]

The relationship between interpretations of myth as history and myth as charter would seem to depend on whether or not the alleged history is consistent with contemporary social life. If inconsistent, the charter theorist is likely to reject the view that the mythical events have a basis in the past and to explain them instead as a ratification of the present (see Durkheim's comment on Frazer, pp. 4–5 above). If consistent, the two interpretations may be seen as mutually-reinforcing. Thus Elkin (1938:250) suggested that natural features now ascribed to mythical culture heroes may have originally been designated as memorials to the social and ritual teachings of real men.

In some instances the two approaches would probably be seen as being in a relationship of indifference. Consider, for example, this story recorded by Tindale in 1938 (referred to earlier, p. 5): Prupe, an old woman going blind, had turned cannibal and eaten most of the children. Koromarange, her clan-sister, had a grand-daughter she wished to protect so she took gifts of food to Prupe's camp. Prupe became suspicious and one day, after she had gone totally blind, found the grand-daughter alone in Koromarange's camp. She seized the child and took her back home. There she was about to remove Koromarange's grand-daughter's eyes, hoping thereby to restore her own sight, when Koromarange arrived in pursuit. Pretending to be pleased that Prupe had found the infant, she asked the old woman to fetch water as she was thirsty from the day's work; and to prolong the task, she tricked her into using a defective baler. During Prupe's absence, Koromarange made a snare, cried piteously to Prupe for the water and then fled with the child. Prupe hastened back and was caught in the snare.

Struggling to free herself, she kicked the camp fire and great flames suddenly engulfed her. A deep pit can be seen today where this happened.

After considering a suggestion that the hole may be a meteorite crater, Tindale (1938:18) said: 'It seems possible that the story, in its present form, may be the dramatisation of an actual meteorite fall at this spot'. But a charter theorist would no doubt regard the historical question as a matter of indifference: the important feature of the story is that it concludes with a punishment of cannibalism.

It is fair to say, I think that neither explanation leaves us with much sense of satisfaction. The trouble is that too much is left unexplained. We are reminded forcibly here of the myth of Mutjingga, the Old Woman (see above p. 11). And, although Stanner (1959–63:45) acknowledges that 'few facts or institutions of living are left without some sort of mythological warrant'[35] and that there 'is also a certain amount of evidence that we are in touch with an historical composite',[36] he undoubtedly regards these aspects as incidental to the central consideration that, in the myths, 'we are clearly dealing with a world-and-life view expressing a metaphysic of life which can and should be elicited'.

Róheim also recognised the socialising and validating function of myths but, like Stanner, was not content with the mere assertion of a functional relationship. In their analyses of Australian myth and rite, both scholars share a concern to go beyond incidental and relational aspects and to come to grips with the material itself. There, however, the similarity appears to end. Stanner, at any rate, has no sympathy with the notion of myth as dream or fantasy (personal communication, 20/5/72),[37] and he speaks with evident distaste of 'the vast cloacal theorem of the *un*conscious' (1965b:232; emphasis in the original). Without attempting to resolve fundamental disagreements between the two approaches (dream versus ontology), I shall indicate a possibility for compromise and cooperation. I do so in the conviction that herein lies the main hope for further progress in the study of Australian religion.[38]

In various places Stanner takes issue with Durkheim's interpretation of religion as a projection of society. For instance, in an unpublished paper describing the aims of his *Oceania* articles, he writes (1961:7): 'I thought it worthwhile to consider another possibility which to me seems more true to human affairs. The social order, and all that goes with it, may very well be the referent of the religious order . . . but the religious order is not the terminal of that relation; it is a sort of intervening relatum, one stated and acted in all the many languages of symbolism; and pointing not back at the social order, but beyond itself, indeed, beyond the two orders. The last thing in the relation, the relatum towards which the relation runs, is a metaphysical object. It is what the Aborigines in their own religions often call the Dreaming'.[39] In the monograph itself, he explains the role of the social order in more detail (1959–63:50–1): 'The art and method of explanation among the aborigines are to find apt likenesses between the familiar and the unfamiliar . . . I conceive that this process of mind occurs in the making of myth. Things of the social order provide them with . . . shapes or images aptly resembling those which their intuitive minds discern in rite. It is an extension of the process by which one subject, an unknown, is likened to another, a known, the likening constituting a type of explanation . . . For my own part I see neither true interest nor significance in dissecting the figurative aspect of the myth for "reflections" or "expressions" of the social structure . . . What I would think remarkable would be to find myths which did *not* contain such reflections or expressions. For what *other* image or idea-language could be used?'[40]

Few would quarrel with the view that human beings use familiar materials for making models to explain the unfamiliar;[41] and it seems plausible to suggest that the social order is used figuratively in the construction of an ontology. Yet, in the four myths Stanner presents in his monograph (1959–63:40–2, 88–94, 127–30, 155),[42] the social order is conspicuous only by its almost complete absence. In many cases, formal relationships and affiliations are left unspecified. And when kinship is mentioned, it is either incidental to the story or there to be violated.

If Stanner is correct on the general principle (that the known is used to make sense of the unknown) but mistaken on the particular one (that the Murinbata commonly use the social order for ontological purposes), then it is important to find an answer to his rhetorical question, 'For what *other* image or idea-language could be used?' I think it is worth considering that the purpose might be served by certain crucial and regular experiences of childhood, occurring prior to an awareness of the social order or as a reaction to its imposition. I am suggesting, in short, that ontogeny might provide a model for ontology.[43]

At the end of the monograph, Stanner summarises his characterisation of Murinbata myth (1959–63:167): 'The myths seemed the first springs of contemplative religion, using allegorical idioms. In several important myths the dominant theme was an irreparable injury to man at the beginning of life under instituted forms. The sense of injury — whether a needless or necessary injury was hard to make out — was expressed in several metaphors, but the common signification seemed to be a paradox, antinomy or dualism common to all the structures of existence.' But nowhere, so far as I can tell, are we given any notion of where this sense of injury comes from or why it should occupy such a key position in Murinbata philosophy. In the circumstances, it seems worth recalling the mature judgement of Róheim that totemism 'as a social institution is a defense organized against the separation anxiety' (1945:249) and that the essential theme of totemic myth 'is the relation of the individual to the object-world, and libidinal cathexis as the defense used by human beings to bear the deprivation of object loss or separation' (*ibid*:17).

If we re-state Róheim's position in less technical language, its bearing on Stanner's ontological formulation becomes inescapable. Infancy among the Aborigines is not merely a period of dependence but also one of indulgence by both parents.[44] The infant is the centre of a circle of devoted attention which provides it unremittingly with sustenance, body contact and amusement. Then, around two years of age, there is a disturbing change: typically, an increasing separation from the mother's body coinciding with a displacement from the centre of attention by a younger sibling.[45] Later, perhaps, the realisation grows that the mother's love was never total, that from the outset she and the doting father shared their bodies in special and exclusive ways with one another. All this creates a primal sense of loss and injury accompanied by feelings of anger and envy. The 'maggots at the centre' are thus not only the frustrations that a person must bear along with the satisfactions of life, but also the hostility existing inside himself towards those he loves. And if reality as a whole is conceived as paradoxical or dualistic, it may be in some degree because the individual's first meaningful experiences are marked by imperfection and ambivalence.[46]

No doubt Róheim would regard this apparent concordance between ontogeny and ontology as confirmation of his view that totemic myths are simply unconscious defences against, or escapes from, the problems of growing up. An equally strong case, however, might be made for the view that they express, in the first instance, a genuine awareness of the nature of these problems. There is a sense in which it is true to say that the Oedipus myth is as much a discovery of the oedipus complex as a symptom of it, and a similar point might be made about some Australian myths. They are not so much dreams as proto-analytic insights into the stuff that dreams are made of. Furthermore, in conjunction with rites separating the young male from his mother, they may be seen as a form of applied psychology in which, to put it perhaps rather too boldly, principles underlying the nightmare are transposed to a conscious and collective level for the purposes of social integration and adaptation (for an account of the terrorising aspects of such myths and rites, see my paper later on). At this level, then, myths may constitute an early step towards the scientific understanding of human ontogeny. But the use of ontogeny as a model for cosmogony and anthropogony is another matter. Here the projection of experience and knowledge gained within the family onto a supernatural plane (where father becomes Father, mother becomes Mother, etc.) may represent, in part, an attempt to deal rationally with genuine metaphysical problems. But in this case, I think it is fair to say, the step was a false one.

The Present Papers

If the present volume can be taken as an indication of future trends, it is apparent that my set of analytic pigeon-holes for reviewing the past already needs renovations and additions.[47] The most urgent requirement would be a box to accommodate the influence of Dutch and French structuralists as manifested here principally in the essays of A.C. van der Leeden and Kenneth Maddock. Its proper location, no doubt, would be adjacent to 'Myth as ontology'; and some space within it might be reserved for approaches like that of Jeremy Beckett which seeks to establish meaningful homologies between myth and social structure.[48] Probably 'Myth as history' could be closed down, at least for the time being, and the space used instead for 'miscellaneous influences', such as current literature on Women's Liberation, in order to house arguments like Isobel White's. Walls between certain compartments would need to be opened up, in order for instance, to make room for Mieke Blow's essay, which uses Lévi-Strauss's procedures to reach Róheimian conclusions; and for my own paper, which seeks to effect a compromise between Róheim and Eliade. Although none of the contributions could reasonably be categorised under 'Myth as charter', most of them in one way or another take the notion for granted during the course of analysis.

For an academic browser with convictions, then, the book will be something of a theoretical lucky-dip: the chances of opening up at a place where the analysis seems fruitful, inconsequential or hopeless might be about equal. If this needs an apology, I will echo G.S. Kirk (1970:v) and say that the collection is not concerned 'to propagate a particular universalistic theory (the very notion of which is in my opinion chimerical) . . .' Rather, it reflects an experimental, undogmatic, and to some extent, eclectic phase in the development of the subject (at least as it stands with reference to the Australian Aborigines). It may turn out, indeed, that the success of one style of analysis rather than another depends in large measure upon which myths (or portions of myths) are chosen for treatment.

Although the essays differ in theoretical inspiration, they share the characteristic of getting down to business on particular jobs. Thus Mieke Blows examines five myths of south-eastern Australia in an attempt to throw new light on a classical problem, namely why are Eaglehawk and Crow regularly depicted as rivals, and what is the significance of their widespread occurrence as moiety emblems? A.C. van der Leeden[49] also seeks to elucidate the relationship between myths and moieties, this time in south-eastern Arnhem Land, by pointing out dualistic contrasts in a variety of registers. A notable feature of his analysis is the attention he pays to that most neglected of factors in myth analysis, the narrator. Kenneth Maddock draws attention to difficulties posed for vernacular taxonomy by the emu and explicates the manner in which certain myths try to resolve them. Isobel White asks why myths of central Australia often describe sexual violence of a kind that is conventionally deplored and concludes that the stories articulate values of male dominance and female submission. My own paper examines the relationship between the motif of 'swallowing and regurgitation' and the induction of youths into secret male cults. Finally, Jeremy Beckett discusses myths accounting for the separation of the living from the dead, mainly in the Torres Strait, but also briefly in Cape York and Papua, thus extending the compass of the collection a little beyond the boundary of Aboriginal Australia.

Burridge (1973:188) has recently said that 'neither in the field of myth nor in religious studies generally, it is fair to say, have anthropologists in the Australian field really begun to reap the harvest of old data transformed by new thinking.' Some of my collaborators in this volume, I venture to say, have now made such a beginning, and it is to be hoped that their efforts will stimulate further demonstrations of agricultural proficiency using the latest models. Other contributors, it is true, seem destined to be left behind, picking over obsolete machinery in farmyard scrapheaps. As a gesture of humanity to them and their like, we publish in the form of an appendix two chapters from Arnold van Gennep's *Mythes et Légendes d'Australie* (1906), translated for the first time into English.

Notes

1. The revision and amplification of the original version of this Introduction, given at the 1972 A.I.A.S. symposium, occupied me for most of my sabbatical year as an Overseas Fellow at Churchill College, Cambridge. I take this opportunity to thank the Master and Fellows for providing me with conditions of inquiry and scholarship that would be hard to surpass. Many people were kind enough to read and comment upon the Introduction at various stages of its preparation. In particular, I must thank J.A. Barnes, Mieke Blows, A.P. Elkin, Meyer Fortes, Jack Goody, Ian Hogbin, G.S. Kirk, K. Maddock, Sheila Mackay, Rodney Needham. Tom Rose, W.E.H. Stanner, and A.C. van der Leeden.

2. Also, the contrast between oral literature and myths in Diagram 2 might be construed as meaning that the latter are transmitted not by word of mouth but by some other means (art, dance, writing, etc.).

3. See pp. 5–7 in the present Introduction.

4. As early as 1906, van Gennep criticised Langloh Parker and others on this last score (van Gennep, 1906: Notice Bibliographique, VII-VIII). A particularly bad example among later works is Ramsay Smith's *Myths and Legends of the Australian Aborigines*; see the Bibliographical notice in *Oceania*, 1, p. 373 (written presumably by Radcliffe-Brown).

5. Van Gennep (1906:CI) must have been one of the first to raise this kind of difficulty, at least in a work on Australian myths. Noting that Hubert and Mauss tended to reserve the term myth for traditions expressed in ritual, he asked: '. . . mais au cours des transformations sociales un rite peut disparaître alors que le mythe qui lui correspondait peut subsister intact: comment, dans ce cas, le nommer . . . ?' (for an English translation, see the Appendix in the present volume, p. 194).

6. In a comment on this point, Professor Elkin (personal communication, 8/6/73) mentions a related difficulty: the sacred/profane criterion might entail that 'inside' (secret male cult) and 'outside' (for women and children) versions of the same story be classified, respectively, as myth and non-myth.

7. It may be noted in passing that both versions up to a point are similar to Stanner's myth of Mutjingga, which sanctions an 'extremely sacred and secret' ceremony in the Northern Territory (see the present Introduction, p. 11).

8. *Cf.* Cohen 1969:337.

9. For an excellent critical review of terminological issues, as well as an interesting suggestion for a qualitative distinction between myth and folktale, see Kirk 1970:ch. 1.

10. See van Gennep (1906:ch. X; English translation in the present volume, pp. 193–201) who shifted between two criteria, viz. nature of the actors, purpose of the story; and Tindale (1946) who attempted to correlate alleged qualitative differences in the narratives with hypothetical migrations of people. Dixon (1916:267–303) and Meggitt (1966:22), though not offering formal Australia-wide typologies, have made statements with typological import. The existence and nature of vernacular categories of oral literature are matters that merit further investigation in Australia (see, for example, Kaberry 1939:202; and *cf.* Malinowski 1926:25–39; Finnegan 1970:78–9).

11. *Cf.* Cohen 1969:338.

12. Mathew would no doubt have been delighted by Thorne's recent discovery at Kow Swamp (Victoria) of crania displaying 'a complex of morphologically archaic features, many of which are modified or absent in modern populations' (1971:87) and his suggestion that differences between the archaic and modern forms might be explained in terms of separate, consecutive migrations (*ibid*:89).

13. See the essay by Mieke Blows, especially pp. 24–28.
14. See also Spencer and Gillen 1904:320–2.
15. For further views on this issue, see Lang (1910:119) and Róheim (1925:ch.4).
16. But see Radcliffe-Brown (1926:21; 1930:343–4) who argued that the supposed crocodile in myths of these areas is really the rainbow-serpent.
17. *Cf.* R. and C. Berndt 1942:329–30 and 1971:83. It should be noted that the latter work includes a chapter entitled 'The Many Faces of Myth' which gives sympathetic consideration to other theoretical approaches.
18. I say this despite the Berndts' assertion that the 'events narrated in these samples of relevant mythology are correlated with normal behaviour in native society today' (1951:178). *Cf.*, for instance, the bizarre sexual fantasy contained in the myth on pp. 174–5.
19. First German edition published in 1900.
20. Freud (English edition, 1950:162) quotes Sophocles' words, 'For many a man hath seen himself in dreams his mother's mate', as evidence for a dream origin of the legend.
21. See 'On Dreams' (1953, first German edition 1901); *The Psychopathology of Everyday Life* (1966, first German edition 1904); 'Creative writers and Day-Dreaming' (1959, first published in German in 1908).
22. Abraham 1955 (first German edition 1909); Rank 1952 (first German edition 1909).
23. The child first sees four legs (the father on all fours), then the two outstretched legs of the mother, and finally the 'third leg' of the father.
24. See also Strehlow 1971:xvi–xvii, where he states his opinion that 'the Freudian school has some excellent suggestions to offer in regard to the elucidation of the aboriginal sacred myths and songs'. Strehlow makes it clear, however, that he is by no means an unqualified admirer of psycho-analytic theory in general or of Róheim's writings in particular (see *op. cit.*, pp. xvii, xlii, 464, 474).
25. For alternative interpretations, see Stanner 1965*a*:166; Hiatt 1971*b*:66.
26. This summary of Eliade's position is derived mainly from the introductory sections of *The Myth of the Eternal Return* (1955) and *Patterns in Comparative Religion* (1958*a*), both first published in French in 1949.
27. See, for example, Elkin 1933; 1938:ch.8 ('Aboriginal Philosophy, Rites and Beliefs').
28. See the essay by L.R. Hiatt, pp. 154–55.
29. See Stanner 1959–63, 1965*a*, 1965*b*. A further difference between Eliade and Stanner is that the former appears to be a convinced dualist, whereas the latter merely speaks of the 'natural facts of human conviction about the ultimates of life' (1959–63:25).
30. Stanner's monograph was first published in 1964 as a reprint of six *Oceania* articles issued between 1959–63. Page references here are to the monograph.
31. See, for example, Meggitt 1966:78, fn. 142.
32. The question may be raised whether 'ontology of life' is a legitimate or even meaningful expression, in so far as ontology is usually defined as that branch of speculation concerned with the most general features of reality. Possibly 'philosophy of life' in the layman's sense would come closer to expressing Stanner's meaning. As a matter of fact, 'myth as philosophy' (*cf.* Elkin 1938) might be a better tag for my own purposes than 'myth as ontology' inasmuch as philosophy is an established umbrella term for speculation in a variety of subjects, including the nature of man and society.
33. Not to be confused with Table 1 on p. 47 or Table 1 on p. 131.
34. Freeman (1969:68 ff.) has recently argued that the theory of the primal deed is a projection into the distant past of Freud's own oedipus complex.

35. The two viewpoints, 'myth as charter' and 'myth as ontology' are obviously complementary (see Eliade 1964:ch.1, where he quotes Malinowski at length and with approval).
36. See also Stanner 1959–63:139–40; Strehlow 1971:705.
37. Though he admits, in a later communication, possibly against himself, having heard Aborigines speak of thinking as being like 'a dream in the head' (personal communication, 25/5/73).
38. See my paper later in this volume, in which I seek to integrate the views of Róheim and Eliade.
39. See also Stanner 1967.
40. Emphasis in the original.
41. See, for instance, Radcliffe-Brown (1922:377–81) on the nature and function of personification; see also Young (1971:137–8) on 'the growth of the model in the brain'.
42. Condensed versions of the first two are given above, p. 11.
43. For this idea, I am indebted to Joseph Campbell 1960:ch.2 ('The Imprints of Experience'). I take this opportunity to thank Professor R. Rappaport for drawing Campbell's work to my attention.
44. See, for example, Stanner 1960:94–5; Hamilton 1970.
45. See Hamilton 1970, especially p. 76 ff., where she describes the violent aggression expressed by infants at the weaning stage towards their mothers. Note also her account of an incident in which a seven-year-old lad was seized by the men for circumcision because he refused to relinquish his mother's breast (*ibid*:75–6).
46. I am merely giving special weight to first experiences, which is not the same as asserting that later experiences and deliberations are caused by them.
47. As a matter of fact, this would have been apparent earlier had I taken into account several papers on Aboriginal mythology that have been published within the last few years; for example, Layton 1970; Maddock 1970; Munn 1969, 1970.
48. *Cf.* Terence Turner (1973:2): 'I attempt to show, on the basis of an analysis of the social system of the tribe from which the myth is taken, that the generative structural model of the myth I propose is isomorphic and homologous with certain key generative processes in the social and cultural domains to which the myth refers'.
49. Dr van der Leeden was not present at the May 1972 Conference but offered his paper shortly afterwards.

References

ABRAHAM, K. 1955 Dreams and myths. In his *Clinical papers and essays on psycho-analysis*, pp. 151–209. London, Hogarth Press.
BERNDT, C.H. *and* R.M. BERNDT 1971 *The barbarians*. London, Watts.
BERNDT, R.M. 1970 Traditional morality as expressed through the medium of an Australian Aboriginal religion. In his *Australian Aboriginal anthropology: modern studies in the social anthropology of the Australian Aborigines*, pp. 216–47. Nedlands, University of Western Australia.
BERNDT, R.M. *and* C.H. BERNDT 1942 A preliminary report of field work in the Ooldea region, western South Australia. *Oceania*, 12(4):305–30.
———— *and* ———— 1946 The eternal ones of the dream. *Oceania*, 17(1):67–78.
———— *and* ———— 1951 *Sexual behaviour in western Arnhem Land*. New York, Viking Fund.
———— *and* ———— 1958 Aborigines: myths and legends. In *The Australian Encyclopaedia*. 2nd ed. v.1:53–55. Sydney, Grolier Society.

────── and ────── 1964 *The world of the first Australians: an introduction to the traditional life of the Australian Aborigines.* Sydney, Ure Smith.

────── and ────── 1970 *Man, land and myth in north Australia: the Gunwinggu people.* Sydney, Ure Smith.

BETTELHEIM, B. 1955 *Symbolic wounds: puberty rites and the envious male.* London, Thames & Hudson.

BURRIDGE, K.O.L. 1973 *Encountering Aborigines. A case study: anthropology and the Australian Aboriginal.* New York, Pergamon Press.

CALLEY, M.J.C. 1958 Three Bandjalang legends. *Mankind*, 5(5):208–14.

CAMPBELL, A.H. 1967 Aboriginal traditions and the prehistory of Australia. *Mankind*, 6(10):476–81.

CAMPBELL, J. 1960 *The masks of God: primitive mythology.* London, Secker and Warburg.

COHEN, P.S. 1969 Theories of myth. *Man*, 4(3):337–53.

DIXON, R.B. 1916 *Oceanic*, v.9 of The mythology of all races, in thirteen volumes, (ed.) L.H. Gray. Boston, Marshall Jones.

DURKHEIM, E. 1915 *The elementary forms of the religious life: a study in religious sociology.* London, Allen & Unwin.

EHRLICH, L. 1922 *Origin of Australian beliefs.* St Gabriel-Mödling (Vienna), Anthropos.

ELIADE, M. 1955 *The myth of the eternal return.* London, Routledge & Kegan Paul.

────── 1958*a* *Patterns in comparative religion.* London, Sheed & Ward.

────── 1958*b* *Birth and rebirth.* New York, Harper.

────── 1960 *Myths, dreams and mysteries.* London, Harvill Press.

────── 1964 *Myth and reality.* London, Allen & Unwin.

────── 1969 *The quest: history and meaning in religion.* Chicago, University of Chicago.

────── 1973 *Australian religions: an introduction.* Ithaca, Cornell University Press.

ELKIN, A.P. 1933 Studies in Australian totemism: the nature of Australian totemism. *Oceania*, 4(2):113–31.

────── 1938 *The Australian Aborigines: how to understand them.* Sydney, Angus and Robertson.

FINNEGAN, R.H. 1970 *Oral literature in Africa.* London, Clarendon Press.

FRAZER, Sir JAMES G. 1910 *Totemism and exogamy: a treatise on certain early forms of superstition and society*, v.1. London, Macmillan.

FREEMAN, D. 1969 Totem and taboo: a reappraisal. In *Man and his culture: psycho-analytic anthropology, after 'Totem and taboo'*, (ed.) Warner Muensterberger, pp. 53–78. London, Rapp & Whiting.

FREUD, S. 1919 *Totem and taboo.* London, Routledge.

────── 1950 *The interpretation of dreams.* New York, Modern Library.

────── 1953 On dreams. In *The standard edition of the complete psychological works of Sigmund Freud*, v.5, (ed.) J. Strachey. London, Hogarth Press and Institute of Psychoanalysis.

────── 1959 Creative writers and day-dreaming. In *The standard edition of the complete psychological works of Sigmund Freud*, v.9, (ed.) J. Strachey, pp. 141–53. London, Hogarth Press and Institute of Psychoanalysis.

────── 1966 *The psychopathology of everyday life.* London, Benn.

GENNEP, A. VAN 1906 *Mythes et légendes d'Australie.* Paris, Librarie Orientale & Américaine.

HAMILTON, A. 1970 Nature and nurture: child rearing in north-central Arnhem Land. M.A. (Hons) thesis, University of Sydney.

HIATT, L.R. 1971*a* Secret pseudo-procreation rites among the Australian Aborigines. In *Anthropology in Oceania: essays presented to Ian Hogbin*, (eds) L.R. Hiatt and C. Jayawardena, pp. 77–88. Sydney, Angus and Robertson.

────── 1971*b* Feminism. *Quadrant*, 15:65–71.

KABERRY, P.M. 1939 *Aboriginal woman: sacred and profane*. London, Routledge.

KIRK, G.S. 1970 *Myth: its meaning and functions in ancient and other cultures.* Cambridge, Cambridge University Press.

LANG, A. 1910 The 'historicity' of Arunta traditions. *Man,* 10(8):118–21.

LAYTON, R. 1970 Myth as language in Aboriginal Arnhem Land. *Man* 5(3): 483–97.

LÉVI-STRAUSS, C. 1964 *Totemism.* London, Merlin Press.

―――― 1966 *The savage mind.* London, Weidenfeld and Nicolson.

McCONNEL, U.H. 1957 *Myths of the Mungkan.* Melbourne, Melbourne University Press.

MADDOCK, K.J. 1970 Myths of the acquisition of fire in northern and eastern Australia. In *Australian Aboriginal anthropology: modern studies in the social anthropology of the Australian Aborigines,* (ed.) R.M. Berndt, pp. 174–99. Nedlands, University of Western Australia Press.

MALINOWSKI, B. 1926 *Myth in primitive psychology.* London, Kegan Paul, Trubner.

―――― 1931 Culture. In *Encyclopaedia of the social sciences,* (ed.) R. Seligman, pp. 621–45. London, Macmillan.

MATHEW, J. 1899 *Eaglehawk and crow: a study of the Australian Aborigines including an inquiry into their origin and a survey of Australian languages.* Melbourne, Melville, Mullen & Slade.

MEGGITT, M.J. 1967 *Gadjari among the Walbiri Aborigines of Central Australia.* Sydney (Oceania monograph no. 14), University of Sydney.

MUNN, N.D. 1969 The effectiveness of symbols in Murngin rite and myth. In *Forms of symbolic action,* (ed.) R.F. Spencer, pp. 178–207. Seattle and London, University of Washington Press.

―――― 1970 The transformation of subjects into objects in Walbiri and Pitjantjatjara myth. In *Australian Aboriginal anthropology: modern studies in the social anthropology of the Australian Aborigines,* (ed.) R.M. Berndt, pp. 141–63. Nedlands, University of Western Australia Press.

PARKER, LANGLOH K. 1896 *Australian legendary tales: folk-lore of the Noongahburrahs as told to the piccaninnies.* London, Nutt.

PIDDINGTON, R. 1950 *An introduction to social anthropology.* Edinburgh, Oliver & Boyd.

RADCLIFFE-BROWN, A.R. 1922 *The Andaman Islanders.* Cambridge, Cambridge University Press.

―――― 1926 The Rainbow-Serpent myth of Australia. In *Royal Anthropological Institute, Journal,* 56:19–25.

―――― 1929 Notes on totemism in eastern Australia. In *Royal Anthropological Institute, Journal,* 59:399–415.

―――― 1930 The Rainbow-Serpent myth in south-east Australia. *Oceania,* 1:342–47.

―――― 1951 The comparative method in social anthropology. In *Royal Anthropological Institute, Journal,* 81:15–22.

RANK, O. 1952 *The myth of the birth of the hero, and other writings,* (ed.) P. Freund. New York, Vintage Books.

RÓHEIM, G. 1925 *Australian totemism: a psycho-analytic study in anthropology.* London, Allen & Unwin.

―――― 1934 *The riddle of the sphinx or human origins.* London, Hogarth Press.

―――― 1941 The psycho-analytic interpretation of culture. *International Journal of Psycho-analysis,* 32:147–69.

―――― 1945 *The eternal ones of the dream: a psychoanalytic interpretation of Australian myth and ritual.* New York, International Universities Press.

SMITH, W.R. 1930 *Myths & legends of the Australian Aboriginals.* London, Harrap.

SPENCER, *Sir* W.B. *and* F.J. GILLEN 1899 *The native tribes of central Australia.* London, Macmillan.

―――― 1904 *The northern tribes of central Australia.* London, Macmillan.

STANNER, W.E.H. 1959–63 *On Aboriginal religion.* Sydney (Oceania monograph no. 11), University of Sydney.

—— 1960 Durmugam, a Nangiomeri. In *In the company of man,* (ed.) J.B. Casagrande, pp. 63–100. New York, Harper.

—— 1961 On the study of Aboriginal religion. Unpublished ms.

—— 1965a The Dreaming. In *Reader in comparative religion,* (ed.) W. Lessa and E. Vogt. New York, Harper.

—— 1965b Religion, totemism and symbolism. In *Aboriginal man in Australia:* essays in honour of Emeritus Professor A P. Elkin, (ed.) R.M. and C.H. Berndt, pp. 207–37. Sydney, Angus and Robertson.

—— 1967 Reflections on Durkheim and Aboriginal religion. In *Social organization,* (ed.) M. Freedman, pp. 217–40. London, Cass.

STREHLOW, T.G.H. 1933 Ankotarinja, an Aranda myth. *Oceania,* 4(2):187–200.

—— 1947 *Aranda traditions.* Melbourne, Melbourne University Press.

—— 1971 *Songs of central Australia.* Sydney, Angus and Robertson.

THORNE, A.G. 1971 Mungo and Kow Swamp: morphological variation in Pleistocene Australians. *Mankind,* 8(2):85–89.

TINDALE, N.B. 1938 Prupe and Koromarange: a legend of the Tanganekald, Coorong, South Australia. In *Royal Society of South Australia, Transactions,* 62:18–24.

—— 1946 Australian (Aborigine). In *Encyclopaedia of literature,* (ed.) J.T. Shipley, pp. 74–78. New York, Philosophical Library.

TURNER, T. 1973 Myth as model: the Kayapo myth of the origin of cooking fire. Unpublished ms.

WARNER, W.L. 1937 *A black civilization: a social study of an Australian tribe.* New York, Harper.

YOUNG, J.Z. 1971 *An introduction to the study of man.* London, Oxford University Press.

Eaglehawk and Crow:
Birds, Myths and Moieties in South-east Australia

Mieke Blows

Myths about a conflict between two characters, Eaglehawk and Crow, have been recorded in widely separated parts of Australia. Probably the most important focus of these stories has been the Darling-Murray river system in South-east Australia. Among the tribes of this area the moieties were named after Eaglehawk and Crow. A short myth connects the moiety names with the tradition of conflict.

M(i): Eaglehawk and Crow[1]

Eaglehawk and Crow were *Nooralie* — beings that existed a very long time ago. There was continual war between them, commemorated in the song: 'Strike the Crow on the knee; I will spear his father.' Finally they made peace and agreed that the Murray people should be divided into two intermarrying classes: Mukwara or Eaglehawk, and Kilpara or Crow.

Three main explanations have been given for the connection between the moiety names and the two mythical characters, as follows (see also Introduction, p.4). First, Mathew (1899) interpreted the myths as distorted or symbolic records of an actual conflict between the original inhabitants of Australia and invaders from the north. He regarded the moiety organisation as an arrangement by which the two groups eventually came to terms. Second, Róheim (1925) interpreted the Eaglehawk-Crow conflict in terms of a primeval struggle between fathers and sons, and explained the formation of moieties as a compromise ultimately reached by the two parties. A third approach, developed by Radcliffe-Brown (1958), treats myth as giving expression to the relationship of opposition, thought to hold both between the birds and between moieties. On account of this common relationship between the pairs, moieties are named after the birds.

I am not concerned here with the two historical hypotheses. Rather, I shall consider Radcliffe-Brown's argument that the pair of birds represents the pair of moieties by virtue of a common relationship of opposition. In view of certain difficulties with this formulation, I shall turn to an examination of the Eaglehawk-Crow myth, which leads to the conclusion, shared with Róheim, that the primary referent of the eaglehawk-crow symbolism is the father-son relationship, which mediates between birds and moieties.

Both Róheim and Radcliffe-Brown saw the problem of the Eaglehawk-Crow moiety names as having far-reaching significance for the theory of totemism. It was this perspective that led Radcliffe-Brown to ask why these species in particular had been selected to represent the moieties. In attempting to answer this question, he used myth to indicate the significant features of the birds, as conceived in Aboriginal thought. Thus he cited a Western Australian myth in which Crow, as the classificatory son-in-law of his mother's brother Eaglehawk, kept for himself the meat which he should have given the latter. After discovering this, Eaglehawk seized Crow and rolled him in the fire, saying: 'You will never be a hunter, but you will for ever be a thief' (1958:115). Radcliffe-Brown related this to the real-life behaviour of the birds: when a hunt is organised by firing a stretch of country, the eaglehawk flies above to hunt the animals as they flee the fire; by contrast, when a camp fire is made, a crow may generally be seen sitting in a tree 'out of reach of a throwing stick', waiting for his chance to thieve a piece of meat. Thus Radcliffe-Brown argued that the myth points up a relationship between the two birds as seen by the Aborigines — both birds are meat-eaters, but one is a hunter, the other, a thief. This contrast of two items sharing a basic resemblance is what makes them a pair of opposites.

Basically, then, Radcliffe-Brown saw the relationship between eaglehawk and crow as one of contrast. Insofar as he described the relationship between moieties, it emerges as one of antagonism mixed with friendship. The first relationship is conceptual, the second, social. How, then, does the first come to stand for the second? For Radcliffe-Brown the gap was bridged by 'the Australian conception of "opposition" [which] combines the idea of a pair of contraries with that of a pair of opponents' (1958:118). Myth translates the resemblances and differences between animal species into social relations of friendship and conflict. Moieties, in their turn, are often named after pairs of contraries. Thus both types of relationship are assimilated to one of 'opposition' in the double sense indicated.

Lévi-Strauss has identified Radcliffe-Brown's argument with one of Bergson, formulated 20 years earlier: 'When therefore they [the members of two clans] declare that they are two species of animals, it is not on the animality but on the duality that they place the stress' (quoted in Lévi-Strauss 1962:95). Duality implies commensurability as well as distinctness. So that on this argument, the relation between eaglehawk and crow as a pair of (possibly multi-faceted) concepts corresponds to the relation between moieties as entities.

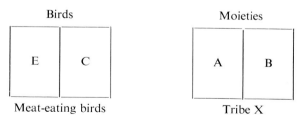

Birds   Moieties

E   C   A   B

Meat-eating birds   Tribe X

A qualitative difference between the birds (hunter/thief) corresponds to a difference in identity of the moieties, while a qualitative similarity in the

25

birds (meat-eaters) corresponds to a common identity of the moieties (tribe X). This correspondence is interesting, and may have been in Radcliffe-Brown's mind, but it does not coincide with the correspondence he invoked between similarity/contrast and friendship/hostility.

Towards the end of his paper, Radcliffe-Brown did attempt to clarify, by reference to other examples, why moieties are often seen as opposites 'in the way in which eaglehawk and crow or black and white are opposites' (1958:125). He cited the case of sex totemism, in which groups of men and women express their opposition by means of the symbolic use of sex totems. In this case, however, unlike that of the moieties, both conflict and contrast are in fact present, a group of men being opposed to a group of women. Another example given is that of the generation division: here 'the group of the fathers, and the group of their sons are in a relation of opposition, not dissimilar from the relation between husbands and their wives' (1958:126). At first sight the generation groups would indeed seem to conform to the type of the sex groups in being qualitatively different — fathers and sons. But in fact the two groups may well be identical in composition in respect of the objective characteristics of its members. Only as seen from inside, will the 'other' group appear different from one's own, as it contains one's fathers and sons, as against one's own group containing one's brothers, grandfathers and grandsons. Applying this viewpoint to the moieties, these may be identified as groups of kin and allies respectively. However, if we may translate these terms as 'we' and 'those we marry', it becomes clear that they entail only social relationships, and that no contrast of qualities is implied.

In the case of the eaglehawk and crow, on the other hand, there is a double bond involved, not merely by 'translation' in myth, but on the basis of observation of the features and behaviour of the actual birds. When examining the behaviour of the birds on which the hunter/thief dichotomy is based, Radcliffe-Brown (1958) looked at each bird separately in its relation to human beings — that is fellow-hunter or thief. But in the myth cited by him, Crow appropriates the meat that belongs to Eaglehawk; in other myths such as M1, Crow tries to obtain the women in Eaglehawk's charge.

Eaglehawk-Crow myths from as far apart as the Flinders Ranges and the extreme south-west of Australia connect mythical conflict with the real-life interaction of the birds. Thus the narrator of the Adnyamatana myth (Mincham 1964:222–3) stated that crows would watch an eagle as it killed its prey, then drive it away by mobbing and take possession of the meat. Similarly, it is mentioned in the Wheelman myth (Hassell 1934:331–4) that eagles dislike crows because 'the latter do not kill for themselves but prefer to follow the Waalich [eagles] and feed on what they leave'; and that, moreover, when the crows notice the eagle becoming tired, they try to drive him away and steal what he has killed. This story in fact concludes with the eagle being driven off by a flock of crows.[2] That these descriptions correspond closely to actual bird behaviour is confirmed by recent research in this field by Rowley, who made the following observation at Geary's Gap, New South Wales, in 1964:

A Wedge-tailed Eagle mobbed by first one and then by two ravens
. . .; the eagle had taken off only recently and was not flying strongly
— it was hampered further by the load it was carrying; the ravens
pressed home their attack so vigorously that the eagle dropped what
turned out to be a threequarter grown rabbit. After I left the ravens
ate the rabbit which had been freshly killed.

Such mobbing, Rowley adds, 'would only take place when ravens
are defending a territory — the fact that they (Corvus) are regular
food items of *Aquila audax* makes this a dangerous confrontation for
the Corvus' (Personal communication).

The relationship between eagle and crow thus becomes quite complex:
there is contrast in the mode of obtaining meat; there is conflict over it;
and there is complementarity in the fact that the crows/ravens tend to
clean up what the eagles leave behind.

These facts must weaken Radcliffe-Brown's argument for the occurrence
of a process of translation of natural similarities and differences into terms
of friendship and hostility, based as it is in the first place on his identification
of this process in the Eaglehawk-Crow myth. Therefore, without assuming
what Radcliffe-Brown aimed to establish, let us compare the relations
between the eagle-crow pair and those between the pair of moieties. Both
combine apparent antagonism and complementarity. The hunter/thief
dichotomy, as well as representing a relationship of contrariety, is anchored
in the behavioural relationship between the birds, one of which takes the
food that the other has obtained by hunting. I have argued that the kin/
ally dichotomy refers to no qualitative contrast between moieties. It could
be suggested, however, that there is a correspondence between the two
dichotomies in the behavioural relations they imply. Discussing social
'opposition' between moieties, Radcliffe-Brown (1958:121) brought out an
element of conflict over women, insofar as the taking of a woman from a
group for marriage represents a loss or injury to that group. Thus with
moieties, as with the birds, the one tries to obtain that which belongs to
the other. Perhaps those from whom a woman is demanded for the moment
experience the relationship as analogous to that of hunter and thief. But
of course, the relationship between moieties is mutual, each being both a
giver and a taker of women.[3] In this respect the relation between moieties,
being symmetrical, differs from that between eagle and crow, which is
asymmetrical. Furthermore, if the moieties have a reciprocal arrangement
in regard to marriage, we may ask, why the antagonism? And indeed,
Radcliffe-Brown himself has suggested that this is to a large extent simply
a conventional attitude (1958:119). Yet myth indicates that antagonism is a
central feature of the eagle-crow symbolism. The lack of fit, within the fit,
between moieties and birds therefore asks to be investigated.

Myth intervenes between birds and moieties. No longer can we regard
the Eaglehawk-Crow myth simply as a means of transforming a logical
relation into a social one, as both of these are based on observation. Radcliffe-Brown, consistently with his general theoretical position, took a
synchronic approach to the analysis of social phenomena, considering in

27

what respects the relationships between the pair of birds and the pair of moieties resemble one another. In asking, however, why these particular birds were chosen to represent the moieties, he implied the existence of this form of social organisation prior to its naming. But moieties, unlike birds, are a cultural artefact. Myth itself [M(i)] claims to explain their formation. Let us see, then, whether analysis of the Eaglehawk-Crow tradition may not yield something beyond formal analogies — an insight into the social forces underlying the moiety system. Such analysis may also throw a new light on the logical problems encountered above.

As myth of reference I propose an Eaglehawk-Crow myth collected by Tindale from the Maraura tribe,[4] near the junction of the Darling and Murray Rivers, around which the Eaglehawk-Crow moiety names were found. Since the theme of conflict is the common denominator of the many myths concerning Eaglehawk and Crow, this conflict, the issues over which it arises, and its outcome, will be examined. The basic question, however, concerns the nature of the relationship between the protagonists. Some of the information relevant to the above questions is easily accessible in the myth of reference. Other aspects of the relationship can be elicited only by a more indirect method.

When we compare any given myth with similar or related myths, common motifs or even episodes[5] at once become apparent. If myth is an organic unity and not just a compilation of unconnected elements, it follows that a motif 'fits' with its context. To draw on Lévi-Strauss's linguistic analogy (1968:208–10), the motifs of a myth may be compared to the words of a sentence. Just as the meaning of a word can be inferred from its various contexts (verbal definitions being the most helpful type), so it should be possible to obtain clues to the meaning of a motif from the set of contexts in which it is found. Elucidation of the word or motif therefore depends on the understanding of the context. If that is not understood, it must be clarified first, by a similar procedure, the process being extended until familiar terms are reached. Direction can then be reversed, each stage being explained by the last, until the original expression is again reached, for example,

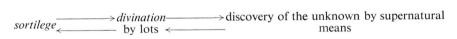

Naturally, we cannot expect to find definitions of motifs in myth, and therefore have to make the best of whatever clues the contexts can provide. But the step-like process of investigation remains the same.

A full analysis of a myth would entail the exegesis of each of its motifs. However, for the purpose of gaining an insight into the nature of the Eaglehawk-Crow conflict, I propose to explore a particular motif — one which at first sight appears quite minor — of the reference myth. As in the verbal illustration, the analysis is taken past the first stage of considering the motif in its various contexts, to a second stage, reaching, in this case, into the realm of ritual, both actual and putative (that is, ritual that is alleged to occur, as in magical operations).

M1 : Eagle and Crow[6]

Crow and Eagle were *nurili* — ancestral beings. They lived at opposite ends of Manara Range (about 75 miles from the Darling River, due east from Menindee). Crow belonged to the Kilpara matrimoiety, and Eagle to Mukwara. Between them lived two sisters, unmarried girls of the Mukwara moiety. They were *tambar*[7] and were in the care of Eagle, who called them 'mother'.

Part I

Crow came to Eagle to ask him for a wife in exchange for the sister he had given him. Eagle told Crow he did not have a sister to give him; whereupon Crow threatened to take the two girls in Eagle's charge, who were his 'mothers-in-law'. Eagle pointed out that Crow's sister's son was present, and should not be allowed to hear such forbidden things.

The next time Crow approached the camp, Eagle immediately sent his son to play somewhere out of earshot. Crow warned Eagle that he would point a bone at him if he did not provide him with a wife. But Eagle could see no way of finding a wife for Crow. However, he promised to be alert for any opportunities, and to keep Crow informed.

Eventually, Crow determined to go and kill his sister's son. On arriving at Eagle's camp, he told the latter his foot was aching from walking; he would stay near the camp with his nephew while Eagle went off to hunt. They would cook the wallaby that was there, leaving him a share.

While Eagle was hunting, Crow forced his nephew to eat far too much of the food, after which he sent him to the river to drink and killed him. Then he made a great many tracks on the ground.

Feeling that something was wrong, Eagle returned to camp. Crow told him he had been attacked by a crowd of people, and that the boy had been killed in the fight. Eagle was not deceived. He told Crow to start digging a hole to bury the boy. He instructed Crow to lie in the hole 'just as your sister's son will be placed', to test it. As Crow lay in the grave, Eagle quickly covered him with earth. Crow, however, dug his way out, but the effort caused him to turn into a bird. Eagle also was transformed into a bird, by lightning.

Part II

From Manara Range, Crow watched the two sisters squatting beside a claypan, to gather food. Singing a magical song, he extended his penis under the ground. It came up first under one woman, then the other.

Both the women became big with child. One day the younger sister left camp alone and gave birth to a male child. She would feed him in the scrub. The elder sister gave birth to a girl. Noticing the women's unusual behaviour, people said: 'They have broken the rules. There is something wrong.'

29

Seeing that they were hated by their own people, the women ran away until they came to the Darling River, at Pooncarie. Here they met Kingfisher. He belonged to Kilpara moiety, and was a fine fisherman, so they took him as their husband.

Crow had followed the women. When he met Kingfisher he asked him why he was able to catch so much fish. Kingfisher showed him the hollow logs lying in the mud. He found a big cod in a specially large hollow tree trunk and invited Crow to dive through the log and spear the fish. Crow, however, noticing bones of men lying in the water, declined. To demonstrate that it was quite safe, Kingfisher himself dived through the log. Crow waited until he emerged, and speared him.

Crow went to Kingfisher's camp, but the women refused his advances. Groaning and complaining of pains, they went to defecate on either side of him, and, by singing, made their faeces grow large. They taught them to say: 'We are coming soon, we have a bellyache and cannot relieve ourselves.'

Then they escaped with the children. When Crow called the women, the faeces answered for them. At last Crow got up and, with his swordstick club, struck first at one of the large objects, then the other. The mess splashed and blinded him. After singing a song to make daylight come quickly, he found the women's tracks and followed them to Limbara. There, although he desired the younger sister, he was able to have intercourse only with the elder one.

Next day he sent the women to fish while he looked after the babies. Still wanting to mate with the younger one, he pinched her baby till it cried; but both sisters came back. Finally he put the babies up in a low gum sapling, and sang to the tree to make it grow up quickly. Halfway up the trunk he made a large gall appear, to prevent the children's rescue.

When the women discovered what had happened, they went for help to the Barkindji people, but no-one could climb the tree. Then someone thought of a clever Maraura youth who was *tambar*—set apart to undergo initiation and therefore red-ochred. He was living with his mother in a cave near Lake Victoria.

The youth was prevailed upon to come. After putting the Barkindji men and the two women to sleep, he magically made the tree grow small again. Then he picked the children off and put them with their mothers. 'When you see a fire blaze up in the distance,' he told them, 'you must cry, "Where is my mother?" ' The youth went away, lit the fire, and the people awoke as he had arranged.

The women continued to travel down the Darling and then along the Murray River. Crow followed them, but, as they had a long start, he was unable to catch up with them.

As the cause of conflict, this myth presents Crow's frustrated wish for a sexual partner, and his subsequent determination to obtain a woman (or two) by fair means or foul. In the first part, Crow is shown in conflict with Eagle over the two women who are his 'mothers-in-law'. In the second part, he kills Kingfisher and attempts to take his wives, the same two women.

Although Kingfisher's nominal relationship to the women differs from that of Eagle, he appears to stand in Eagle's place, as the man in charge of them. Supporting evidence is provided by a Ualarai Eaglehawk-Crow myth (Parker 1953:60) in which the hollow-log fisherman killed by Crow is Eaglehawk himself.

When Crow appears about to succeed in gaining sexual access to the women, he is foiled by their trick of leaving behind, to impersonate them, a set of talking faeces. What can be the meaning of this strange motif? I shall try to elucidate this question, for I believe it holds the key — or one of the keys, as myths contain a good deal of redundancy — to the nature of the conflict between Eaglehawk and Crow.

The three myths which follow share with M1 the theme of the talking faeces. M2 also shares the theme of the tree that is made to grow tall by magic, in this case accounting for the origin of the moon.

M2: Moon and his Nephew[8]

Moon and his nephew were hunting emu. The nephew ably assisted Moon in capturing the bird and preparing it for cooking. When it was cooked, he asked for a piece of meat, but was refused. His uncle said: 'Go away — eat pig-face!'[9] The boy did so and returned to camp.

Moon came back with two or three emus and he and his two wives ate emu meat. While the old man went away for a while, the women gave the boy a little piece of emu meat.

Next day, the boy and his uncle went out to hunt emu again. 'I feel ill,' said the boy. He went further away. When he looked up, he saw grubs in the nearby tree. He told Moon, who came and climbed up the tree. Then, the youth blew on the tree to make it grow tall. Having done this several times, he asked his uncle: 'What's up there?' 'It's the sky.' 'Grip it hard.' And the boy made the tree grow small again. That's how the moon came to be in the sky.

The boy went back to the camp and told the wives of Moon he would be their husband. He slept with them. They got up and defecated and instructed the faeces to answer him. Following them, the youth put his foot in the faeces. He shouted: 'You two fucking cunts, you shitty cunts, you red cunts!'

Another myth on this subject comes from the neighbouring Wongaibon:

M3: Two Young Men and the Moon[10]

Moon had two young male relatives living with him. He was a greedy man, and if the boys caught male possums, he would cut off the scrotal pouch, heal the wound, and claim that the animal was a doe, which the youths were forbidden to eat.

The boys decided to leave Moon, using the talking faeces method.

After a time, they caught an emu. Remembering that they were not allowed to eat emu, they ordered the faeces now to be silent, and called Moon so that he could hear them from afar.

The youths stood on a flat rock, on which they had lit a fire to roast the emu. As the old man, Moon, approached, they magically raised the rock by some twenty feet. 'Look, grandfather, what we have here,' they called to Moon. 'Throw it to me,' came the reply. They cut off a bit from the fattest part, and threw it down. Moon caught it, but, seeing it was mostly fat, threw it back to the youths. This was just what the boys wanted, for they were not permitted to eat the flesh of the emu until given a piece by an old man.[11] They greased their mouths with the fat, and ate the morsel of flesh that was attached to it. They were now released from their taboo.

The youths told Moon to obtain a sapling to lean against the rock, so that he could climb up to join in the feast. But while he was away, they raised the rock another ten feet, so that, when Moon brought along his sapling, it did not reach the top. They told him to get a larger pole, but raised the rock again. The third time, they left the rock as it was. Moon managed to climb the pole nearly to the top, although his hands were greasy from emu fat. Then the youths caught hold of the pole, and twisted it rapidly around. Moon fell heavily on his back. As he lay there, he sang the song which has to be sung to the present day when anyone is allowed to eat emu flesh for the first time. For some days after he fell, Moon walked with a great stoop, which is why the new moon always appears bent.

In this case, the motif of the tree-that-grows is absent, but we do find what appear to be its constituent elements, in separate form — a rock made to grow tall by magic, and a tree used to reach it. We may note at this stage that both Moon myths share a concern with the eating of emu flesh. The fourth myth which incorporates the talking-faeces motif also shares this concern with the Moon myths.

M4: Porcupine[12]

Porcupine and Crow went hunting for emu. They caught one and cooked it. When it was ready they took it out of the hole and Porcupine told Crow to fetch some leaves to put it on. Crow approached a tree: 'This one?' 'No, further on.' Porcupine went off with the meat, but left behind a talking turd to tell the boy to go on. When out of earshot, the boy turned back and found his *gariga* (grandfather/cross-cousin) gone. Returning to camp, he told the others what had happened, and they joined Crow in tracking Porcupine to the other side of the Darling River.

Porcupine knew he was being pursued, and hid himself in the root of a hollow tree. They found him there and they all speared him. That is how he got his spines.

These three myths may now be compared with Part II of the Eaglehawk-Crow myth, M1. All four stories depict a conflict between two males over either women or food. This basic similarity allows us to set out a table showing for each myth the personae, the issue over which conflict occurs, and the outcome of the conflict.

TABLE 1

Myths sharing the talking-faeces motif

Myth	Leading Actors		Issue	Outcome
M1, Part II	Kingfisher	Crow	Women	Crow kills Kingfisher Success in obtaining women prevented by talking faeces Crow continues to pursue women
M2	Moon	Nephew	Food (emu)	Nephew puts Moon up to sky Transformation of Moon Success in obtaining women vitiated by talking faeces
M3	Moon	Youths	Food (possum)	Youths cause Moon injury Transformation of Moon Youths obtain right to eat emu
M4	Porcupine	Crow	Food (emu)	Crow (with others) spears Porcupine Transformation of Porcupine

In each of the last three cases, the second character is evidently the junior partner, for he is denied food by the other person, who is in charge of the situation to begin with. The boys in M3 seem to have been recently initiated, as they are forbidden to eat emu and female possums — two of the restrictions on post-initiation diet mentioned by Howitt for the Kurnai (1885:316) and other south-eastern tribes (1884:455). In M1, Crow is probably the younger partner, for Kingfisher is married, as is Eagle whom he replaces, while Crow is not.

These myths, then, feature a conflict between an older and a younger male, the former being defeated by the latter in each case. In the first two myths, the younger male then attempts to take possession of the other's wives. There is thus a close similarity between the action of Crow (M1) and Moon's nephew (M2). In the other two cases, M3 and M4, but also in M2, a transformation of the older male is brought about by the younger male(s). Here again the action of Moon's nephew or young relatives (M2, M3) corresponds to an action by Crow (M4). These correspondences suggest an equation between Moon's nephew or young relatives and Crow. Supporting evidence is provided by a Ualarai myth (Parker 1905:24) in which it is Crow who puts Moon up to the sky, causing his transformation.

In M2, M3 and M4 conflict between the male actors arises over food. Specifically, in M2 and M4 it concerns the eating of emu flesh; while in M3, although the food first mentioned is possum meat, the principal concern is evidently the eating of emu meat. The main issue in M1 is the possession of women. There is no mention of emu in this myth. M3 and M4 do not touch on the subject of women. But M2 unites the two subjects, for, although the issue is the eating of emu meat, the adventure culminates in the young man taking possesssion of Moon's wives — and then being repelled by the talking faeces. If it is reasonable to assume continuity between the object

33

of contention and the object gained, then the wish for emu meat and the young man's desire for the women are symbolically equivalent. And indeed, in M2 the equation is stated directly: Moon's wives give the youth some emu meat, although this is evidently not permitted; they also cohabit with him.

Is there any connection between the talking-faeces theme and the subject of these myths? The use to which the talking faeces are put in each case may be summarised as follows:

> M1 Women use talking faeces to escape from Crow.
> M2 Women use talking faeces to escape from young man.
> M3 Young men use talking faeces so that they shall have emu meat.
> M4 Porcupine uses talking faeces to avoid sharing emu meat.

Although the myths appear to differ in the ultimate end for which the talking faeces are used, the immediate effect is the same in each case: to separate, or put a distance between, people. This is allegedly achieved by magic, but in the Bagundji Moon myth (M2) we find a clue to the underlying meaning. The youth has already copulated with the women; contact with their faeces raises in him a feeling of disgust towards them. His terms of abuse to the women, 'you shitty cunts', give pithy expression to the vitiation of attraction and pleasure by repulsion. But if this incident sheds some light on the women's use of talking faeces, it does not account for their use by males in M3 and M4.

A lead is provided by M3: the song sung by Moon as he fell, is the song that 'has to be sung to the present day when anyone is allowed to eat emu flesh for the first time' (Mathews 1904:361). Therefore this myth — and presumably M2 as well — relates to the emu-meat taboo and its ritual lifting. Some ideas and practices associated with this taboo and its lifting among the Wongaibon[13] are discussed by Berndt (1947:353). The emu was associated with two spirit beings, *Kurikuta* and *Ngurimelan*; it was also said to be under the direct protection of Baiami. Infringement of the emu-meat taboo was believed to incur supernatural punishment in the form of severe illness. To cure the transgressor, a medicine man would be called in, and he would ask the patient whether he had eaten emu meat. If the answer was yes, the doctor's task would be to extract the emu feathers and nails, said to have entered the eater with the meat. He would hold to the patient's nostrils a *Nginberan* — a bunch of emu anal feathers having a particularly obnoxious odour. Repeated applications would eventually enable the doctor to extract the emu feathers and nails from the man's anus. The ritual lifting of the emu-meat taboo was performed some time after initiation into manhood. It required that the novice practise *coitus interruptus* with a particular woman, the semen being collected in a wooden bowl, to be drunk by the other men.

Interpreting this material fairly freely, one may regard the 'treatment' by means of obnoxious-smelling emu anal feathers as a sanction against the premature eating of emu meat.[14] Evil smelling anus feathers would 'put the patient off' emu meat, just as the talking faeces in myth are used to deter the women's pursuer (M1, M2). A close association between the eating of emu meat and sexual activity is revealed by the ritual itself: for the emu-meat taboo is terminated by the performance of the sex act! And so a parallel emerges between the youth who copulates with the woman but is not allowed to ejaculate except into a bowl, whose contents are to be drunk by the men, and the youth of myth (M2, M4) who helps to hunt emu, but is not permitted to eat it, while the older men do so. It may be concluded that the emu symbolises woman and that the eating of emu meat represents coitus. This interpretation helps to make sense of a curious Ualarai custom described by Parker (1904:24): 'When a boy, after his first Boorah, killed his first emu, whether it was his Dhé or totem, or not, his father made him lie on the bird before it was cooked.'[15] It seems, then, that not only do we have the relationship, anal feathers : emu : : faeces : woman, but that the emu stands directly for woman, while in myth, faeces are used similarly to emu anal feathers, to prevent specific other persons from eating emu (M3, M4).

Another use of the anus feathers is described in Berndt's account of the putative experience of the rainmaker or 'clever man' in *Wantanggengura*, the country beyond the sky (Berndt 1947:362). When the rainmaker goes to *Pali:ma*, in the *Wantanggegnura* country, he first has to pass Moon, with long beard and extraordinarily long penis, and Sun, with a similarly elongated clitoris. Next, he meets two ancestral beings, Ngintu-ngintu and Kunapapa, who dance and sing humorously. Should the onlooker laugh or smile, he would be killed. When these beings give up, some women perform erotic dances in front of the 'clever man', to which he must show no sign of responding. If he succeeds in this, they too, eventually cease, and only Ngintu-ngintu remains. The 'clever man' now produces a bunch of emu anal feathers and throws it into the distance while singing, thereby transforming it into a phantom emu. He says to Ngintu-ngintu: 'There goes an emu!' and the latter collects his spears and goes towards his hut for his dog. Meanwhile, the rainmaker rushes for the hut containing the water bags and pierces one with his spear. Immediately this is done he runs for the opening through which he entered, for by now Ngintu-ngintu is in pursuit of him, having noticed that the emu is not a real one. He escapes just in time. The water is poured through the clouds to be purified; for, having been so long in these bags, it has become 'stinking' and bad.

In relation to the emu-meat taboo, anus feathers are used to counteract the attractiveness of emu flesh. In *Wantanggengura*, it is used to stave off the danger which Ngintu-ngintu represents, which may be identified with that previously represented by the licentious dancing and singing — that is, sexual temptation, succumbing to which means death. The anus feathers, embodying the negative aspect of the much-desired emu, offer protection against this temptation, again confirming that the eating of emu meat is symbolically equivalent to coitus with a woman.

The question raised earlier, concerning the connection between the talking-faeces motif and the subject of the four myths sharing it, can now be answered. M1 features the sexual desire of Crow for two women who are controlled by Kingfisher (replacing the original Eagle); M2, M3 and M4 feature the desire of a youth (or two youths) for emu meat, controlled by an older relative. In the emu taboo-lifting ritual, the two themes of the hunt for emus and the sexual quest are united, the initiate corresponding to both Moon's nephew or relatives and Crow. Thus the sharing of the motif is indicative of an area of meaning shared by these myths and the ritual to which they refer: modification or restraint of the desire for woman/emu by the 'off-putting' effect of the talking faeces/emu anal feathers.

The association of talking-faeces with the hunt for emu has revealed the important connection of these myths with initiation, through the emu taboo-lifting ceremony. Independent evidence of a link with initiation ritual exists for M1, with which was connected a set of songs owned by four men, and performed only when these men met for initiation (Tindale 1939:245). A new myth will extend our interpretation of both myth and ritual.

M5: Crow's Mother[16]

One night, Wakend [Crow] was sitting down eating with his wife. Kurikuta was sitting in the same camp, waiting for her share of the food; but her son and daughter-in-law continued to eat without giving her any. She began to 'growl' about this. Wakend, who was annoyed by his mother's constant grumbling, took hold of his spear, and going over to her speared her in the knee. Instead of pulling out the spear he left it in the wound. It was upon this that she climbed up and went into the sky to *Wantanggengura*; she has still got that spear in her knee, being unable to remove it.

Berndt (1947:77) explained that Kurikuta was an ancestral being 'who had lived in the past, was still living in the present, and would continue to live in the future; in that sense she was eternal.' She was completely covered with quartz crystals, so that, as she turned, light would flash in every direction. Beautiful in form, she appeared always as 'particularly youthful and virile, because she is the wife of Baiami' (*ibid*:77). The emu, with which she was identified, was her assistant totem.[17] The latter is the 'spirit animal' which was 'sung into' the trainee doctor at about the age of 12, by the doctor training him or her. Although the doctors were most frequently men, female practitioners also existed (Berndt 1947:331, 333).

Kurikuta was the wife of Baiami, usually referred to, according to Elkin (1964:254) as father or all-father. He was 'often pictured as the hero who led the tribe to its present habitat, and made the natural features as they are today. In addition, he bestowed on men their various items of material culture, gave them their social laws, and above all, instituted the initiation rites' (*ibid*:252). Berndt (1947:334fn.) observed that 'all power, whether religious or magical, emanated from Baiami.' It is to this supreme personage that Kurikuta was the wife. Parker (1905:7) stated that Baiami's chief wife, whom the Ualarai called Birrahgnooloo, was 'claimed as the mother of all.'

In his discussion of the emu-meat taboo, Berndt named two spirit-beings, Kurikuta and Ngurimelan, having a special relation to the emu. Of these two, the second may be identified with a star called 'Moiree Mulleirn' meaning emu,[18] according to another statement by Biggs (Robinson 1966: 107). A doubling of the same identity therefore seems to be involved. The emu-meat taboo, then, is closely tied up with Kurikuta, Emu, woman, wife of Baiami, mother of all, and, specifically, mother of Crow.

An account by Howitt of the food restrictions of novices in the initiation ceremony of the Coast Murring reveals the first three of these meanings of emu: food, woman, and wife of the chief culture hero or deity. The youths were not allowed to kill and eat various animals which would recall aspects of the ritual. Howitt went on to say: 'Nor, above all, the Emu, for this is *Ngalalbal*, the wife of Daramulun,[19] and, at the same time, "the woman"; for the novice during his probation is not permitted even so much as to look at a woman, not to speak to one . . . Yet on one occasion during his probation he is shown to his mother, in order that her mind may be set at rest concerning him' (Howitt 1884:456). Ngalalbal, Emu and wife of Daramulun among the Yuin tribes, evidently corresponds to Kurikuta among the Wongaibon.

M5 relates how Crow speared his mother, Kurikuta, and placed her in the sky. The spear joined earth and sky, as did the tree by which Moon's nephew sent his uncle to the sky (M2), with which the tree in M1 is cognate. In both these cases the action of causing the tree's magical growth springs from the young man's desire — for women (M1) or for emu (M2). Similarly, in M3 the youths' magical raising of the rock is motivated by their desire for emu meat. That the impetus for these magical extensions lies in the nature of the desire they serve, is further confirmed by the observation that the magical growth of the tree in M1 echoes the magical extension of Crow's penis to such a length that it enters the women at a distance. Crow's spear shows the same capacity for magical extension as do the rock, the tree, and his penis. Thus we may infer that the spear, appropriate to the emu aspect of Kurikuta, is used in relation to her human aspect as a symbol of the penis. M5 therefore gives symbolic expression to the idea of mother-son incest.

Myth and ritual jointly indicate that Kurikuta is Emu *par excellence*. Let us look at the significance of this for each in turn. As far as myth is concerned, we now have the key to M1–M4: Kurikuta is *both* woman and emu; it is she, Crow's mother, who is the object of his desire. That the younger partner(s) in M2 and M3 may be identified with Crow, I have argued earlier. Where the object of the young man's desire is represented as women, that is in M1 and partly in M2, the young man kills or transforms their husband and pursues the women. It is, then, Crow's mother, Emu, he wants; and to get her, he has to destroy the man who owns or controls her, her husband — that is, his father. This, therefore, is the nature of the Eaglehawk-Crow conflict.

Turning now to the ritual concomitant, we may infer that Kurikuta is both the emu which the youth is for the first time allowed to eat, and the woman with whom he may copulate for the first time. So that if, as I have argued, the novice corresponds to Crow, then Kurikuta is more than just a woman to him: she is his mother — and his action echoes that of Crow in M5. But because Kurikuta is mother not only to the novice, but to all men, the basically anti-social act of incest is socialised: it is symbolic, insofar as the woman representing Kurikuta is not the youth's real mother;[20] and its outcome is deflected, enabling the group of men symbolically to participate — or even to have that, in a sense, which the youth was denied. If the myths express the oedipal wish, then this ritual enacts a modified wish-fulfilment, with the men determining the nature and extent of the gratification permitted the youth.

Thus the latent meaning of myth finds its expression in ritual. Let me briefly retrace the line of thought leading to the present interpretation. The Eaglehawk-Crow myth, M1, represents a conflict between two men over women, with whom Crow has illegitimate sexual relations. Starting from this point, the analysis was extended by taking up the talking-faeces motif, which brought a further set of myths within our ambit. The recurrence in these myths of emu as the desired object in place of women, and the reference to the emu taboo-lifting, led into the field of ritual, which revealed the figure of Kurikuta — emu, woman, wife of Baiami, and therefore mother of all. A final myth, M5, completed the circle by identifying Kurikuta as the mother of Crow, its symbolism confirming the sexual nature of Crow's quest. This myth therefore helps to unite the set of myths with ritual, and Crow with his ritual counterpart, the novice.

If Crow has his ritual counterpart in the novice, is there a similar counterpart for Eaglehawk? I suggest that indeed there is, but that the correspondence in this case is to be found at the manifest level of myth. Having given Eagle his sister for wife, Crow expects a wife in return, on the principle of sister-exchange.[21] Initiation rituals in south-east Australia followed the pattern of a separation of the boy from his mother and his subsequent placing in the charge of a guardian. Where moieties existed, the latter must belong to the other moiety from that of the novice, for example, among the Maljangaba (Beckett 1967:462).[22] But beyond this, the guardian often belonged to the group — moiety or section and totemic clan — into which the novice was entitled to marry. For the Wiradjuri, Wolgal, Ngarigo, Theddora and Coast Murring, Howitt (1884:436fn.) stated that 'a youth is directly under the charge and instruction, during his initiation, of a man who is either the husband of his sister or who is the brother of the girl who has been promised to him as his future wife. If there is no "own" sister's husband, or any "betrothed", then a "tribal" sister's husband or brother of a "tribal" wife is selected.' Mathews' statements concerning the Wiradjuri[23] and Kamilaroi agree with this (1895:420; 1896:308; 1897:273). Similarly among the Wongaibon, Beckett states, the guardian was 'a cross-cousin who might be sister's husband' to the novice (personal communication).

The correspondence between the novice-guardian pair of initiation, and the pair of antagonists of myth, is clear for M1, where Eagle and Crow are brothers-in-law. In M2, where Moon is mother's brother to the youth, it does not apply. Crow, in M4, calls Porcupine *gariga*, grandfather or cousin (Beckett 1959:201). Of the four Wongaibon classes of kin, it is this one in which a person finds his brother-in-law, and therefore, wife. Indeed, Berndt (1947:354) has translated the term as brother-in-law. To the nature of the relationship between Moon and his relatives in M3, there is only one clue, for the youths call Moon 'grandfather'. As the Wongaibon classified father's father with brothers, Moon should be mother's father to the boys, that is, *gariga*, as Porcupine is to Crow in M4. Thus, in three of the four myths the relationship between the protagonists belongs to the same category as that between novice and guardian in initiation.

Both in myth and in ritual the oppositeness in moiety membership of the two leading actors, or between novice and guardian, appears important. Thus Howitt (1904:608) has stated that invariably 'the men of one moiety of the tribe initiate the youths of the other moiety.' Howitt linked this fact with the provision of a wife: 'As his wife comes to him from the other moiety, it is men of that moiety who must be satisfied that he is . . . able to take his place as the provider for, and protector of, the woman, their sister, who is to be his wife' (*ibid*:608). Moiety membership is also crucial in the Eaglehawk-Crow myth, M1, which specifies that Crow was Kilpara and Eagle, Mukwara. It is against this background that we must see Crow's demand for a wife in exchange for the sister he has given Eagle.

How can this aspect of the Eaglehawk-Crow myth be reconciled with the interpretation in terms of latent meaning? Manifestly, Crow is Eagle's young brother-in-law, and the women are his 'mothers-in-law'; while at the latent level, it seems that the women symbolise Crow's mother, and Eagle, his father. I suggest that what we have here is not so much a matter of contradiction as one of dialectic. Initially, M1 is phrased in terms of the reciprocal relationship between moieties: the difficulty appears to be the lack of a sister whom Eagle can give Crow as wife, in exchange for the sister received by him from Crow. Crow thereupon decides to pursue his 'mothers-in-law'. A change of scene occurs, so that Crow's antagonist becomes Kingfisher, who has married the women, and who belongs, not to the opposite moiety, but to Crow's own, Kilpara. Only then does there develop the rivalry situation which is implicit in the eagle-crow imagery, and which recurs in M2, as well as in the Ualarai Eaglehawk-Crow myth referred to above (p.31). As long as Eagle is of the opposite moiety to Crow, real rivalry cannot properly occur. I would argue, accordingly, that the conflict does not belong to the context set by the manifest relations, but to the context of familial relations as interpreted. To this conflict, the organisation of society into matrimoieties may be seen as a response, preventing its recurrence; for the son, being in his mother's moiety, must marry into the other, where he can provide no rivalry to his father. This mode of social organisation is reflected in the manifest relation between Eagle and Crow.

The hypothesis that this is the nature of the connection between the moieties and the Eaglehawk-Crow myth is supported by the high incidence of matrilineal moieties named after these birds among the tribes of the Darling River (Maraura, Bagundji) and westward (Bandjigali, Maljangaba), and the Murray between Wentworth and Swan Hill (Tatathi, Kerami, etc.) as well as further eastward (Ngarigo, Wolgal) (Howitt 1904:98–100, 195). However, between Swan Hill and Albury, on the Murray River, were several tribes, notably the Bangerang, with patrilineal moieties named

Bunjil and Waang (also meaning Eagle and Crow), like the Kulin tribes to the south, with whom they intermarried (Howitt 1904:257).

These tribes, then, seem to have been more closely related to the Kulin group than to the group sharing the Mukwara/Kilpara moiety names of the Eaglehawk-Crow myth, M1.[24] A Kulin myth tells how Bunjil (the Kulin chief culture hero or deity whose name means Eagle) speared Crane, the first man made by him, causing his transformation. Again, the cause of conflict is women, but in this case it is Bunjil, the senior partner, who takes them from the junior (Smyth 1878, vol. I:425). In this respect, the Eaglehawk-Crow myth is here inverted. Thus the patrilineal Kulin represent the older male as taking possession of the younger man's wives, while the matrilineal moiety tribes of the Darling-Murray rivers region attribute the illegitimate taking of women to the younger man. In view of this correlation, it is interesting to recall Róheim's observation that while, as primary marriage rule, matrimoieties would prevent mother-son marriage, patri-moieties would prevent a father being able to marry his daughter, due to their common moiety membership (Róheim 1925:426fn.).

In the light of this analysis, let us return to the question of the relation between birds, myth and moieties.

That the eagle and crow represent a contrasting pair has been generally accepted, although the specific contrasts emphasised vary from one writer to another. I have argued that the hunter/thief dichotomy deduced by Radcliffe-Brown derives, not simply from the behaviour of each bird considered in isolation, but from their interaction, as crows/ravens eat the remains of animals killed by the eagle, at times involving overt conflict. The contrast and the conflict between the birds are therefore inextricably intermingled, so that here we have a real-life case of 'opposition' in the double sense. I would suggest, however, that the most spectacular contrast between the birds lies in their respective size and strength, and that this lends force to the hunter/thief contrast: the large, powerful being hunts while the small, weak one must use his native cunning to obtain what he wants.

By analysing the myth-symbolism, we arrived at the conclusion that Eagle and Crow represent the father-son relationship. And indeed, in regard to contrast in qualities, a beautiful fit may be discerned: father and son, like eagle and crow, are large and strong, and weak and small respectively; while in addition, the first is a hunter and the second, a taker of food. This latter aspect of the relationship resembles the hunter/thief relationship between the eagle and crow, since it involves both a contrast in behaviour, and a relationship between two persons, insofar as the son obtains (meat) food from his father. But myth does not simply establish this analogy; rather, it uses it to express an aspect of the father-son relationship that is not normally acknowledged, that is the aspect of sexual rivalry, which it places at the centre of the conflict it depicts.

It may well be because of the potentially disruptive nature of father-son rivalry that it is not openly stated. Yet the very expression of this basic pattern of attachment and antagonism may be a necessary step in the incorporation of the youth in the society of adults. For myth and ritual seem to express the incest wish and the consequent father-son rivalry in such a way as to channel these tendencies into a socially acceptable pattern of behaviour. Thus in the initiation ritual the boy is taken away from his mother and placed in the charge of a guardian — who, I have suggested, represents Eagle to the novice's own Crow — from, or through, whom he will receive a wife. An (ideally) reciprocal relationship thereby replaces the rivalrous and asymmetrical father-son pair. In this process of redirection of the youth's sexual striving, the 'talking-faeces' of myth, and the emu anal feathers in ritual, have their use in deterring the youth from making an unacceptable object choice.

This brings us back to the objection raised earlier to the view that eagle and crow represent the moieties by virtue of a common relationship between the pairs. The objection was that in one case, the relation is asymmetrical, being based on a qualitative contrast, while in the second, it is symmetrical or reciprocal, without any qualitative contrast. Although there are some resemblances between the eagle-crow relation and that between moieties, I would conclude that the connection is not direct, but is mediated by the father-son relationship. As to the reason why moieties are so often named after logical opposites, it is tempting to conjecture that it is due to the pressure of the underlying relationship of father-son opposition, which combines the double sense of contrast and conflict. By careful analysis of particular cases with their associated myth and ritual, it should be possible to throw further light on this question.

Acknowledgements

I am grateful to Dr L.R. Hiatt for his constructive criticism; I also wish to thank Dr M.R. Allen, Dr J.R. Beckett and Prof. I. Hogbin for their comments and suggestions.

Notes

1. Smyth 1878, vol. I:423–4. Origin stated as northern Victoria; however, this myth is evidently closely related to the Maraura Eaglehawk-Crow myth, M1, not only by the moiety associations of the birds, but also by the use of the word *Nooralie*, rendered by Tindale (1939:245) as *nurili*, 'ancestral beings'. I have labelled this introductory myth M(i) so that the myth of reference may be labelled M1, in accordance with the custom established by Lévi-Strauss (1970). With the exception of M5, the myths presented here have been condensed and paraphrased from their source. Where direct speech is quoted, however, the original is followed exactly.
2. Although the myths invariably refer to Eaglehawk, or Eagle, and Crow, the latter term almost certainly includes both ravens and crows. These birds in Australia are very similar in appearance, the ravens generally being somewhat larger and lack the white feather bases characteristic of crows (Rowley 1970:36, 67). As for Eaglehawk, this name seems generally to refer to the Wedge-tailed Eagle. This is the species to which Cayley (1958) refers the reader in his index entry under 'eaglehawk'; in the text he comments on the inappropriateness of this name for a bird which is the fourth-largest species of eagle in the world. Average wingspread, he states, is 7 ft 6 in.
3. In south-east Australian tribes reciprocity was commonly emphasised with the custom, or at least the ideal, of sister-exchange, on which, see note 21.

4. Closely related to this version are the Bagundji and Maljangaba Eaglehawk-Crow stories recorded by Beckett (1957); connected also are the Ualarai account (Parker 1953:60–6) and the Madimadi version collected by Hercus (1971) as well as the short myth cited as M(i) and two other brief, probably residual, accounts identified only as coming from the Murray River (Smyth 1878 vol. 1:430, 451).

5. My use of the terms 'motif' and 'episode' follows Lévi-Strauss's usage in *The Raw and the Cooked* (1970). I am interested here in the raw material which provides the starting point for analysis, rather than in 'mythemes' involving abstraction from a number of variations (see 'The Structural Study of Myth', in Lévi-Strauss 1968).

6. Maraura tribe. Tindale, 1939. The division of the myth into two parts is Tindale's.

7. Tindale explains this term as meaning 'set apart, forbidden, almost sacred' (1939:245). The same word is used for the novice set apart for initiation, whose body was plastered with red ochre and oil, (*ibid*:257).

8. Informant: George Dutton; Bagundji tribe. Beckett, 1957. I wish to acknowledge my debt to Dr Beckett, who has allowed me to use unpublished myths collected by him in western New South Wales in 1957.

9. Probably *Carprobotus rossii*. Earlier, pig-face was classified under the old genus, *Mesembryanthemum*. (Australian Encyclopaedia, 1965.)

10. Wongaibon tribe. Mathews, 1904:358.

11. Howitt (1884:316) described the release of novices from taboos on eating the flesh of various animals by 'one of the old men suddenly and unexpectedly smearing some of the cooked fat over his face.' However, for some species the procedure was more elaborate, as in the case of the kangaroo in Kurnai initiation (*ibid*:318).

12. Informant: Fred Biggs; Wongaibon tribe. Beckett, 1957.

13. Berndt evidently included an area north-west of the Lachlan River in Wiradjuri territory; thus he classified Fred Biggs, born at Ivanhoe, as Wiradjuri; Beckett states, however, that Biggs identified himself and King, who were Berndt's main informants (Berndt 1947:327), as Wongaibon (personal communication). Having already followed Beckett in identifying Biggs as Wongaibon, I shall adhere to this viewpoint.

14. Or, possibly, its symbolic equivalent, sexual intercourse.

15. Róheim (1925:44) has earlier drawn attention to this description in a footnote in support of his interpretation, on other grounds, of the emu figure as woman and mother.

16. Informant: probably either Fred Biggs or Jack King; Wongaibon tribe (see note 13 above). Berndt 1947:77. This myth is quoted verbatim.

17. Confirming the connection between Kurikuta and emu, Beckett reports the tradition that if someone griddled emu in the bush instead of bringing it back to camp to be roasted, Kurikuta would come down in a thunder cloud to punish him (personal communication). In Biggs' words, 'She opens up the world and comes like a scythe to eat you.' (Beckett, 1957).

18. If we accept Berndt's spelling as the better representation, then the above interpretation is borne out by the fact that *nguri* is the Wongaibon word for emu (Beckett, personal communication).

19. Daramulun in the Yuin tribes (including the Coast Murring) corresponds closely to Baiami among the Wiradjuri, Wongaibon, Bagundji and Kamilaroi. Howitt referred to both when he wrote: 'The attributes of these Supreme beings are those of an unbounded power, including, of course, the most potent magic, which is imparted by them to the wizards; the power of "doing anything and going anywhere" and of seeing all that is done by the tribesmen.' (Howitt 1885:321). While among the Wiradjuri, Daramulun was

a secondary figure, son of Baiami, among the coastal Yuin he was supreme (Howitt 1884:452fn., 453).

20. The actual relationship between the youth and the woman concerned is not specified in Berndt's paper (1947), but we can assume that it was not that of true mother and son.

21. Howitt referred to the practice of sister-exchange in a number of south-east Australian tribes. Of the tribes around the Darling and Murray rivers he specifically mentioned the Wiradjuri and Wollaroi (Ualarai) as having the practice. About the southern Wiradjuri, he stated: 'When a boy is old enough to marry, that is when his beard has grown again after the Burbung ceremony, and the consent of the kindred on both sides has been given, he fetches his promised wife, and usually her brother returns with him to his part of the tribe, and receives the sister in exchange. This exchange of sisters was called "Gun-gun-mur"' (Howitt (1904:210–1). Beveridge, writing of the Aborigines of the Lower Murray (Victoria) and Riverina district, went as far as to say that 'No man can get a wife unless he be the possessor of a sister or ward, whom he can give in exchange' (1889:22); and 'As wives are always obtained by exchange, the relationship of brother-in-law and sister-in-law is usually double' (1889:24). Discussing Maljangaba marriage customs, Beckett has stated: 'Marriage was first explained to me in the familiar form of an exchange of sisters. In the betrothal ceremony two pairs of brothers and sisters sat side by side, facing their respective partners. The brother and sister involved in this transaction, who might be actual or close kin, called one another budinja. The dissolution of one marriage resulted in the dissolution of the other . . .' Beckett argued that actual sister exchange was probably infrequent in Australia because of the considerable age difference between spouses, but adds that 'Dutton [the informant] asserted that among the Maljangaba age differences were not very great'. (Beckett 1967:458). It seems that at least the model, and probably the practice, of sister-exchange was fairly common in the tribes around the Darling and Murray rivers.

22. Beckett (1967:457) has stated that matriclans of opposite moieties were linked by the mutual provision of guardians. Thus linked were Snake and Goanna, Kangaroo and Emu, Dog and Snake clans. It would be interesting to know whether these same links applied to intermarriage. There is some suggestion of this in Howitt's (1904:194) statement that, among the 'Itchumundi' (which included the Maljangaba), 'Mukwara eaglehawk married Kilpara bone-fish; Mukwara kangaroo married Kilpara emu; Mukwara dog married Kilpara padi-melon.' Only the middle pair corresponds exactly, so that the evidence for a link between the guardian-novice relationship in initiation, and marriage, is inconclusive. A further hint of a possible connection emerges from two separate statements by Beckett: that a youth's guardian in initiation was a real or classificatory cross-cousin, and that cross-cousins who were not too closely related could become brothers-in-law (1967:460).

23. Mathews apparently intended to include the Wongaibon in the 'Wiradthuri tribes', for he wrote that the speakers of the Wailwan, Wongaibon and Wiradjuri 'dialects' all belonged to the 'Wiradthuri community' (1896:312) whose initiation ceremonies are the subject of his paper (ibid:295).

24. All the other tribes mentioned above had matrimoieties whose names, except in the last two cases, were closely related to the Mukwara/Kilpara names of the Maraura and Bagundji tribes on the Darling River. For the Maljangaba, the names are recorded as Magungera/Dilungera by Beckett (1967:45), while Howitt (1904:98) rendered as Mukwara/Kilpara the moiety names of the 'Itchumundie' group of tribes located north-west of the Darling and west of the Paroo River in New South Wales, which includes the Maljangaba. The Mukwara/Kilpara moiety names also extended from the Darling-Murray rivers junction eastward as far as the Loddon River (Howitt 1904:195).

The Madimadi (Balranald district) had Magwara/Gilbara (Hercus 1970:43). Between the Darling and Lachlan rivers, the Wongaibon sections were grouped into Kilpungara and Makangara moieties (Radcliffe-Brown 1923:425). The Ngarigo and Wolgal, separated from the above groups by the Bangerang, had Merung/Yukembruk and Malian/Umbe, both meaning Eagle/Crow, as their matrimoiety names (Howitt 1904:101–2).

References

BECKETT, J.R. 1957 Aboriginal myths from western New South Wales. Unpublished ms.
———— 1959 Further notes on the social organization of the Wongaibon of western New South Wales. *Oceania*, 29(3):200–207.
———— 1967 Marriage, circumcision and avoidance among the Maljangaba of north-west New South Wales. *Mankind*, 6(10):456–64.
BERNDT, R.M. 1947 Wuradjeri magic and 'clever men'. *Oceania*, 17(4):327–65; 18(1):60–86.
BEVERIDGE, P. 1889 *The Aborigines of Victoria and Riverina*. Melbourne, Hutchinson.
CAYLEY, N.W. 1958 *What bird is that?: a guide to the birds of Australia . . .* rev. and enlarged by A.H. Chisholm, K.A. Hindwood and A.R. McGill. 2nd ed., Sydney, Angus and Robertson.
ELKIN, A.P. 1964 *The Australian Aborigines: how to understand them.* 4th ed., Sydney, Angus and Robertson.
HASSELL, E. 1934 Myths and folktales of the Wheelman tribe of south-western Australia: selected and revised by D.S. Davidson. *Folk-lore*, 45(3):232–48; 45(4):317–41.
HERCUS, L.A. 1970 A note on Madimadi. *Victorian Naturalist*, 87(2):43–47.
———— 1971 Eaglehawk and crow: a Madimadi version. *Mankind*, 8(2):137–40.
HOWITT, A.W. 1884 On some Australian ceremonies of initiation. In *Royal Anthropological Institute, Journal*, 13(4):432–59.
———— 1885 The Jeraeil, or initiation ceremonies of the Kurnai tribe. In *Royal Anthropological Institute, Journal*, 14:301–25.
———— 1904 *The native tribes of south-east Australia.* London, Macmillan.
LÉVI-STRAUSS, C. 1962 *Totemism.* London, Merlin Press.
———— 1963 *Structural anthropology.* London, Allen Lane.
———— 1970 *The raw and the cooked.* London, Jonathan Cape.
MATHEW, J. 1899 *Eaglehawk and crow; a study of the Australian Aborigines including an inquiry into their origin and a survey of Australian languages.* Melbourne, Melville, Mullen & Slade.
MATHEWS, R.H. 1895 The Bora, or initiation ceremonies of the Kamilaroi tribe. In *Royal Anthropological Institute, Journal*, 24:411–27.
———— 1896–97 The Burbung of the Wiradthuri tribes. In *Royal Anthropological Institute, Journal*, 25:295–318; 26:272–85.
———— 1904 Ethnological notes on the Aboriginal tribes of New South Wales and Victoria. In *Royal Society of New South Wales, Journal and proceedings*, 38:203–381.
MINCHAM, H. 1964 *The story of the Flinders Ranges.* Adelaide, Rigby.
PARKER, LANGLOH K. 1905 *The Euahlayi tribe: a study of Aboriginal life in Australia.* London, Constable.
———— 1953 *Australian legendary tales;* selected and edited by H. Drake-Brockman. Sydney, Angus and Robertson.
RADCLIFFE-BROWN, A.R. 1923 Notes on the social organization of Australian tribes. Part II. The Wongaibon tribe. In *Royal Anthropological Institute, Journal*, 53:424–47.
———— 1958 The comparative method in social anthropology. In his *Method in social anthropology: selected essays*, pp. 108–29. Chicago, University of Chicago Press.

ROBINSON, R. 1966 *Aboriginal myths and legends.* Melbourne, Sun Books.

RÓHEIM, G. 1925 *Australian totemism: a psycho-analytic study in anthropology.* London, Allen & Unwin.

ROWLEY, I. 1970 The genus *Corvus* (Aves: Corvidae) in Australia. *CSIRO Wildlife Research,* 15:27–71.

SMYTH, R.B. 1878 *The Aborigines of Victoria: with notes relating to the habits of the natives of other parts of Australia and Tasmania, compiled from various sources for the government of Victoria,* v.1. Melbourne, Government Printer.

TINDALE, N.B. 1939 Eagle and crow myths of the Maraura tribe, lower Darling River, New South Wales. In *South Australian Museum, Records,* 6(3):243–61.

Thundering Gecko and Emu:
Mythological Structuring of Nunggubuyu Patrimoieties

A.C. van der Leeden

*I have taken the Lizard, an Animal said to be Endow'd by nature
with an instinctive Love of Mankind, as my Device, & have Caus'd
it to be Engrav'd as my Seal, as a Perpetual Remembrance that
a man is never so well Employ'd, as when he is laboring for the
advantage of the Public; without the Expectation, the Hope or
Even a wish to derive advantage of any Kind from the Result of
his exertions.*

Joseph Banks in Newfoundland and Labrador, 1766; His Diary,
Manuscripts and Collections (Banks 1971:58).

Introduction

In a recent publication, Guiart (1972:113–4) says: 'myth, then, contains
at the very least two messages: the one the structuralist deciphers, studying
his text as a vehicle of the culture as a whole, and the one the narrator
impresses on it, which is the summary of his social position, affirming a
disappointed ambition or one on the point of success, protesting the wrong
done him'.

I would add that the two 'messages' are not necessarily opposed to each
other, and that the interplay between these levels becomes especially apparent when a fair knowledge is available of the factors which in particular
instances lead up to story-telling and mythological argumentation. This
applies particularly to myths meant to explain sociological phenomena, in
situations impelling the narrators to refer purposefully to their own and/or
their opponents' social positions. In such circumstances, mythological
research may and should start with an analysis of the practical functions of
the myths. The resulting conclusions would thus not only derive from the
participants' reflections of 'an anonymous collectivity which determines his
every act', but would also be supported by the 'specific named individuals',
who carry out Guiart's second 'message' (p.123). From this viewpoint,
structuralistic analysis may contribute substantially to an elucidation of
the interplay between the unconscious and conscious levels of mythological
thought, or of the dynamics of mythological transformation. Members of
a society may under circumstances necessitating particular intellectual
alertness become quite conscious of the possibilities of mythological symbolism for defending or improving individually or collectively maintained
positions.

46

Although far from complete, parts of my mythological and sociological material from the Nunggubuyu in south-eastern Arnhem Land may be used to illustrate my point.[1] This is true of the six stories selected here for examination. They refer explicitly to the patrilineal moieties, a dominant feature of Nunggubuyu social organisation. Furthermore, all except the first served either as criticism or to enlarge upon earlier stories in the series. I myself unintentionally caused the development of these mythological discussions and sequences of story-telling in so far as my initial questions about the structuring of the moieties unexpectedly induced the man, Gumi, to narrate a myth (story A below). When I played it back for other Nunggubuyu, some of them disagreed with Gumi's interpretation or considered that he had forgotten important details. They wished to explain the mythological theme further by adding other stories to the one Gumi had told.

Furthermore, since the stories deal with dual oppositions as a basic feature of Nunggubuyu culture and social organisation, it is no exaggeration to say that Nunggubuyu views concerning these oppositions strongly reflect the binary principles which have been the subject of Dutch and French research into mythology. With regard to the former, although a demonstration of the typically local features of mythology in south-eastern Arnhem Land is the main object of this essay, my analysis will show the particular influences of the views of J.P.B. de Josselin de Jong (1929), Locher (1932) and Ouwehand (1964) on the ambivalence of mythological heroes and tricksters.[2] With regard to Lévi-Strauss, I shall refer particularly to his 'Les organisations dualistes existent-elles?' (1956), an inspiring discussion of concentric and diametric forms of dualism relevant to Nunggubuyu mythology and ceremonies.

However, I should from the outset emphasise that other theoretical approaches (psychological or otherwise) would not necessarily contradict the structuralistic approach adopted here. Apart from a consideration of Hiatt's (1971) view of secret pseudo-procreation rites in the conclusion, I shall in fact refer several times to Stanner's 'operational-transactional' views (1959–63) as they bear directly upon phenomena to be discussed. The connections the Nunggubuyu themselves see between their myths, and the feedback process I referred to above, are consistent with Stanner's approach. Moreover, like Stanner, I do not see myths from an exclusively social-structural viewpoint, but rather as 'efforts at self-understanding', the allegoric themes having implications which go beyond purely sociological considerations (p.99). That the Nunggubuyu regard their myths as symbolising the structuring of the moieties does not contradict this, for the moiety organisation evidently is part of a much more general cultural process.

Having made these theoretical points, I shall now summarise those features of the Nunggubuyu social structure that are relevant for an understanding of my six myths.[3] Unlike most of their neighbours, the Nunggubuyu do not recognise such kinship categories as sections or subsections.[4] They have patrilineal clans, divided between patrilineal moieties, Mandayung and Mandaridja, hereafter for practical reasons to be called Dua and Yiridja,

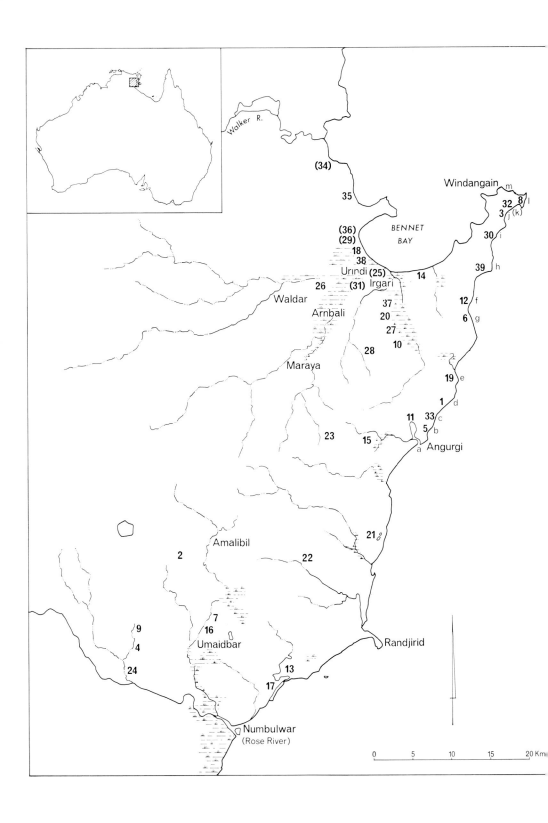

Walker R.

(34)

35

Windangain m
32 8 l
3 j (k)
30 i

BENNET
BAY

(36)
(29)
18
38
Urindi (25)
26 (31) Irgari
Waldar
Arnbali
37
20
27
28 10

14

39 h

12 f
6 g

Maraya

19 e

1 d

11 33 c
5 b
23 15 a Angurgi

21

Amalibil
2
22

7
9 16
4 Umaidbar
24
13
17

Randjirid

0   5   10   15   20 Km

Numbulwar
(Rose River)

their respective and better known equivalents elsewhere in Arnhem Land. In addition to the two-fold division, a four-fold subdivision (of 'companies', as Nunggubuyu say in English) is also operative in ritual. The clans discussed in this paper are enumerated in Figure 1 with their totemic affiliations and are arranged according to their positions in the four ritual subdivisions or sub-moieties. To simplify the highly complex territorial clan names, I shall use mainly abbreviations (*cf.* italicised word parts in Figure 1). The sub-moieties will be referred to as M_aI, M_bI, M_aII and M_bII respectively.[5]

The four-fold ritual subdivision reflects different orientations towards Gunabibi, a cult 'owned' by Dua and 'managed' by Yiridja, and Ru:l,[6] a cult ascribed principally to Yiridja and 'managed' by Dua.[7] The Gunabibi is of course widespread in Arnhem Land. Ru:l is a local variant of Maraian. Elkin (1964:258) describes it as 'the basic cult of Arnhem Land', the myth of which describes 'the journeyings of cult-heroes, often in animal form, in particular of a great python, the rainbow serpent or its representative'. His information is important for the analysis of the present mythological theme. It brings to mind that Water Python is the principal totem of the Irga clan in Ru:l of M_aII (*cf.* Figure 1).

A distinction has to be made between two different Gunabibi traditions, that is, Murungun and Mambali, which are associated with the two Dua sub-moieties, and two other, as far as I know unnamed, Ru:l traditions of the Yiridja sub-moieties[8]. Murungun relates the journey of the mythological Muru crowd (*cf.* Figure 1: M_aI) from Lulmara (somewhere near Jalma Bay; northern part of Blue Mud Bay) southwards through coastal countries such as Windangain and Guluruid (see map) to the Roper River. The last part of this myth describes how mosquitos attacked the Muru people at Wargudjadja, northern bank of the Roper River. Only two men

---

Sketch map of the region of the Nunggubuyu between Walker River and Rose River, south-eastern Arnhem Land. It is based upon the sketch map in Hughes (1971-ii-iii). The locations are mostly approximate, particularly when put in parentheses. The numbers refer to the following territories:

1 Ailalag	14 Yurang	27 Ugui
2 Aindur	15 Lhalainbaid	28 Uldji
3 Alhargang	16 Lharlamadji	29 Ulmngul
4 Alil	17 Mabanadjaruid	30 Ului
5 Alhuara	18 Magandaruid	31 Ululami
6 Amadhardin	19 Malgayangu	32 Undungundarngina
7 Amayadiruid	20 Manimurua or Mainmurua	33 Urulhulu
8 Amardumbi	21 Miul	34 Walgawalga
9 Anarbarin	22 Murndabala	35 Warain
10 Arayabia	23 Nimalhurwaruid	36 Wargala
11 Arbul	24 Niwangala	37 Warnbarn
12 Darari	25 Udjudjalngan	38 Warndawarnda
13 Guluruid	26 Ugugandar	39 Wilili

FIGURE 1

Nunggubuyu clans with some of their totemic implications,
and arranged according to the sub-moiety system[10]

Moiety of Mandajung (Dua)

Sub-moieties	Clans*	Some important totemic implications
M_aI	*Winda*ngain, *Malga*jangu, *Gulu*ruid *Winda*ngain	*a* Murungun tradition of Gunabibi: *Muru*murungun crowd, bringers of Gunabibi from Lulmara southwards. *b* Little Boy. Exo-connection with M_bI and *Angu*rgi (M_bII) through Thundering Gecko and Emu theme. *c* Dugong.
M_bI	*Ama*libil *Arnba*li	*a* Mambali tradition of Gunabibi: Scrub Python, with Rainbow Serpent implications. Endo-connection with *Arnba*li. *b* Thundering Gecko (Yamindji). Endo-connection with *Arnba*li. Exo-connection with *Winda*ngain (M_aI) and *Angu*rgi (M_bII) through Thundering Gecko and Emu theme. *c* Ru:l cult of Arnbali: with some highly esoteric totems implying a strong exo-connection with the Ru:l cult of *Uri*ndi-*Irga*ri (M_aII). *d* Common Brown Snake. Rainbow Serpent implications, exo-connecting *Arnba*li through *Irga*ri with the Ru:l cult of M_aII. *e* Stingray (Rabariala). Endo-connection with identical clans at Bickerton Island and Groote Eylandt. *f* Brolga or Crane (Gudargu). Endo-connection with Mara clans, the Roper River area.

FIGURE 1— *continued*

Moiety of Mandaridja (Yiridja)

Sub-moieties	Clans*	Some important totemic implications
M$_a$II	*Uri*ndi, *Irga*ri	*a* Ru:l cult of *Uri*ndi-*Irga*ri: Old Man, bringer of a number of secret and profane tokens (bandicoot amongst them) from Groote Eylandt westwards. Bandicoot is important for endo-connection with *Walda*r. *b* Goanna. Endo-connection with Mara clans, the Roper River area, and with the Jabadurua cult. *c* Water Python from *Irga*ri. High Rainbow Serpent, important for Ru:l cult. Exo-connection with *Arnba*li (M$_b$I) through Ru:l cult. *d* Fire. Endo-connection with *Walda*r through Ru:l cult. *e* Water — as *c*.
	*Walda*r	*f* Sugar Bag (stinging Bee). Endo-connection with *Uri*ndi-*Irga*ri through Ru:l cult. *g* Dog. *h* Kangaroo (Ardjambal).
M$_b$II	*Angur*gi, *Umai*dbar	*a* Ru:l cult of *Umai*dbar. Tradition different from that of *Uri*ndi-*Irga*ri. Old Man started from Larlamadji, near *Umai*dbar, and went westwards, bringing secret tokens along with him. *b* Emu. Endo-connection with Mara clans, the Roper River area. Exo-connection with *Winda*ngain (M$_a$I) and M$_b$I through Thundering Gecko and Emu theme. *c* Groper Fish. Endo-connection with Mara clans, the Roper River area. *d* Scaly Mackerel (Walgara). *Umai*dbar only.
	*Numbu*lwar (Rose River)	*a* Salmon. *Numbu*lwar only. *b* Leatherskin, (Walbalg).

* Clan references on a territorial basis.
Italicised parts indicate abbreviations to be used further in test.
Identifications Hughes, 1971.

FIGURE 2

Position of the Arnba clan with regard to the ritual sub-moiety system

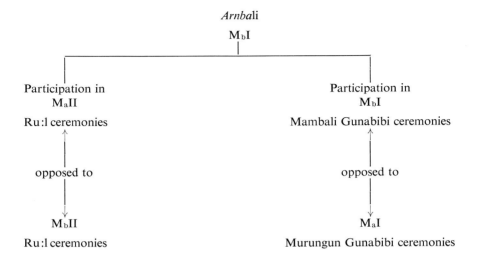

*Arnba*li

M$_b$I

Participation in	Participation in
M$_a$II	M$_b$I
Ru:l ceremonies	Mambali Gunabibi ceremonies
opposed to	opposed to
M$_b$II	M$_a$I
Ru:l ceremonies	Murungun Gunabibi ceremonies

FIGURE 3

Concentric opposition between inland and coast

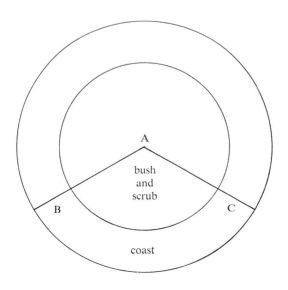

A
bush
and
scrub

B   C

coast

A: Nimalhurwaruid   B: *Angu*rgi   C: *Winda*ngain

FIGURE 4

Triadic effect of combining the concentric and diametric oppositions

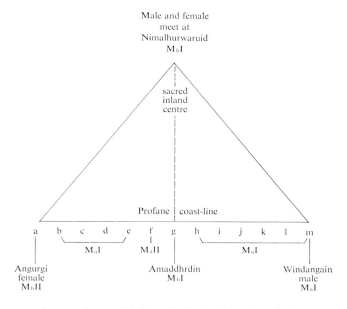

Letters and numerals indicate distribution of the clan territories
according to sub-moiety division along the coast.

FIGURE 5

Diagram of diminishing oppositions between inland and coast

Inland
    Thundering Gecko

— sacred centre
    Nimalhurwaruid;

concentric rope through
hole connection with   — shooting *gooseberries*
coast   with *spear*

                              lowered through   *The*
                              the *ground* like a *stone*   *Little*
                              at the end of a *rope*   *Boy*

— profane centre   — being caught like
    Arbul-Angurgi;   a *tadpole*

— diametric downstream —
    upstream connection
    with inland
    Emu
Coast

	1	2	3
A	Emu and Yamindji camp at Nimalhurwaruid. They sleep together. Emu goes away daily, at sunrise. Comes back at sunset.	Emu collects tadpoles for children, downstream, with basket.	Little Boy follows behind parents. Plays, saunters, runs. Calls out for them to locate them. Shoots with spears at gooseberries which fall down. Opens up and eats these. Circles bushes.
B		**1.** As A/2. Motherly engagement emphasised.	
C			**1.** As A/3. **4.** Little Boy tricks Old Woman and holds on to her pandanus drag. Drawn upstream behind the drag.
D	**1.** *Inversion:* Emu and Brolga camp at inland Lhalainbaid. Grinds pandanus roots together. Each sunrise Brolga leaves, to come back at sunset. **5.** Emu and Brolga grind and eat pandanus roots together.		**3.** Brolga collects pandanus roots daily at Warndawarnda, Ulmungul, Jurang, Malgajangu. All (sub)coastal territories. Three first ones in Blue Mud Bay direction from Windangain. Last one Rose River direction. Two last ones: Windangain clan. Brolga cuts roots. Roasts these in hot ashes (beside fire). **6.** Looking for good roots, busy Brolga moves from one place to another. **8.** Brolga busy looking for roots, cuts these.

8	9	10
	8. Spirit gets up after Jamindji's blow. Follows him.	**13.** Yamindji remains underwater at Anarbarin Bill. Keeps an eye on Spirit from this position. She has finally given up chasing Yamindji in the water. Goes up at sand bank, tired. Continues looking for him.
	9. Spirit throws spear with spear-thrower to hit Yamindji. Misses.	
	10. Spirit chases Yamindji, all the way throwing spears. Hides and rolls under grass. Passes Alil.	
	12. Spirit chases Yamindji down to the water, discovering his hiding place. Drags in vain with net, only to catch some dying fish. Discovers his grass trick and northward movement. Catches up with prints again. Continues chase.	
	13. Spirit tries to follow Yamindji in Anarbarin Bill, but gives up because of deep water. Almost drowns. Has to get out.	
12. Spirit discovers Woman's trick of travesty by smelling at fly with her sweat.	**13.** Spirit follows Woman. Tracks her by smelling the camp. Runs. Swims. Goes up river-bank. Walks. Goes inside Woman's paperbark cover.	**10.** (Suggestion that Woman commands dog to go and bite Spirit.)
		14. Waking her up dance circumcision ceremony Woman's sister discovers Spirit. Goes back to get people to kill Spirit with spears. They cut Spirit open to eat him. Find a little salty flesh left of Spirit only.

survived to cross the Roper River via Kangaroo Island (Yarara). They are said to have taken Gunabibi southwards through Djingili country as far as Daly Waters. A link may well exist here with the Gadjari cult of the Walbiri (Meggitt 1966).[9]

In addition to the notion of a big crowd of people, the Murungun tradition includes an Old Woman initiation motif[10] suggesting a structural connection with the Wawalag-Yulunggul Python beliefs in north-eastern Arnhem Land (Warner 1964:225–326; R.M. Berndt 1951), and with the Murinbata myths about Mutjingga, Rainbow Serpent and Black Snake-Woman (Stanner 1959–63).

Mambali, the other and more secret Gunabibi tradition, relates the journey of a male culture bearer from Borroloola and Walhalha westwards along the Roper River (and consequently crossing the Murungun route somewhere) and on to Katherine. Mambali is therefore not properly Nunggubuyu. In Nunggubuyu country, it is represented by the Ama clan (M_bI; see map and Figure 1), but most other Mambali clans belong to the Mara and Warndarang south of the Rose River.[11] However, Mambali does play an essential part in Nunggubuyu performances of Gunabibi.

The distinctive ritual functions of the two Yiridja sub-moieties are less precisely established. Ru:l of the Uri-Irga clan (M_aII) is traced back to Amagulhu (Dalhagurba according to other versions), south-eastern Groote Eylandt, from where a male culture bearer started on his westward journey to the continent. He took several esoteric and profane tokens with him to Bickerton Island, Irgari and Urindi (see map), and further along the Waldar or Harris Creek as far inland as Rarawa, a Ridharngu territory covering the upper reaches of Walker River and Harris Creek.

The important thing to remember also, is that elements such as Fire and Water are important totems of the Ru:l clans of this northern Yiridja M_aII sub-moiety. This does not apply to the Angu-Umai and Numbu clans of M_bII (see Figure 1). Their claim to Ru:l is based upon a journey of a culture bearer from Lharlamadji, near Umaidbar (see map), in a north-western direction to Badjungara, another Ridharngu territory.

It is impossible to understand the mythological and ritual structuring of the Dua and Yiridja moieties without taking the sub-moieties into account. In many ways they resemble the Mara semi-moieties (Radcliffe-Brown 1930–31b:41). For example, the Dua couple amongst the Mara also bear the names of Murungun and Mambali, though I do not recall that the Mara names Burdal and Guyal (or Purdal and Kuial) were ever used for the corresponding Nunggubuyu Yiridja sub-moieties. For this and other reasons, I hesitate to identify the Nunggubuyu four-fold subdivision as a fully-fledged semi-moiety class system, at least if one may with Maddock (1972:84–94) use the concept of a class system in this connection. More particularly, the Nunggubuyu marriage regulations are primarily based upon interpersonal kinship ties, marriage choices never being expressed in terms of relations between particular sub-moieties. I mention this here to explain why I prefer to use sub-moiety symbols different from the letters (P, Q, R and S) which have since Radcliffe-Brown's days been conventional semi-moiety symbols.

To understand the myths, it is necessary also to take into account the special position of the Arnba clan (M_bI) to both moieties. Figure 2 shows that it is the only Dua clan which combines participation in a Gunabibi tradition, that is Mambali of M_bI, with a right to Ru:l of M_aII. In other words, while sociologically Dua, the Arnba clan plays a double role: *managing* (as indeed expected from Dua) one part of Ru:l, and *owning* (as if it were Yiridja) another part. I hope to be able to show that this double role, as summarised in Figure 2, is reflected in the mythological Thundering Gecko and Emu theme. Since it implies Ru:l to be shared, so to say, by both moieties, some connection may exist with the structurally comparable Narra ceremonies in north-eastern Arnhem Land. Both Warner (1964: 325–60) and R.M. Berndt (1952) have pointed to the existence of Dua Narra *and* Yiridja Narra ceremonies, which both belong to the Djunkgao (or Djanggawul) complex.

As to the narrators, the six stories given here were told by five Nunggubuyu men. I recorded the myths in Nunggubuyu[12] in the Rose River area during the second half of 1964, and analysed them linguistically as well as anthropologically with two permanent assistants, the narrators and the occasional listeners who always were present. Story A was told by Gumi (Angu clan, M_bII), B by Gara (Arnba clan, M_bI), C and D by Mabu (Winda clan, M_aI), E by Manga (Warndarang clan of Ujagiba, M_bI) and F by Marbu (Waldar clan, M_aII).

A pronounced difference in marriage orientation between some of the narrators' clans seems also to be relevant to the mythological interpretations. Although every clan maintains marriage relations with all other mentioned clans in the opposite moiety, more or less regular alliances are noticeable only between the northern Uri-Irga and Waldar Yiridja clans on the one hand, and the northern Winda-Malga-Gulu Dua clans on the other. The preference of most southern clans to marry with Mara, Ridharngu or Ngarndi people outside the Nunggubuyu area is consistent with the importance of their totemic relations with these population groups. Clans like Ama and Numbu have indeed very few members surviving at Rose River. Their territorial and totemic affairs are 'minded', as the Aboriginals say, by dominant local clans of the same ritual sub-moiety. Thus, the Angu clan takes an interest in matters concerning the Umai and Numbu clans, whereas Manga acted as narrator of story E of the Ama clan, as his Warndarang clan of Ujagiba 'minds' Ama clan business at the Rose River Mission Station.

The Angu clan is the only southern Yiridja clan with a noticeable interest in marriages with northern Dua clans, principally clans of Bickerton Island and Groote Eylandt which are considered as identical to the Arnba clan. Gumi, narrator of story A, is a noticeable exception to this, for he married Mabu's sister (hence, from the Winda clan), who is his real mother's brother's daughter. This is properly speaking a wrong marriage, for the Nunggubuyu prescribe or prefer either second cousin marriages (close or distant) of the Aranda type or marriages with distant patrilateral cross cousins. Gumi's marriage is a typical example of so-called 'wrong' marriages resulting from a feed-back process because of a former series of aberrant marriages. In Gumi's case, 'wrong' marriages of some of Mabu's older 'brothers', of the Winda clan, introduced a pronounced change of marriage orientation amongst men of the Angu and of other Yiridja clans interested in marrying Winda clan girls.

A final introductory remark concerns the predominantly chronological order in which I shall analyse the six stories. Although perhaps not in all regards the most logical order (the first story being the most complicated one of the whole series), it does demonstrate the development of the mythological argument amongst my Nunggubuyu instructors since my original question to Gumi (see above). Most important of all, it brings out the 'relations of similarity' (Stanner 1959–63:132) seen by Nunggubuyu themselves between different components of the stories, which they definitely considered to be interrelated or even, in some regards, identical.

It is an additional advantage that the relatively differentiated picture of operations in Gumi's story is a good starting-point from which to analyse the transformational reductions found in the other stories. The operations are summarised in Figure 6 (see fold-out), which in spite of some manifest differences is very much a 'contraction and restatement of the sequences of incidents' in Stanner's fashion (p.100).

Story A

Gumi and I were alone when he told me his story during a discussion about the significant features of the moieties. Uninterrupted by the interjections that are so usual when a story is told in the camp, Gumi succeeded in narrating a very well-balanced story — one of the best I recorded.

The story relates a quarrel between Thundering Gecko (Yamindji) and Emu (Wa:in) about Little Boy. It is hardly necessary to introduce Emu as representing Australia's largest though flightless bird (*Dromaeus novaehollandiae*; Cayley 1959:7, Plate I), but Thundering Gecko presents a difficulty. The name Yamindji refers to a number of species and subspecies of more than one genus of the lizard family of *Geckonidae* (covered with granulated scales) according to Western zoological classification (Worrell 1970:19–30). I do not know exactly which of these the Nunggubuyu classify as Yamindji, but it refers anyhow to Gehyra species such as the House Gecko and Variegated Gecko (*Gehyra variagata* and *australis* respectively; *ibid*:24, Plate 14) and several *Diplodactylus* and *Phyllodactylus* species (pp.20–3,29, Plates 8–10,14). They live in rocky areas and in trees, and their squeaking sounds may offer some indication of their association in Nunggubuyu mythology with lightning and thunder, although this would be too simple an explanation of Gecko's qualities as an incarnation of Lightning and Thunder. Defining the concept of Thundering Gecko, which is as vague as the connected concept of Rainbow Serpent (*cf.* Maddock 1970a:444–6; 1972:120–6), is in fact one of the purposes of this mythological analysis.

Variants of the Thundering Gecko theme are to be found in the literature about Arnhem Land. Mountford (1969:66) refers to it and uses as illustration Ainsly Roberts' beautiful painting of Thundering Gecko. Capell (1960:33–6) mentions it, though only in the opening line of a short version of the Murungun myth of Gunabibi: 'It was Lizard who made the two moieties, Mandaridja and Mandajung' (p.35). Nevertheless, the connection between the Thundering Gecko theme and Gunabibi will prove to be highly significant and it is equally interesting to notice Capell's sigh that 'At the same time it has been a difficult story to record, and considerable discussion amongst the narrators took place before a text was arrived at' (p.33). It seems that Capell's assistants were also unable to agree on a correct version.

(1)   Once upon a time, Emu and Thundering Gecko lived together at the rocky place of Nimalhurwaruid [south of Arnbali and Maraya; no. 23 on the map].

(2)   Early each morning Emu would leave the camp to collect tadpoles down the river. On one of her collecting trips, she suddenly heard the noise of Little Boy who was following his mother and father. Emu, too, started to follow them.

(3)   Little Boy sauntered some distance behind his parents, trying to catch gooseberries with his spear. Each time he hit his target, he picked up and consumed the fallen gooseberries, in the mean time keeping in touch with his parents by calling: 'Mother! Father!'. 'They are not far away', he kept thinking as long as he could hear their reply from afar: 'Gu : : : : :'. This game went on for quite a while, Little Boy sauntering, running along as soon as he fell too far behind, and shooting, picking up and eating gooseberries.

(4)   In the mean time, Emu thought of a trick to carry Little Boy off. Bending her head behind the gooseberry bushes at which he threw his spear, she remained unnoticed as long as she kept to the opposite side. However, he could not help but catch her eye when he started to run around the bushes. He now started to call for his parents again:
    'Mo : : : : ther! Fa : : : : ther!'
    'Here I am', Emu said, 'I am your mother, so don't be afraid.'
    Speaking in this friendly and soothing way, Emu succeeded in persuading Little Boy to leave his parents and to follow her. Carrying him on her back, she hurried to her camp.

(5)   Thundering Gecko was startled by her arrival. He thought: 'What on earth is she carrying Little Boy around for?'
Reproaching her, he said, 'What a greedy thief you are. The boy is theirs!'
    Emu stammered in reply: 'I . . . . e . . . . I really found him quite by chance. He crossed my path while I was looking for food. He is so different from us.'
    'No, you stole the boy', Thundering Gecko said.
    After arguing in this way for a while, the two of them went to sleep.

(6)   Early next morning, Emu started out again with a basket to catch tadpoles for the children. Thundering Gecko now thought of a way to return Little Boy secretly to his family. He started to dig a hole and to make a rope of bark. He made the rope every

day a little longer. Every afternoon he listened for the peculiar footsteps, *arararararara*, indicating Emu's daily return:

'Here she comes', he thought; and he started camouflaging the hole with the rope in it, so she would not see it. Thundering Gecko would then lay down with his knees drawn up, pretending to be fully relaxed. After sunset the two of them would go to sleep as if nothing had happened at all, and each morning Emu would get up again for her daily wanderings.

After some time, Thundering Gecko checked whether the rope was long enough to carry Little Boy down through the hole and free him from Emu. To this end, he tied a stone to it and lowered it so as to make sure it touched the bottom of the hole. After pulling up the stone again, he instructed Little Boy to sit down and keep one end of the rope between his legs.

'Hold it tight', he told him, and Little Boy bent down to cling to the rope. Having tied the other end of the rope half-way-up a tree, Thundering Gecko started to lower Little Boy down through the hole. Upon reaching the bottom, the latter swung the rope so as to signal his arrival: *gagagagaga*.

'He must be there now. He reached the bottom!', Thundering Gecko thought. He hauled up the rope and put it in another hole so as to hide it from Emu.

(7)   After his liberation, Little Boy hurried home to Windangain. Starting from Angurgi River, he went along the coast and successively passed through Alhuara, Urulhulu, Airlalag, Malgajangu, Darari, Amadhardin, Wilili, Ului, Alhargang, Undungundarngina and Amardumbi. After Amardumbi he only had to cross the bush (of the interior part of Cape Barrow) to arrive at Windangain, where people saw him coming out from the scrub. His arrival caused great excitement:

'Thank Heavens! He is back again. Good for him that he managed to follow his parents back home', they said.

His mother cuddled him, and he was covered with grass[13] to hide him from Emu who would have found out about his disappearance by this time, and who would certainly be following his tracks.

(8)   And how surprised Emu was! She started looking around as soon as she had noticed Little Boy's absence.

'Where is Little Boy?', she asked Thundering Gecko.

'You did look after him, didn't you?' She searched the ground carefully for footprints to reconstruct the past events.

'Here are his footprints, and here . . ., and here . . . and here, and here they disappear', she observed. 'Good Heavens! He seems to have fastened the rope to the tree over here so as to lower Little Boy through the hole over there. I might sing out for the sky!'.[14]

(9)   After some argument Emu left the camp to trace Little Boy's whereabouts down the river. This journey brought her finally to Windangain, where she started another argument:

'You people must give him back to me', Emu urged. 'You must give Little Boy back to me. He is mine. I found him. I am in the right. Let him come out and give him back to me!'

Emu thus obliged the people of Windangain to return Little
Boy to her. She speedily carried him back upstream to
Nimalhurwaruid.

(10)   At Nimalhurwaruid, it was Thundering Gecko's turn again
to get angry and to start scolding when Emu entered the camp:
   'Good Heavens! A greedy thief, that's what you have been
again!'
   The two of them started a fight during which Thundering
Gecko burnt Emu all over her body. It took some time to break
up their fight.

A number of oppositions are at once apparent which bear directly on
the moiety system. Leaving aside Little Boy's admittedly important
characteristics for a moment, Emu is a big 'female'[15] terrestrial bird representing Yiridja sub-moiety M_bII (see Figure 1). In contrast to her, Thundering
Gecko, during the translation of this particular text consistently called
'Gecko' only, is a little 'male'[16] terrestrial and arboreal lizard, and a typical
Dua M_bI representative.

I shall presently have more to say about the complicated territorial
oppositions in this story, but may further point out here that Emu has

FIGURE 7

Intersection of the concentric and territorial oppositions

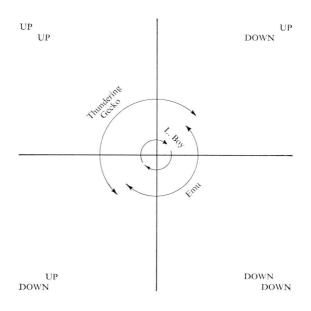

```
up   sky    — earth   down
up   inland — coast   down
```

61

properly a coastal background, for Arbul (no. 11 on the map) of the Angu clan of M_bII is her principal dreaming place. On the other hand, the attitude and manners of Thundering Gecko are determined fully by inland Nimalhurwaruid (no. 23 on the map), which is an Arnba clan territory, and therefore M_bI. This implies that in this story the moiety system is approached from the viewpoints of the two sub-moieties Yiridja M_bII and Dua M_bI only. In this connection, it is worthwhile mentioning that Gumi told me during the translation that Emu went as far south as Murndabala (no. 22 on the map) to collect her tadpoles. This is another sub-coastal territory of the Angu clan.

Another set of dualistic contrasts concerns Emu and Thundering Gecko's respective activities. Emu is a highly mobile mythological trickster. She roams about as a real bushranger, not only collecting tadpoles but also taking anything catching her imagination. On the other hand, Thundering Gecko is a typical culture hero, far less mobile than Emu and using Nimalhurwaruid as the basis of his coolly calculated operations, designed to remedy the wrong done to Little Boy and return him to the place where he belongs. Moreover, this happens in a vertical direction, through a hole in the ground, indicating a partial opposition to Emu's upstream-downstream journeys; partial, since these directions will presently be shown to be trans-formations (albeit highly significant ones) of the same general idea. Thundering Gecko makes himself a rope and uses a stone to carry out his secret scheme, whereas Emu uses a basket for catching tadpoles and does not play any trick to capture Little Boy other than approaching him surreptitiously.

Dualism is emphasised further in the sequence of events, and particularly in the truly dialectic alternation of the contrasting acts of Emu and Thundering Gecko with Little Boy's appearance both as principal cause and as pivotal *trait d'union* in between.

The dualistic moiety symbolism culminates in the fight between Emu and Thundering Gecko. However, their concern with Little Boy also conveys a strong initiation notion. Indubitably present are at least four (if not all) of the six main operations formulated by Stanner (1959–63:esp.4–16,47,53, 101–3) in his analysis of Murinbata initiation rites: 'setting apart' (of Little Boy under the care of Thundering Gecko); 'making into beasts' (he is bereft of his parents and put in a secret place); 'destruction and trans-formation' (esp. p. 53; he is swallowed, that is, goes through a hole in the ground, to act a grown-up man as soon as he reaches the 'bottom'); and 'return to life' (he is welcomed home, 'adorned' with grass, but partially excluded again; compare Drawing 3).

These points, together with possible sacrificial implications as pointed out by Stanner (pp.2–21), will be taken up in the discussion of the other stories. As is classically the case in the symbolism of ambivalent inter-moiety relations, the Nunggubuyu myth expresses not only antagonism and opposition but also collaboration and even marriage. Indeed, Emu and Thundering Gecko are fostered as symbolising the totality of human existence as characters who do not stand up against each other as truly independent representatives of radically opposed ideas and moral codes, but as closely interrelated and therefore inter-dependent persons. The story makes it clear that they live and sleep together and that Emu looks for food and feeds her children. Although a 'riteless myth' (*cf.* Stanner, 1959–63:81–106), Gumi's story deals nevertheless with some fundamental aspects of Nunggubuyu society and culture.

The attitudes of Emu and Thundering Gecko as 'adoptive parents' of Little Boy confirm this further. The emotional aspects of Nunggubuyu kinship relations are first of all apparent from the 'motherly' engagement of Emu who, after all, and in spite of her initial injustice to Little Boy, does not do him any real harm. To the contrary, her attitude towards him corresponds to the way in which a Nunggubuyu mother and, particularly from a ritual viewpoint, also mother's brother respond to their (sisters's) 'sons'[17] (*waraminimarayung*).

For these reasons, the meaning of Emu's persistence in a mother-role involves much more than a simple and seemingly capricious trick to get hold of Little Boy. Two important messages at least would seem to be conveyed. First, the myth offers additional confirmation of the relevance of the inherent notion of initiation. Secondly, since the myth deals explicitly with the structuring of the moieties, the mythological emphasis on this maternal feature may also be taken to indicate the obliqueness of the inter-moiety relations and the important functions which matrilineal filiation has in this regard. Thus, to mention a concrete example, it is true in a general way to say that the Dua moiety within the framework of the existing pattern of inter-moiety cooperation 'manages' or organises Ru:l performances of Yiridja. However, this 'management' is in actual practice dominated by patrilineal clan patterning[18] on the one hand, and by matrilineal filiation on the other hand, so as to imply (a) that a distinction is made between different parts of Ru:l as owned by different patrilineal Yiridja clans within different Yiridja sub-moieties (see Figure 1); (b) that, as among the Gidjingali (Hiatt 1965:54–67)[19], the 'management' of these different parts rests on persons who are Dua, but whose respective mothers are members by birth of these respective Yiridja clans; and (c) that members of a particular Dua clan may be seen to participate in the 'management' of Ru:l affairs of different Yiridja clans because of differences in clan membership between their mothers. As the Nunggubuyu themselves emphasise this 'mother' aspect of their great moiety ceremonies (Gunabibi being 'managed' by Yiridja in return), there can in my opinion be little doubt about the reflection of this phenomenon in Emu's maternal engagement.

On the other hand, the paternal aspects of Thundering Gecko's attitude towards Little Boy tallies with the patrilineal structure of clans and moieties. Thundering Gecko is Little Boy's 'adoptive father' (and can in fact be so as both of them are Dua) and instructs him to do things in very much the same fashion as a real Nunggubuyu father would instruct his (brothers') 'sons' (*naniwiayung*). From the viewpoint of the inherent notion of initiation it might be added that Thundering Gecko effects the 'swallowing' of Little Boy by letting him down through a hole in the ground, using to this end a rope which, like the hole, had been made by Thundering Gecko.

Thundering Gecko also acts as Good Protector or guardian of Little

Boy from Emu's 'over-mothering'. Considering the limitation of the present discussion to a mytho-ritual level on which phenomena undifferentiated in daily life may become significant symbols, Thundering Gecko's protectorship may be taken as an ambiguous feature as it is something one would, ritually speaking, expect only from a 'mother's brother'.

This ambiguity is in my opinion to be explained by the heterogeneity of the occurring oppositions, that is, by the interplay of continuous and discontinuous symbols. I borrow this terminology from Lévi-Strauss (1956: 119–200) who makes this distinction to indicate the subtlety of the dialectics of dualistic symbols and to demonstrate further that some discontinuous oppositions have an asymmetrical and triadic plan rather than the plainly symmetrical and diadic structure of fully continuous oppositions.[20]

I consider the interplay between symmetrical and asymmetrical oppositions as highly characteristic of the Nunggubuyu myths under discussion. As a first indication, besides such continuous oppositions as the male-female contrast between Emu and Thundering Gecko, the latter's ambiguous appearance refers to apparent discontinuous or asymmetrical traits as well in his relation to Emu. These concern the central theme of the relation between a malignant trickster and a benign hero.

Polarising these positions as 'radically bad' versus 'radically good' would be to turn a discontinuity into a continuity again and would detract both from Emu's maternal side and from Thundering Gecko's use of tricks and force to attain his ends. However, even without such an exaggeration it is clear that the myth puts Emu plainly on the egoistic and profane side as a Ruler of Bush and Scrub, in which nothing is safe from her; whereas Thundering Gecko dominates as Master of the Sacred Ground, ritually balancing Emu's evil moves and finally inflicting the burnt complexion upon her as a punishment for her persistence in egoism.

A second asymmetrical indication regards another apparently major theme, that is, the mediating functions of the main characters of the myth. To begin with, Emu and Thundering Gecko are engaged in establishing a connection between the inland and the coast. They do this in different ways, for different purposes and *seemingly* in different directions. Emu runs downstream in a semi-horizontal direction in search of food (and incidentally to steal Little Boy). For reasons of secrecy, Thundering Gecko chooses to dig a hole in the ground and to return Little Boy to the coastal area in a vertical direction (see Drawing No. 1).

I emphasise 'seemingly' to indicate that the different directions are actually transformations of each other, symbolising the one fundamental connection between inland and coast. The correctness of this conclusion appears not only from Little Boy's landing at coastal Angurgi (see map) upon reaching the bottom of the hole, but quite clearly also from the appearance of the word *lhiribalhaui*, meaning 'downstream' as well as (vertically) 'down(ward)', in the respective parts of the Nunggubuyu text of the myth. In contrast, the word *arwar* may mean either 'upstream' or (vertically) 'up(ward)'.

If the horizontal notion may therefore be assumed to symbolise the inland-coast connection from Emu's viewpoint, so to say, and the vertical

DRAWING 1

Thundering Gecko's rope trick in story A. Pen drawing by Magun,
January 1965.

DRAWING 2

Two versions of Thundering Gecko's rope trick, in stories A and B.

Pen drawing by Magun, January 1965.

Field notes in handwriting of fieldworker.

DRAWING 3
Little Boy covered and hidden from Emu upon his return to Windangain.
Stories A and B. Pen drawings by Magun, January 1965.
Field notes in handwriting of fieldworker.

one the same connection from Thundering Gecko's viewpoint, it becomes possible to bring out the asymmetrical implications of this connection in full relief by translating the notions in 'diametric' and 'concentric' terms (*cf*. Lévi-Strauss 1956:102–20) respectively. This is to suggest that Emu's view of the environment is static and diametric. Thundering Gecko would, on the other hand, conceive it as much more dynamically and concentrically structured (Figure 3), with Nimalhurwaruid (principally his domain) as a sacred centre surrounded by dangerous bush and scrub country (Emu's domain) and too sacred, in a manner of speaking, for ordinary life which dominates the outer circle. Here, all central forces are reconciled and socially elaborated. The outer circle is the societal counterpart of principles sacredly focussed in the centre. It would seem to be significant in this regard that Little Boy behaves undecidedly as long as he is out in the bush or stays at Nimalhurwaruid, but acts in the much more confident fashion of somebody initiated into a higher social status as soon as he comes out at Angurgi and runs straight 'along the outer circle' to Windangain (see map).

A number of other indications testify to the applicability of this concentric plan. First, in view of the connection between the myth and the principle of initiation, it is relevant to point to actual secret initiation ceremonies, for which the initiates are brought to an isolated sacred ground surrounded, like Nimalhurwaruid, by bush and scrub country. Here, the initiates receive ritual instruction, see the (male *and* female) ceremonial attributes, and are 'swallowed' to come back 'reborn' to the general camp with which the connection has all the time been ritually maintained.

Secondly, it does not seem to be coincidental that Little Boy's home journey takes him to 13 explicitly mentioned places (territories *a* to *m* on the map) of clans or sub-clans of all four sub-moieties (*cf*. Figure 1): that is, in the order of occurrence in the test, territory *a*, of the Angu clan in Yiridja $M_b II$; territories *b* to *e* of a Winda sub-clan in Dua $M_a I$; territory *f*, of the Uri-Irga clan in Yiridja $M_a II$; territory *g*, of a coastal Arnba sub-clan in Dua $M_b I$; and again territories *h* to *m* of the Winda clan in Dua $M_a I$.

The geographical order of these territories leaves out a few places on the sketch-map and moreover reverses the order of two (*f* and *g*) of the three middle territories (*f*, *g* and *h*) so as to turn territory *g* of the Arnba clan in central position between Angurgi (*a*) and Windangain (*m*). This may be due either to geographical misinformation or to a mistake in narration. Nevertheless, the central position of territory *g* of an Arnba sub-clan (*cf*. Figure 4) does emphasise the central significance of Nimalhurwaruid, another territory of the Arnba clan, as the sole inland or upstream centre and existential *raison d'être* where all essential socio-cultural processes are focussed in the relation between the male Thundering Gecko and the female trickster Emu.

The triadic representation (as in Lévi-Strauss 1956:118,120) of Figure 4 also exposes the transformational connection between (or identity of) Thundering Gecko and Emu's views, and leads up to two further conclusions.[21] Thus, the triadic plan of Figure 4 is fully in line with, and consequently confirms, the central position of the Arnba clan in the great moiety ceremonies as indicated in Figure 2. Then, all former asymmetrical indications lead to the conclusion that the mythological relation between Nimalhurwaruid and the coastal region, *and ipso facto the interpretation by this myth of the structuring of the moieties*, results from an interplay between a diametric and concentric view of all oppositions involved in the myth. This explains why Emu's diametric plans are crossed, so to say, at con-centric Nimalhurwaruid. In reverse, it explains why the concentric implica-tions are unfolded or 'stretched out' at a limited part of a relatively straight coast line only, with Angurgi as the predominantly female (Emu) end, and Windangain as the predominantly male (Little Boy) end of this profane and societal base-line. Ultimately, this mixture of diametric and concentric elements accounts for the pronounced ambiguity of the main characters of the myth.

To introduce further details of this ambiguity I should also point out that Gumi's story does not limit itself to a mere description of the intrinsic qualities of the basic mythological categories as such, but presents a dynamic view of their interrelations. Thundering Gecko digs a hole for making this connection. Emu is expressly said to travel 'down the river', a detail indi-cating incidentally how important the rivers are for the mythological con-nection between inland and coast.

These observations at the same time confirm the impossibility of defining the main mythological characters in terms of single categories. They combine traits of several categories. It is true that Thundering Gecko and Emu each dominates in a particular area and category, for example, the former at inland Nimalhurwaruid (literally, 'at the place where he made the rope') and the latter at Arbul near coastal Angurgi. But there are also indications that each regularly and deliberately steps across bounds and thus manifests basically opposite notions. Reference has already been made to the am-biguity of Thundering Gecko *vis-à-vis* Little Boy and to his role in connecting the inland with the coast. Their dual features might even be thought to follow from their innate qualities.[22] This is most apparent from the case of the hero of the story, Thundering Gecko, whose name connects 'upward' phenomena, especially 'lightning' and 'thunder' with this 'downward' little creature that nevertheless makes it an arboreal habit of *moving up and down* trees and rocks, that is, living half-way. Indeed physical traits may also in the case of the trickster Emu underline an innate ambiguity, for this big and often ridiculed bird cannot fly and is doomed, as story B explains, to a restless and wandering existence in bush and scrub.

Let us turn now to the third actor in our mythological cast, Little Boy. Without doubt he is the most polymorphous and sphinx-like character of them all. On the one hand, although representing the 'crowd' of Windangain (probably the Muru crowd of $M_a I$ Gunabibi; *cf.* Figure 1), throughout most of the myth he acts like a youngster dependent on his parents, Emu's caprices and on Thundering Gecko's intentions. He is engaged originally in a seemingly harmless and child-like game, which nevertheless attracts the attention of Emu. His initial passivity and obedience towards Emu, who tricks him, and Thundering Gecko, who instructs him and lets him be swallowed by the earth, again suggests the atmosphere of initiation. More-over, we may recall that Emu is out collecting tadpoles when she sees Little

Boy. As tadpoles are young and harmless creatures in *statu nascendi*, and as they are not in reality part of an Emu's diet, a transformational link between Little Boy and the tadpoles is accordingly probable.

On the other hand, the polymorphous nature of tadpoles, as well as the dialectics of the evoked initiation procedures, bring out the other side of Little Boy's dualistic nature. Just as tadpoles turn into real frogs, and Nunggubuyu initiates return to normal life in a higher social position, so Little Boy shakes off his passivity to act decisively when he leaves the hole and rope behind at Angurgi. The temporary and partial isolation to which he is subjected upon his home-coming does not detract much from this change in his personality, for it is a normal way of finishing initiation ceremonies.

Although dependent upon, and therefore intimately associated with, Emu and Thundering Gecko, Little Boy is superior to them in so far as he alone moves both along the horizontal (upstream-downstream) and vertical (through the earth) axes of the inland-coast opposition. He enters the inland region 'diametrically' on Emu's back to leave it again via Thundering Gecko's concentric conception.

Combining his presence and duality with his significance both as the focus of interest of the two other personalities and as the immediate cause of their final separation (and thus of the ultimate disjunctive structuring of the moieties), Little Boy is the true product of all forces unleashed by Emu and Thundering Gecko. His central position with regard to both of them has been summarised in Figure 5, a Lévi-Straussian diagram of diminishing oppositions and increasing resolution (1958:248).

The following two conclusions may be drawn from this discussion. To begin with, the vagueness of Little Boy's appearance does not at all contradict the central position ascribed to him but may indeed be considered as a general characteristic of relatively neutral mythological beings who stand in the centre of contrasting forces and embody their combined qualities. Further, Little Boy's significance as a mythological being goes far beyond his position as a descendant of a Windangain couple. He shares the characteristics of those impersonal and highly dualistic beings who so often form a triad with a hero and trickster as concomitant characters (J.P.B. de Josselin de Jong, 1929). Also from this viewpoint, it is not surprising to find him engaged in and subjected to a series of initiation-like activities of central interest.

The mythological theme of culture hero, trickster and supreme being is known to occur in many transformations, with varying accents on the different figures, and not uncommonly with one or two of them omitted or combined, as will appear also from the stories presently to be dealt with. The elaborateness and consistency with which Gumi put all three types of characters on the stage make his story a valuable starting-point for discussing these transformations.

Story B

Gara, the narrator of story B, is a member of the senior generation of the Arnba clan. He is a man of importance and one of the highly gifted and inventive singers for whom his clan is rightly famous. Besides song items about Crane or Brolga (Gudargu; *cf.* story D), items about Thunder are amongst the song items which have made songs of the Arnba clan very popular at Rose River.

Gara's story is very like Gumi's but contains a number of variations confirming the influence of territorial and clan affiliation on views of the moiety organisation. It therefore merits separate consideration. Also, Gara told his story under quite different circumstances while he, other Nunggubuyu, and I, were visiting his totemic homeland, Arnbali Creek (see map). Mabu, narrator of stories C and D, repeatedly interrupted Gara, particularly during his description of Little Boy's homeward journey. Mabu is a member of the Winda clan and takes the view that this journey occurred on the other side of Windangain, i.e. along the coast-line of Bennet Bay. Inconsistencies in Gara's version, and the absence of a systematic enumeration of the territories through which Little Boy passed along the coast before reaching Windangain, may be partly the result of Mabu's unsettling interruptions. Parts of the text where the narrator argued with Mabu about the correctness of his interpretation are almost unintelligible.

Another difference is that Gara was addressing a larger audience, and this induced him to elaborate the comical elements. Although Gumi, by contrast, told his version rather prosaically, we may note that the myth is supposed to be a 'funny story'.

In view of the many identical passages, particularly in the beginning of the story, it will be sufficient to take up Gara's story where he starts to relate Thundering Gecko's plan to lower Little Boy with a rope. The preceding episode about Emu's trick of hiding behind gooseberry bushes is described in much less detail than by Gumi who is after all a member of the Emu clan. Gara concentrated upon the role of Thundering Gecko, which is readily explained by his close totemic association with people from the proper Gecko clan as fellow-member of the Dua sub-moiety M_bI (*cf.* Figure 1).

Here, the successive operations do not start with the number 1, but with 4, which corresponds (see Figure 6) with operation 6 of Story A.

> (4)   Next morning Thundering Gecko was determined to carry out his plan: 'Today I shall send down Little Boy', he thought.
>
> He worked on the rope a little longer, and then lowered it through the hole, with Little Boy at the end of it, to make sure that his plan would work. At first, the rope proved to be too short, and Thundering Gecko had to pull up Little Boy, as the latter had passed only about half-way down. Afterwards he was more successful. Singing his song, he let Little Boy down from the sky by the rope until he reached the sand. Upon landing, Little Boy swung the rope. Thundering Gecko then knew he had arrived and hauled up the rope.
>
> (5)   Little Boy now hurried home to Randjuguyugaid, the point of Windangain. As soon as he had found his family, they hid him from Emu.
>   'She will probably come soon', they said as they put Little Boy in a piece of paperbark.

(6)   And come soon she did, indeed, arriving after a fast run from her own camp.

'Where is the boy, my son, Little Boy?' demanded Emu. 'He is not here', the Windangain crowd replied, 'he is not here'.

'It isn't true that he is not here. I am sure you are hiding him', Emu insisted, 'I might call out for the sky to cover us up'.

Frightened by these threats, the Windangain people let Little Boy come out. Emu took him and ran back. The Windangain crowd sent dugong flesh, sacred meat, to Thundering Gecko. Emu's meat was not sacred. It was of a different kind.

(7)   Emu's return angered Thundering Gecko. 'Good Heavens! How greedy you are', he said.

'No, I found him myself. He pleases me. I have found him.' Emu's unrepentant attitude made Thundering Gecko so furious that he decided to burn her with a torch made of a bundle of stringybark which he hid for a later moment.

'How greedy you are', he said while watching Emu. 'No, she keeps talking strongly', he concluded, lighting the torch, 'she keeps talking strongly. Her tongue moves too fast. What in earth is wrong with her?'

Thundering Gecko now hit Emu with his torch all over her body and caused her to burn like a fire. Then he spoke up, making it clear that he would for ever carry on hitting the trees with his lightning and frighten people with his thundering voice because of Emu's bad behaviour.

'I shall hit the trees, and my power will be heard as I make my sound!'

Emu forecast her own less fortunate destiny: 'I shall keep to the plain. I shall go through the scrub where I shall hurt myself. The scrub will stick into me. That is what it will do. I shall get hurt because of the scrub. I shall keep to the plain'. This is the way in which Emu spoke up.

'I shall make my power sound. I shall hit the trees', Thundering Gecko repeated, 'I shall be lightning and I shall thunder'.

And so Thundering Gecko and Emu split up, Emu taking to the bush and Thundering Gecko going his way.

The most striking variation on Gumi's version is that Gara introduces another transformation of the already well-established territorial opposition between inland and coast, that is, the opposition between sky and earth. Gara leaves no doubt about Thundering Gecko's intention of lowering Little Boy from the sky to the earth. Drawing No. 2, made during the discussion of the text, confirms this and indicates also the transformational link between Thundering Gecko's terrestrial and arboreal methods in story A and his aerial solution in story B. In view of this situation it would seem to be no coincidence that the translators of story B constantly referred to the hero as 'Thunder', and never as 'Gecko' as was the case during the discussion of story A.

The structural identity of terrestrial and aerial positions is also apparent from the fact that inland Nimalhurwaruid remained Thundering Gecko's and Emu's camp and meeting-place, and Windangain Little Boy's home-country. It is true that story B also contains a reference to the digging of a hole during the period of preparations by Thundering Gecko for Little Boy's escape. We may assume that, in story B, Gara was torn between two possibilities, which of course is consistent with the transformational identity of inland and sky on the one hand and of coast and earth on the other.

In addition, Gara's version seems more radical than that of Gumi. Besides the polarising effect of the contrast between sky and earth, the fire symbolism (so reminiscent of the use of torches during Gunabibi or other initiation ceremonies with Rainbow Serpent associations) and the final prophecy bring out the irrevocability of the disjunction between Thundering Gecko and Emu after the fight much more strongly than story A has done.

A number of factors seems to underly this radicalism (always in a relative way, of course). It may thus be reasoned that the position of the Angu clan as the clan of the plainly terrestrial Emu explains why Gumi literally took a 'down-to-earth' view on the main oppositions of the myth, for example, implying why he did not let Thundering Gecko (a lizard) reach higher than half-way up a tree to tie a rope with which to lower Little Boy *through the ground*. In contrast, it is equally understandable that the central position of the Arnba clan with regard to the Angu and Winda clans is strengthened by the introduction of the notion of the sky, the preference for which is also apparent from the emotional involvement of Arnba clan members in Brolga (Crane), whose aerial implications are of course evident. In fact, and also in anticipation of story D, it may be that thinking in pronounced oppositions is particularly attractive for Arnba people (in general, for people who for some reason or another take an Arnba clan viewpoint in the subject of Thundering Gecko), since their principal totems comprise terrestrial animals (e.g. Brown Snake) and aquatic animals (e.g. Stingray) as well as aerial creatures (e.g. Brolga). The tendency to apply a properly Arnba totemic plan would further follow from the fact that according to the myths all three of these totems followed the same direction, from the inland (in all three cases from Ridharngu territories) to the coast. In contrast to Brolga, Brown Snake and Stingray did so partly *along* the Arnbali Creek, partly *through the ground*. During its journey, the male Brown Snake met the female Water Python (of the Uri-Irga clan; *cf.* Figure 1), who travelled upstream along the Irgari River (see map). Upon meeting, the snakes went back again in the direction from which they had come. Their combined efforts make up much of the Nunggubuyu concept of Rainbow Serpent.

All three totems are typical Arnba clan totems whereas Thundering Gecko is first of all an Ama clan totem (*cf.* Figure 1). Accordingly, even though he does not deal with her explicitly, it is not surprising that Gara takes Brolga's 'bird's eye' view of things. Moreover, Brolga will be seen to appear in story D as the principal character and substitute for both Thundering Gecko and Little Boy.

So far, the radicalism of Gara's story has been approached only from internal totemic Arnba clan affiliations. In addition we may fruitfully consider its structural implications as resulting from a model of two inter-secting axes, displayed in Figure 7 and supplementing Figure 4, and indicating the interplay between the vertical and horizontal transformations of the inland-coast opposition. Figure 7 resembles Van Wouden's diagram (1935:110) concerning 'cosmic' versus 'social' dualistic implications of mythological systems as found in the Timor Archipelago, eastern Indonesia. In fact, almost the same terminology seems to be applicable to the Thundering Gecko theme in south-eastern Arnhem Land, for the vertical and concentric view of Thundering Gecko does show explicit cosmic features setting it off from Emu's role in the mythological system as a *cosmic* versus *territorial* viewpoint.

In justification of Figure 7 it is important to recall that Thundering Gecko and Emu's plans cross quite literally (story A) and that their dualistic views are essentially transformations of one basic opposition, that is, between inland and coast. From both viewpoints, vertical and horizontal, the inland has been shown to be the upward pole as opposed to the coast or downward pole.

From the combination of the two dualistic viewpoints in Figure 7 it follows that the relative radicalism of Gara's story and his unmistakable references to Thundering Gecko's sky features are fully consistent with the doubling of Thundering Gecko's upward orientation in the diagram. In this respect, too, Gara's interpretation balances that of Gumi, for it is easy to see that Emu's doubled downward orientation in Figure 7 confirms earlier indications of Gumi's 'down-to-earth' Angu clan version of the myth.

All the same, Figure 7 also visualises the mediatory functions of the three mythological figures, and the impossibility of characterising them to represent single categories. In this regard it is worth mentioning that Figure 7 has much in common with the cross-like diagrams which Ouwehand (1964: 227,229) used for recapitulating ambivalent relations between Thunder God, Catfish and Monkey as mythological concepts in Japanese folk culture.

Finally, a few words ought to be said about the sacrificial offering of ceremonial dugong flesh ('holy beef', Nunggubuyu assistants explained in English, contrasting it with the 'different kind' of meat from Emu) by Winda clan people to Thundering Gecko. Explaining this offering further, the translators made a comparison with the Christian Holy Communion.[23] Drawing an analogy with their own cultural traditions, they pointed to similar procedures during Gunabibi and Ru:l ceremonies.

If this may be taken as a reference to the rather general Arnhem Land tradition of communion to finish up the great ceremonies (Warner 1964:366) or 'to make one people', as Murngin told Warner in connection with Dua Narra ceremonies in north-eastern Arnhem Land (p.346), this passage of Gara's story corroborates the special relationship between the Winda and Arnba clans (the former of which has Dugong as a totem) as representatives of the two Dua sub-moieties M_aI and M_bI (*cf.* Figure 1). At the same time, it strengthens the significance of the notion of initiation. This concerns particularly the return of the initiates, who are now in a higher social status, to the general camp towards the end of the initiation ceremonies.

On the other hand, if this ceremonial gift-giving also, or perhaps primarily, symbolises the offerings to the snake that appears during Gunabibi initiation ceremonies, the operation may offer a clue to the structural connection between initiation and sacrificial symbolism as discussed by Stanner (1959–63:2–21). A general study of Nunggubuyu mythology would be necessary to demonstrate all aspects of this connection. Suffice here to mention this sacrificial notion as a further indication of the importance of the Thundering Gecko theme for an understanding of basic Nunggubuyu cultural values.

Story C

Mabu, the narrator of stories C and D, is not only a gifted story-teller but also an important ritual leader of the Winda clan, particularly with regard to the Murungun tradition of Gunabibi (*cf.* Figure 1). In general, Mabu is a widely respected source of information concerning all Nunggubuyu ritual affairs.

However, his pride as a story-teller leads him quickly to disagree with or correct deviating mythological and ritual interpretations by his fellow Nunggubuyu philosophers. Both of Mabu's stories illustrate this point and offer further examples of the influence of territorial and clan affiliation on mythological formulation. Story C, in particular, was told in immediate response to a play-back of Gumi's story A, which Mabu considered mistaken on the ground that 'Little Boy came from the ground, not from above'. I did not understand his argument at first, but after a comparison of the three texts drew the conclusion that it is based on a difference in regional orientation and has both ritual and sociological implications.

Ritually speaking, it seems important that Gumi's Angu clan interests are dominated by its relations with southern (inland and coastal) Nunggubuyu clans and with Warndarang and Mara clans south of the Rose River. Thundering Gecko reminds Gumi first of all of the Ama clan even though Amalibil (see map) makes up the Dua sub-moiety M_bI together with Arnbali (*cf.* Figure 1). On the other hand, the ritual and mythological information Mabu supplied me with, suggests that he is biased ritually towards territories in the environment of Blue Mud Bay. His clan's Murungun tradition, as I mentioned before, originated from Lulmara. Nor should we forget that Mabu's mother was a Dai woman from a Murngin language group north of the Walker River.

This territorial point will be worked out further in the analysis of story D. It is necessary to point out here that this orientation is strikingly brought out by the fact that Mabu told the Reverend Earl Hughes a story, largely identical to story A but with the important difference that all mythological operations are suggested to have occurred in Blue Mud Bay territories also mentioned in his story D about Brolga and Emu.[24] It seems as if Mabu prefers to relate a rather different variation of the Thundering Gecko theme (story C) when he has to consider its implications for Yiridja territories of the Angu clan south of his own Windangain country. In story C about Little Boy and Old Woman at Miul (no. 21 on the map), Little Boy shows himself indeed from a different viewpoint, that is, from both a terrestrial and an arboreal side; 'from the ground', as Mabu would probably say.

Gumi of course also knows this story which is about one of his own clan territories. On another occasion I actually recorded his interpretation of it. To understand Mabu's prompt reaction to story A and insistence on the correctness of story C, I would mention again (see pp. 53, 57) that the two men are at the same time full cross-cousins and brothers-in-law, an unorthodox combination in terms of Nunggubuyu marriage rules. Although in general they are on good terms, this irregularity in their relationship may well have influenced Mabu's reaction to Gumi's first story.

(1)   A mother and father were on walkabout with their small son. The parents went in front, and Little Boy followed behind, throwing his spear at wild gooseberries and regularly calling 'Mother! Father!' to keep in touch with them. His play caused him to cross the path of Old Woman, who thought of a trick to catch him. Unaware of her presence, Little Boy kept circling around the bushes, shooting at the gooseberries, picking them up, eating them, and from time to time crying 'Mother! Father!'

(2)   Old Woman now started to attract his attention: 'Come on! Come on!' But Little Boy ran away, so she had to chase after him.

(3)   Approaching Miul Billabong (no. 21 on the map), Little Boy took a sharp turn and jumped into the water.

(4)   Old Woman tried to follow him but had to give up, as the water was too deep and the billabong too wide for her. Thinking of another trick to get him, she cut down a pandanus tree and dragged it upside down through the water, hoping thus to catch Little Boy. In vain. Little Boy was even able to play his own little trick by holding the pandanus so that Old Woman actually drew him through the water behind the drag. Stopping to examine her catch (Little Boy at this point releasing his hold) she found only some small expiring fish: 'Look here! I only caught some *alalid, walgara, buyal, warngardurwa* and some *mudhung* and *lhuru*!'

(5)   She continued the chase down the river, looking around without finding any sign of Little Boy.

(6)   The latter was already running away. Still near Miul Billabong, he crept inside a Mill-tree.[25]

(7)   After another try with the pandanus drag, Old Woman went up the river bank where she stood up to look around.

(8)   *Gi ː ː ː.* 'That way now', she thought when she heard the sound of a little bird. She at once ran forward to look for Little Boy's tracks in the direction indicated.
    'Mmmm. Here are his footprints again. And here.' Following the tracks, Old Woman finally found Little Boy's hiding place inside the tree.
    'There he is. His eyes are shining', she thought after inspecting the hole in the tree. *Liːn.* This was the sound of Old Woman fearsomely cutting the tree after her discovery.

(9)   She started to cut the part of the tree underneath Little Boy.
    'Don't do that! Don't do that!' Little Boy told her from his hiding place, playing a trick upon her. Knocking the wood above his head to suggest a better place for cutting the tree, he continued: 'Cut there! Cut there!' And so Old Woman did. She tried to put her hand through the new and still narrow hole.

'No, no', Little Boy went on, 'it has got to be bigger if you want to pull me out by the legs. Make it wider over here!'

After widening the hole in the tree a bit further, Old Woman was able to put her arm right up to her elbow inside the tree.

'Yes, you are doing fine.' Little Boy continued to encourage Old Woman. As soon as she stretched her hand, he said: 'No, no! Turn the back of your hand and your fingers upwards! That's it! A little more yet. Now, if you lift your arm a little bit to that side, you can grip my leg and pull me out!'

Ga:rd. The next moment Little Boy bit Old Woman's elbow so she cried of pain: *Gigigigigigigi.* 'Ow! Ow! Ow! Ow!'

Little Boy stopped biting as soon as Old Woman began to fall down. *Bdu:l.* She landed on the ground with a crash. On his guard against the possibility of another trick, Little Boy reached several times cautiously out of the tree with his head so as to make sure that she was dead. A big fly, picking Old Woman's teeth, removed his last doubts.

(10)   Little Boy now came out of the tree, hit Old Woman once more and ran after his parents.

Without entirely losing his childish traits, Little Boy in this story assumes a different personality. On the whole, he has taken over Thundering Gecko's functions and heroic attitude from story A. He runs off and hides from Emu, tricking her twice and finally killing her.

Little Boy's metamorphosis is explicable from the viewpoint developed before — that he is a generalised spiritual being capable of assuming various attitudes and faces which together make up his total image. Comparative mythological research (J.P.B. de Josselin de Jong, 1929) suggests this to be a regular phenomenon which is quite adequately explained by the structural interchangeability and unity of figures of the hero-trickster-supreme being triad. In this connection it is not surprising to see Little Boy combining his heroism with the role of a trickster.

Other details indicate that Little Boy keeps his dualistic and omnipresent qualities. Some of these, such as the partly missing footprints, are familiar from story A. Story C introduces his *association with water and trees*, which adds another halt to the already established series of coast-inland, earth-sky and downward-upward transformations of the myth's dualistic theme.

In story C the opposition of water and tree actually replaces all former ones, Little Boy also in this instance being connected with both poles. On the one hand, he seems to feel literally like a fish in the water. On the other hand, he deliberately chooses a tree for his plan to kill Old Woman.

Little Boy's succession to Thundering Gecko's position results in yet another transformation. Since story C deals intentionally (although in a reduced way) with the same mythological theme as A and B, and since Little Boy's invisibility or, rather, 'tracklessness' in water establishes his superiority in rivers and billabongs (Emu is 'helpless' in deep water), a definite connection seems to exist between the hole Thundering Gecko made at Nimalhurwaruid (story A, operation 6, and B/4) and Little Boy's underwater position in Miul Billabong (C3 and 4). In other words, in spite of the reversed clan and moiety affiliations of these places, the camp at Nimalhurwaruid (A and B) and Miul Billabong (C) may be considered as transformations of the one central notion in a concentric dualistic view on inland and coast.

It seems similarly possible to trace a structural connection between, on the one hand, Thundering Gecko's actions of tying a 'life-line' half-way up a tree (again A/6, B/4) and thrashing Emu with a torch (*cf*. particularly B/7) and, on the other hand, Little Boy's hiding half-way up a tree and his act of biting Old Woman's elbow (C/9). Little Boy's adventures thus make it possible to trace an association of Thundering Gecko (personified as Little Boy in C) with the contrasting notions of water and tree (on land).

Furthermore, these 'extreme' associations seem to indicate a fundamental connection between the Thundering Gecko and Rainbow Serpent themes. This conclusion is based partly on general knowledge of Australian concepts of Rainbow Serpent as a perennial inhabitant of deep and permanent water (Radcliffe-Brown 1926, 1930; Elkin 1964:260–1; Stanner 1959–63:81–106; Maddock 1970*a*, 1972:118–9), and partly on the evidence of R.M. and C.H. Berndt (1964:209) about the close relationship of Rainbow Serpent and 'Lightning Snake' in eastern Arnhem Land.

In this connection it should also be mentioned that the Arnba and Ama clans (*cf*. Figure 1) possess important though separate Rainbow Serpent myths. I have already referred to Rainbow Serpent implications of the Arnba clan's Brown Snake. There is also an Ama clan myth about Scrub Python who, after swallowing two newly initiated boys is tracked down and cut open by an Aboriginal doctor with a stone axe (*cf*. story E). This is a typical Rainbow Serpent motif.

An additional point of interest is the reduction from a triadic structure in stories A and B to a diadic structure (Little Boy and Old Woman) in story C. An atmosphere of directness, simplification and generalisation is thereby created. For example, and with further reference to Figure 6, Little Boy's final operation of hiding in a tree to bite Old Woman's elbow (C/9) reminds us not only of his secret journey with the rope (particularly his journey through the ground, A/6) but also of his hiding place at Windangain (A/7 and B/5) and, lastly, of Thundering Gecko thrashing Emu with the torch (A/10, B/7). As a result of the reduction from three to two main characters, and of Thundering Gecko's transformation into Little Boy of story C, three separate former operations are combined in one.

Another and closely related reductive effect of the diadic plan of story C concerns the absence of a true fight (without any real killing) and of a terminating prophecy. Instead, story C lets Old Woman die, and it fades away with Little Boy catching up with his parents (C/10); that is, a Windangain scene occurring in stories A and B as an intermediate operation only (A/7 and B/5). In story C these events are the logical conclusion of the plain antagonism of all of its simple dialectic movements. For this reason they symbolise the disjunction of the moieties as unmistakably as the prophetic words of Thundering Gecko and Emu upon their ultimate separation in B/7.

Mabu, as I have said, reacted to Gumi's story A (and Gara's story B) by telling the stories C and D. Anticipating the analysis of story D, these stories may be considered to have offered him different possibilities of expressing his views and criticism of story A. As to story C, it enabled him to concentrate all positive functions of story A (and *ipso facto* of B) in the one figure of Little Boy from his own Winda clan (*cf.* Figure 1), and to replace Miul for Nimalhurwaruid as a transformation of the concentric dualism of story A.

The notion of Rainbow Serpent, so tangible in story C, does not contradict this as it is not an exclusive Mambali concept of sub-moiety M_bI (*cf.* Figure 1). It is at least as important for Murungun and Mabu's sub-moiety M_aI. Moreover, of their two traditions Murungun compares best with Yurlunggur Snake and Rainbow Serpent implications of Gunabibi ceremonies in north-eastern Arnhem Land[26] (Warner 1964:372–4; R.M. Berndt 1951; R.M. and C.H. Berndt 1964:213).

Story D

Although told at Arnbali Creek at a much later date, the first few lines of Mabu's second story bear witness to his critical attitude towards the Thundering Gecko theme as first told by Gumi. Mabu actually started narrating as soon as Gara had finished story B and Arnba clan stories about Brown Snake and Stingray. Other Nunggubuyu narrators, also Gumi, have on other occasions also told me stories similar to story D about Brolga and Emu. In Mabu's case, the typical Arnbali location and atmosphere of story-telling seemed to induce him to choose the Brolga viewpoint of the Arnba clan to express, as will presently become apparent, his mythological orientation towards territories around Blue Mud Bay.

Mabu began by saying: 'I shall tell the story of Lhalainbaid which they [the first narrators; vdL] have missed. They did not tell the story about Mandaridja and Mandayung in *that* direction [of Blue Mud Bay and territories north of it; vdL]'.

He then continued:

(1)   The two of them, Brolga and Emu, stayed at Lhalainbaid (no. 15 on the map).

(2)   It is the place where Emu used to hide pandanus roots from Brolga.

(3)   It is also the place from where Brolga would start off to collect pandanus roots at Warndawarnda, Ulmungurl, Yurang and Malgayangu (nos. 38, 29, 14 and 19 on the map). Working hard to collect the roots, she would afterwards roast them in hot ashes. She would run away as far as Yurang. At sunset she would return home.

(4)   'Here she comes.' At Lhalainbaid Emu would await Brolga's daily return.

(5)   Upon Brolga's return, the two of them would grind flour and eat.

(6)   Each sunrise Brolga would run off to look busily for food. She would extend her search for pandanus roots to other places, such as Warndawarnda, as soon as small roots only were left elsewhere.

(7)   In the mean time, Emu would stay behind at Lhalainbaid and hide roots from Brolga.

(8)   One day, Emu thought of a trick she could play upon Brolga during the latter's daily collecting journeys.

(9)   'She comes back.' Thus anticipating Brolga's return, Emu started grinding flour to satisfy her hunger all alone. Still feeling hungry, she wanted also to swallow Brolga's grinding stone. 'Yes. Let me take the stone and hide it from her. Let me swallow it.' *Dab!* This sound affirmed that she suited the action to the word and that Brolga's grinding stone disappeared in Emu's stomach. The good stone thus disappeared. Emu's own stone, which was no good, was the only one left behind.

(10)   *Ararararararara!* Brolga's footsteps announced her homecoming after a long day's work. From afar she started to look for the grinding stone; but it wasn't there.
    'Dear me! Where is my stone? I say! Who hid it from me?'
    'How would I know?', Emu replied.
    'Who hid the stone from me? Where is it? I am sure it was there, but I don't see it any more. You hid it from me, didn't you?' Brolga thus turned her question directly towards Emu.
    'No, I don't know anything about it', Emu kept saying.
    'Yes, you took it away from me. I am sure you hid it from me,' Brolga insisted.

(11)   Suddenly picking up a stick, Brolga ran towards Emu and tried to hit her on the head.

Ih, ih, ih, ih. 'No, no, no, no! Stop hitting me on the head. There, there! Hit me on the back, right there! Hit me on the back!' Emu told Brolga. Brolga then aimed her blows at Emu's back. *Baid!* They caused the stone, that Emu had swallowed to hide it from Brolga, to jump out, so it lay down on the ground again.

Afterwards it was Emu's turn to thrash Brolga, and this time right on the latter's head. The marks that brolgas nowadays have on the heads and emus on their backs reflect the violence of their conflict.

When the fight was over, Emu began to evoke the territories in which she would for ever after roam about:
    'I shall come out at Lhalainbaid, Arbul, Uldji, Manimurua, Warnbarn and Ugui (nos. 15, 11, 28, 20, 37 and 27 on the map). I shall go to any place, to billabongs; I shall go everywhere. I shall touch the scrub wherever I pass. I shall disappear in the scrub and stray through it. The scrub will hide me.'

In this way Emu evoked the territories of her destiny: 'I shall come out from the scrub at Uldji, and Arajabia!' (no. 10 on the map).

In a similar way Brolga, too, evoked her destiny: 'I fly away.
The wind will freshen me. I shall fly away and circle in the sky.
I fly away when I see people. I shall fly to Ululami and
Udjudjalngan (nos. 31 and 25 on the map). I shall fly to the
billabongs. I shall stand up and eat *amamuyugu* roots,
amarlala roots, and *amaurialyal* roots. I fly away when I see people,
to Ugugandar (no. 26 on the map), to the billabongs, to Ululami.
I shall go everywhere. I shall fly away from Warlgawarlga
(no. 34 on the map) when I see people, and go to Ulmungurl,
Warndawarnda, Wara:in, Magandaruid and Wargala (nos. 29, 38,
35, 18 and 36 on the map). I fly away when I see people!'

Brolga spoke in this way. In this way she spoke up for herself.

Mabu's introductory remarks, and Brolga's heroic part in this story,
make it clear that this is the story of the Arnba clan. In spite of the differences
and the narrator's doubts as to the relevance of stories A and B, the connection between story D and the general Thundering Gecko theme is easy
to see. Thus we note the recurrence of such elements as the collecting of
food by one character, her daily return to another character in a relatively
permanent camp, the hero-trickster relation, the terminating fight and
evocations explaining the ultimate separation of the principal characters
(and, of course, the disjunction of the moieties), the implicit initiation
symbolism and, not to forget, an only seemingly insignificant detail as the
recurrence of a (grinding) stone.

It would be no exaggeration to say that Mabu's stories jointly reveal all
principal operations of the stories A and B. But it is also clear that story D
looks at the common theme from a different viewpoint. For one thing,
the change in regional setting (all named territories lie around or directly
south of Blue Mud Bay) demonstrates Mabu's mythological orientation
towards this area, which has been mentioned as an important motive for
his criticism of Gumi's Thundering Gecko story. In contrast to Gumi's
'terrestrial' viewpoint, Brolga's flights between several of these territories,
away from frightening people and suggestively evoked in the final part of
story D, supply additional evidence of the aerial implication of Mabu's view.
Also in the case of story D, the doubling effect of the crossing axes of
Figure 7 seem to explain the emphasis on Brolga's aerial capacities and, in
fact, the apparent ease with which Thundering Gecko of stories A and B
and Little Boy of story C have been replaced by this popular Arnba clan
totem.

Again, in a different and partly inverted way the naming of territories
of all four Nunggubuyu sub-moieties recalls the conclusions concerning
the combined concentric and diametric implications of the territories mentioned in story A. As a difference some of these are mentioned at the beginning of the text. The diadic emphasis in story D manifests itself further
in the fact that Brolga evokes Dua territories and Emu Yiridja territories
only; the former ones mainly along the coast of Bennet Bay and the latter
ones further south near Irgari River (see map). However, the affiliation of
all former ones with the essentially interior Arnba clan once more confirms
the central position of this clan with regard to the moiety ceremonies.

Lastly, an inversion seems to put Lhalainbaid, a territory of the Angu clan (no. 15 on the map) in the same concentric position as Nimalhurwaruid, Arnba clan territory of stories A and B (no. 23 on the map).

Without really affecting the basic inland-coast opposition (or the upward-downward, and ultimately, hero-trickster opposition), the change in principal characters coincides with a number of other transformations deserving special attention. For example, Brolga and Emu are both 'female'. In this myth, the opposition between them refers primarily to differences in physical appearance, habits and habitat. As an explanatory myth, story D accounts for the characteristic spots on Brolga's head and Emu's back. More importantly, and in spite of the suggestion that Brolga alternatively flies and 'stands up' to look for her favourite roots,[27] their final evocations leave no doubt about Brolga's preponderantly aerial inclinations and Emu's terrestrial habits. I would not consider Brolga's dualistic tendencies as contradicting this but rather as indicating her mediatory functions and her central position in the totemic system of the Arnba clan. In this regard, Brolga's exclusive association with fire is also worth mentioning, as one would rather have expected a close relation between the Yiridja Emu and this likewise Yiridja fire totem (*cf.* Figure 1).

As another characteristic of the story, Brolga's and Emu's female qualities accompany typically female (human) activities of collecting and grinding roots. An inversion makes itself felt with regard to the division of labour: this time the hero walks about daily to collect food, while the trickster steals the grinding stone in the camp at Lhalainbaid.

Continuing this survey of reductory transformations I have also to mention the reappearance of the polymorphous Little Boy, this time in the form of a grinding stone. The identification, Little Boy = grinding stone, is suggested by the reduction of Thundering Gecko's rope trick (A/6 and B/6) and the handling of the torch (A/10 and B/7) to Brolga's thrashing of Emu in D/11. Emu, of course, stole Little Boy in stories A and B, and Brolga's grinding stone in D. Furthermore, Little Boy in stories A and B, and the grinding stone in D, are rescued from their 'imprisonment' in the same way in so far as *both pass through a narrow passage.* In story A (and suggested in B), Thundering Gecko lowers Little Boy through a hole in the ground after checking the length of the rope *by means of a stone.* In story D Brolga thrashes the stone literally out of Emu's stomach until it drops on the ground.

Besides their significance for this complex structural identification, these observations also suggest that the principle of initiation is a significant motif here, as in the previous stories.

Apart from these reductions and changes, story D contrasts with all former ones in that it is the first to deal with fire to the exclusion of water. Billabongs are mentioned towards the end of the story in Brolga's evocations, but never as part of operations leading up to the final separation. Implicitly, Brolga acts as a guardian of fire, which in this story results in a new and apparently highly significant opposition, that is, 'the raw and the cooked', referring directly to the relation between the trickster and the hero. Proof can be found in Brolga's habit of roasting the roots *secretly*, just as Thundering Gecko, in stories A and B, made a rope and lowered Little Boy *secretly*, and as Little Boy of story C *hid* in the tree to bite Old Woman *unexpectedly*.

Though by-passing in this essay the apparent consequences of the myth for a comparative analysis of the 'fire-fireless' and 'raw-cooked' oppositions (Maddock 1970*b*:196–8), I would, in conclusion, point out that the element of fire, rather than contradicting the evidence of the water in story C, provides further proof of a fundamental connection with Rainbow Serpent. As before, I base this conclusion partly on the literature about this notion in Australian mythology, in particular on Stanner's discussion of the Murinbata myth of Rainbow Serpent (1959–63:81–120; *cf.* also Maddock 1970*b*:197). But the regional setting of the myth is also significant, for it concerns the meeting place of the male and female Rainbow Serpent concepts of the Arnba and Uri-Irga clans respectively (*cf.* Figure 1, and the analysis of story B).

Story E

This is a story from the clan of Amalibil (an inland territory just north of the Rose River; see map). In the absence of proper Ama clan narrators, it was told by Manga, whose own Warndarang clan has a coastal area south of the Rose River and near the mouth of the Roper River as its principal territory. However, Manga's clan belongs to the same Dua $M_b I$ sub-moiety.

Our story is about Thundering Gecko, proper totem of the Ama clan (*cf.* Figure 1), who is chased by a Spirit. Apart from the difference in characters, this well-balanced story lays equal weight upon qualities and possibilities of both characters and is strikingly similar in plan to Mabu's story C. It was told to me actually on the suggestion of Gumi who, for reasons not quite clear to me, was somewhat cryptic and referred to it as a profane Ru:l story. This much is certain that Gumi's interior Umai sub-clan (Yiridja $M_b II$; *cf.* Figure 1) borders upon Amalibil and maintains close totemic ties with it. Amalibil is the southern Nunggubuyu Rainbow Serpent centre, and may be to the neighbouring clans what Arnbali means to the northern Nunggubuyu clans and territories. Besides, story E explains why Anarbarin is considered as a 'devil-place', haunted by Spirit who in its turn is constantly being watched by Thundering Gecko from his deep hiding-place at the bottom of the billabong.

For all these reasons the story conveys a strong covert notion which may very well have induced Gumi to consider it as a suitable counter-balance to story C as told by Mabu, his rival in story-telling. Also, the narrator's territorial and clan affiliation will be seen to dominate his view of the Thundering Gecko theme just as much as in all former cases.

(1)   Spirit looked around. It came from Aindur (no. 2 on the map) and listened.

(2)   It listened acutely and heard Thundering Gecko sharpening his stone axe.

(3)   Indeed, Thundering Gecko was sharpening his stone axe.

(4)   Spirit stood still to listen acutely when it caught the sound of Thundering Gecko sharpening his axe: *i:r, i:r, i:r, i:r,* Alternately, Spirit ran, stood still, and listened, so it could follow the direction of the sound of Thundering Gecko's stone axe: *i:r, i:r, i:r, i:r.* It saw Thundering Gecko once it got quite close to him, and it made a plan to approach him surreptitiously, from behind.

(5)   However, a fly flew from Spirit to Thundering Gecko and landed upon his shoulder. Sitting with his back towards Spirit, Thundering Gecko killed the fly, sniffed at it and so deduced from the smell that it had come from a spirit. He wondered what kind of spirit it would be. A good one? A bad one? So he turned around suddenly to look at it.

'It is hiding. It is hiding from me', he concluded. And then, quickly rising and once again turning sharply: 'There you are! I see you alright.'

(6)   Spirit felt ashamed. It looked up and saw that Thundering Gecko was starting to run away. It ran after him and tried to catch him.

(7)   *Mi:nim!* Using his stone axe, Thundering Gecko suddenly flashed lightning, so Spirit fell down on the ground. It went down alright. *Da, da, da, da, da!* A thundering sound followed Thundering Gecko's lightning blow which hit Spirit.

(8)   Thundering Gecko ran again and Spirit got up to follow him. *Dulmug!* The sound of Thundering Gecko's running could be heard as he went in a westerly direction, looking back regularly and noting that he couldn't shake off Spirit. 'There it is!'

(9)   Indeed, Spirit did not give up the chase and kept following right behind Thundering Gecko, with a spear hooked in the spear-thrower ready to throw as soon as he stood still.

(10)   *Minim! Da, da, da, da, da!* Thundering Gecko flashed lightning and thundered again, but he missed his target. Spirit kept following, hiding under the grass and rolling in all directions to escape Thundering Gecko's blows.

In his turn, Thundering Gecko kept running until he reached Alil (no. 4 on the map). Spirit was still after him. *Minim!* Thundering Gecko aimed his lightning blows in all directions around him. *Dulmug!* Off he ran to the other side of Alil Billabong.

'There he is.' Spirit did not lose sight of him and balanced the spear in its hand, preparing to shoot. *Minim!* Another terrible lightning blow from Thundering Gecko once again sent Spirit to the ground. From the other side of the billabong Thundering Gecko flashed lightning in all directions. Then again he ran away, with Spirit still in pursuit.

(11)   This went on for a while until Thundering Gecko, after hitting Spirit with a last lightning blow, buried his stone axe in the ground half-way up the route to Niwangala (no. 24 on the map). *Djadbur!* He went into the water upon reaching the billabong so as to hide from Spirit. Reaching a shallow, he jumped along with his feet on the grass, careful not to leave traces which might put Spirit on his track.

(12)   On reaching Niwangala Billabong, Spirit started indeed
to look around for footprints. 'He went into the water over here',
it concluded, and it fetched a net with which to drag Thundering
Gecko up from the billabong. However, it caught only some small
and mostly expiring *wara-lhuru* and *anarlalid* fish.

Thundering Gecko now started to run eastwards, but Spirit did
not give up the pursuit and succeeded finally in finding the
track again. 'He must have put his feet on the grass over here,
to jump along and hide his prints from me. Oh, he did indeed
run eastwards!' Following the track, Spirit tirelessly continued
the chase.

(13)   In the mean time Thundering Gecko reached Anarbarin
Billabong (no. 9 on the map). He went into the water, this time
disappearing completely by diving into the deeper part.
    'His footprints vanish into the water', Spirit noted a second time.
It walked into the billabong, but hurried on to the dry again,
as it almost drowned. It went up the sandbank. This time
the pursuit had tired Spirit. So now it keeps looking for
Thundering Gecko from the sandbank, whereas Thundering Gecko
watches Spirit from the bottom of the billabong, where he stays
for ever.

Story E is the last story of this series that deals overtly with the Thundering
Gecko theme, this time with Thundering Gecko *in optima forma* as the
sole hero of the story.

The structural similarity of stories C and E is manifested in such details
as the discovery by the hero of the concealed approach of the attacker, and
the flight of the hero into deep water which the attacker is unable to enter,
but from which the latter tries to drag him up. Story E, to be sure, does
not end fatally like story C, although it does use the theme of a running
battle to convey its message. On the other hand, it exhibits the same simple
scheme and dialectic order of sequences and breathes the same atmosphere
of directness and generalisation that was shown to be characteristic also
of story C. In story E this atmosphere is enhanced by the almost equal and
symmetrical weight put upon the qualities and possibilities of the antagonists.

In fact, stories C and E are so similar in plan that both of them demonstrate the maximal reducibility of the operations of story A (and of the
Thundering Gecko and Emu theme in general), particularly of A/2 and 4
(and 9), A/3 and 6, and A/6 and 10 (*cf.* Figure 6). From this viewpoint
stories C and E may be seen as forming a sub-type of Thundering Gecko
and Emu stories in which the hero carries out two series of actions to escape
from the pursuer's evil intentions, the first unsuccessful and the second
successful. In both stories one series entails the notion of secrecy and disappearance, and the other that of aggression. In story C, the disappearance
of the principal figure comes first (and is indeed unsuccessful). In comparison
with story A, this act simplifies the structure of (the story) E, for it replaces (or
generalises) the operations A/3 and 6. However, disappearance in the same
manner is the purpose of Thundering Gecko's second activity in story E.
In this story it substitutes A/6 and 10. Stories C and E differ as to the ag-
gressive activity, which concerns the second trick of Little Boy in C (sub-

stituting A/6 and 10) but the first reaction of Thundering Gecko in E (substituting A/3 and 6). It seems important that this reversal of scenes implies also that Little Boy and Thundering Gecko move in opposite directions, that is, the first one *upwards* (from water to a tree) and the latter *downwards* (from lightning into water).

These notes make it redundant perhaps to conclude that the close resemblance of stories C and E allows us to consider Spirit of E as the substitute for Old Woman of C, and Thundering Gecko for Little Boy of C. To be more explicit about the latter replacement, we may consider it as a further indication of the inseparability of the two characters. Just as Thundering Gecko appeared symbolically in Little Boy's actions in story C, so Thundering Gecko's sovereignty in story E does not suggest it to be devoid wholly of symbolical references to Little Boy. Thus, previous information enables him to be recognised in Thundering Gecko's stone axe which is buried underground so as to hide it from Spirit. This may be correlated with Little Boy's mysterious disappearance through the ground in story A as well as with the disappearance of Brolga's grinding stone in Emu's stomach and, not to forget, its forced return in story D. Since Thundering Gecko also follows Little Boy's example of diving into a billabong, their inseparability permits us to conclude that Thundering Gecko's actions and attributes function structurally to refer to Little Boy and, in reverse, Little Boy's deeds automatically (in story C) refer to Thundering Gecko.

These observations throw additional light on the mentioned opposite effects of Thundering Gecko's and Little Boy's vertical movements in both stories. Thundering Gecko and Little Boy have both been revealed as typically dualistic characters with vertically focussed mediatory functions (which Little Boy alone combines with horizontal functions). From this viewpoint, Little Boy's tree trick (and the little bird's putting Old Woman on his track) in story C symbolises Thundering Gecko's *upward* and aerial affinity, whereas Thundering Gecko makes up for Little Boy's absence in story E by repeating the latter's *downward* movement into water (small fish being his dreaming-spirits) and in fact maintaining an underwater position. Here again, each seems to speak symbolically about his alter ego.

Here, it is unavoidable to generalise a bit further and to point out that Little Boy's simultaneous horizontal movements also indicate an important association with Emu (alias Old Woman or Spirit), even though Emu's (or her replacers') unalterable inclination towards theft and pursuit seem difficult to bracket with Thundering Gecko's more nuanced Little Boy symbolism. Traces of Little Boy symbolism in Emu's or her successors' behaviour are indeed present in all stories. As examples I need only refer to the collecting of tadpoles in story A, the use of a pandanus drag (with which she catches small fish) in story C (and repeated in E), and the theft and consumption of roots (of the pandanus again) as well as the swallowing of the grinding stone in story D. Apart from the dragging scene, Spirit's spear in story E also refers quite possibly to him. In addition, Spirit chases Thundering Gecko (Little Boy's substitute) and does so in a westerly direction. This happens to be also the direction in which Emu brought Little

Boy to Nimalhurwaruid (the intersection of her and Thundering Gecko's dualistic conceptions) in stories A and B.

In its turn, this last information recalls the asymmetrical nature of these dualistic relations, in particular the combined concentric and diametric structuring of the Thundering Gecko and Emu theme which has been discussed in relation to stories A and B. In story E this combination appears from Spirit's 'diametric' pursuit and Thundering Gecko's 'concentric' dive into deep (too deep for Spirit) water. Just as in the case of Thundering Gecko at Nimalhurwaruid in stories A and B, so story E leaves no doubt about Thundering Gecko's sovereignty in Anarbarin Billabong where the emphasis lies on the downward and sub-aquatic side of Thundering Gecko's ambiguous personality.

Figure 7 has proved to be useful in sounding Thundering Gecko's structural depth and transformational possibilities. Its use has been limited so far to an analysis of the significance of his aerial implications for narrators from northern Dua clans, but leads to similar conclusions regarding his downward orientation in the southern Dua view of the Ama clan. This contrasts with (and balances) that of the Arnbali clan (stories B and D) because of its basically terrestrial starting point.

This is not to neglect the joint participation of the joint Arnba and Ama clans in the Mambali ritual of Dua $M_b I$ (Figure 1). Owing to this ritual partnership Thundering Gecko acted also as a key figure in story B from Gara, for whom Thundering Gecko does not constitute a proper clan dreaming. But shifting the inquiry to the interplay of the concentric and diametric implications of the myths introduces a different level of structural abstraction. On this level, the Dua interests of the southern Ama clan do no longer run parallel with those of the northern Arnba clan, but tallies rather with the radically terrestrial bias of the southern group of Yiridja clans (down/down section in Figure 7).

Yielding an additional reason for Gumi's preference for Manga's Dua $M_b I$ interpretation, these considerations are far from suggesting a hard and fast line between the northern and southern views. On the other hand, it does seem to be fortunate to have several readings of these views, for they present necessary material for generalisations, to be given in the conclusion, that cover all aspects of the many-sided Thundering Gecko and his companions in this mythological drama.

Lastly, and for reasons familiar by now, Thundering Gecko's withdrawal underwater at the 'devil-place' of Anarbarin Billabong reminds us of initiation and Rainbow Serpent symbolism which have been corroborated time and again as central notions behind the Thundering Gecko and Emu theme. As Nunggubuyu say, the whole region around Amalibil is 'snake country', with Scrub Python (swallower and regurgitator of initiates) as the most spectacular aspect of Rainbow Serpent in this interior part of the Rose·River.

Story F

Marbu told his story on the same occasion and immediately after Mabu's story C. Exhibiting a different design, with a spirit (reminiscent of the first one, but referred to with another vernacular term) on the face of it as the only link with story E of the proper Thundering Gecko series, it was inspired nevertheless by Gumi's story. On a closer look, and if we take into account that the narrator is a member of the northern Waldar clan of Yiridja M_aII (Figure 1), it does reveal the same 'inside truth' as all former stories. According to Marbu's information, story F is regarded as an original story from the Ridharngu people in the source areas of the Rose, Waldar and Walker rivers.

(1)　Woman went hunting wallaby.

(2)　To this end she left the camp.

(3)　and paddled across the river in a stringybark canoe, which she left (or anchored) on the other side of the river. She went.

(4)　She killed a wallaby bitten by a dog.

(5)　Woman returned with the wallaby.

(6)　She made a big fire to roast the wallaby, which she cleaved in two. She then covered the halves with hot ashes.

(7)　A noise suddenly caught her attention and made her listen sharply. On her guard against possible danger she cut her hair and attached it to her chin and upper lip so as to look like a bearded man with whiskers and a moustache. She also dug a hole in the ground, in which she covered herself half-way up to her breasts with sand.

(8)　How right she was. Spirit, who was attracted by the smell of Woman's fire, came out at the fire-place to find her in this position.

(9)　'Here it is!' Speaking up like a man she said: 'Sit down over there, and wait a moment so I may get hold of the dog.' And afterwards: 'Now take the wallaby from the ashes.' So Spirit did. 'Cut off one half of it', Woman continued. And Spirit cut off one half of it. 'I shall hold this dog.' Woman kept saying, 'I shall hold it as it is dangerous. It might bite you'. Talking in this way, Woman prevented Spirit from coming close to her.
　'Now keep one half of the wallaby yourself and go while I watch you', Woman went on.

(10)　Spirit did leave the place. When it was far away, Woman fetched the other part of the wallaby and told the dog to go off: *Gu:rd!* 'Hurry up! Hurry up!'

(11)　Woman left the fire-place too, and ran back to the river. She took the canoe and paddled back across the river, to anchor the boat on the other side. In the camp she found the crowd dancing and performing a circumcision *(mandiwala)* ceremony. However, instead of joining the dancers, she covered herself with a piece of paperbark and went to sleep.

(12)　In the meantime a fly that had touched Woman now visited Spirit. The latter killed it and sniffed at it. In this way Spirit discovered that it had been tricked into thinking that Woman was a man.

(13)   Spirit at once returned and ran to the fire-place to look around and find out where Woman had gone. It ran down to the river and swam to the other side. It walked to the place where Woman was asleep and crept under the paperbark (wanting to copulate with her).

(14)   However, Woman's sister discovered Spirit when she tried to call her to the dancing ground.
      'Wake up, you! Wake up! You should also be dancing!'
Lifting up the paperbark cover, she found out about Spirit's presence and hurried back to warn the men and women and ask them to kill it.

Having killed it with their spears, they cut it open, but only to find a bit of salty meat left,[28] that they could eat.

In contrast to other stories, a river marks off two different locations — a fire-place as centre of hunting and cooking scenes on one side, and a camp with a crowd of people, a circumcision ceremony and a sleeping scene on the other side of the river. At both places, the principal character is confronted with an uninvited bad spirit. The principal character, furthermore, is a woman who crosses the river twice in a canoe, kills a wallaby bitten by a dog, turns transvestite to play a trick, shares the meat with her opponent who finally seeks revenge by trying to sleep with her when she is back in the camp.

As mentioned before, a correct evaluation of this design makes it necessary to start from Marbu's Yiridja sub-moiety M_aII background. For a start this is most obvious with regard to the elements of fire and water which are proper Ru:l cult dreamings of clans belonging to this sub-moiety (*cf.* Figure 1). These elements occur also in the other stories but their occurrence as important symbols in the same myth is new.

More conjecturally, though not without reason, we may explain the female nature of the principal character as the mirror effect of a transformational inversion because of the special ritual relationship between Yiridja M_aII clans and the Arnba clan from Dua M_bI (*cf.* Figure 2). This unique position of the Arnba clan as participant in a Dua cult of Gunabibi as well as in Ru:l of Yiridja M_aII has been shown before (Figures 3 and 4) to be an important factor in the Thundering Gecko and Emu theme.

Considering further that Marbu himself sees a connection with story A, we are justified in applying a transformational viewpoint. In particular, story F shows a strong tendency to generalisation of characters and operations of all former Thundering Gecko and Emu myths. As for the principal character of F, this time it is as if the narrator modelled his heroine not on the example of Thundering Gecko but after the generalised image of Little Boy as a supreme and omnipresent being. Like Little Boy of stories A and B, Woman appears as a total figure. On the one hand, in some parts of my field translation of the Nunggubuyu text she is referred to as a vague and transparent spiritual being even though the linguistic evidence leaves no doubt about her qualities as a woman in the flesh.[29] On the other hand, Woman combines this transparency with practically unlimited capacities for different actions. She changes herself in travesty into a man, and moves in all directions including downwards into a hole. Above all *she controls both elements of fire and water*, for she crosses a river paddling a boat (a specialised water technique) and roasts a wallaby in the hot ashes of a fire (an equally specialised fire technique). In all these respects she combines the qualities of Thundering Gecko and Little Boy. Her particular connection with Little Boy is brought out further by the symbolism of the fundamental stages of the initiation cycle that have also been met in story A. To recall these by borrowing Stanner's (1959–63:4–16,53) terminology: 'setting apart' (across the river), 'making into beasts' (Spirit approaches), 'destruction and transformation' (transvestite; turning raw into cooked meat), 'gift to the sign' (offering part to the wallaby) and 'return to life' (in the camp where people perform a circumcision ceremony and partially exclude her. She sleeps under a paperbark cover). For all of these reasons Woman may be put on a par with Little Boy in and around the centre of the diagram of Figure 7.

However, this central kind of symbolism is not limited to Woman alone. A comparison of typical Little Boy operations from stories A, B and C (*cf.* Figure 6) suggests a further association between Little Boy and the dog who bit a wallaby and in this way enabled Woman to kill it. In the first place, there is the parallel with Little Boy's act of biting Old Woman to death in C/9. Further, without going so far as to identify Little Boy and the dog (who merely functions as a mediating accessory), one may consider the dog as a dreaming-spirit of Woman (alias Little Boy), comparable with the spear used by Little Boy to 'shoot' gooseberries in stories A and B. The following equations may serve to illuminate this point:

A, B, C: Little Boy: shooting gooseberries: with a spear.
    F: Woman   : killing a wallaby   : bitten by a dog.

As a further implication, the equation of gooseberries and wallaby in this summary also reflects the transformational part of the wallaby in the central Little Boy symbolism of the Thundering Gecko and Emu theme.

Three more notes are needed to conclude the analysis of story F. The first concerns the combination of a diametric and concentric view which makes itself felt just as much here as in all other stories. The diametric dualism is reflected in the opposition between the two sides of the river, with a crowd of people gathered in a camp (comparable to the coast in A and B) on one side, and a hunting territory with a fire-place with secret implications (like the inland from A and B) on the other. In combination with the initiation (and Rainbow Serpent) symbolism of the vertically focussed transvestite trick in the hole in the ground, this notion of secrecy at the same time characterises the 'upward' position of the fire-place in its concentric relation to Woman's 'downward' return position when she sleeps under her paperbark cover on the opposite side of the river. Also in this respect, and particularly in consideration of Woman's partial exclusion, the analogy of Little Boy's adventures and home-coming at Windangain in stories A and B is striking. Moreover, in A and B as in F both views, diametric and concentric, signify relations between the same territorial or local categories.

In the second place, and still in connection with the two dualistic principles, the crossing of the river occurs as a concentric and diametric device for moving from one opposite to the other. On the surface suggesting a deviation from the different concentric and diametric ways of connecting the opposites in stories A and B, it does not indicate a real difference between the three stories, for Spirit and Woman do cross the river in strikingly different ways, Spirit in the rather uncomplicated way of swimming and Woman using the complex technique of paddling a boat. To my mind the river has to be considered, first of all, as a piece of Rainbow Serpent symbolism to be connected particularly with the female Water Python of Ru:l of Yiridja M_aII, which is the pendant of Brown Snake of the Arnba clan (Figure 1). This symbolism characterises the river as a central notion running through all dualistic movements of the story. Translated in terms of Figure 7, it may be taken as a further indication that Marbu's story elucidates the crossing of all dualistic 'barriers' along the inner circle where the concept of Little Boy (and so of Woman) fades into that of Rainbow Serpent.

In the third place, as a difference in emphasis the crucial events appear to be more equally distributed in story F than in stories A and B. In the latter ones these events take place mostly at inland Nimalhurwaruid. In story F, the final execution is not carried out at the same place as the transvestite act but at the camp side of the river, and by performers of an initiation ceremony who in this respect replace Thundering Gecko. This phenomenon mirrors one possibility of reducing the mythological triad, story C conveying another possibility, that is, Little Boy taking all responsibilities for himself. But it may be also partly due to the 'downward' orientation of Marbu as a member of a Yiridja M_aII clan. In this instance story A from Gumi of M_bII has been shown to reflect another terrestrial solution.

Conclusion

A mythological analysis of this kind unavoidably amounts only to a first step in a continuous process of inquiry into an ever widening field of interconnected mythological themes and operations in the Rose River area as well as elsewhere in Arnhem Land. However, it seems possible and worthwhile to conclude my study at this stage with some more generalisations about the Thundering Gecko and Emu theme. Before doing so, in an attempt at combining the structuralistic approach followed in this essay with a psychological interpretation of Australian Aboriginal religious phenomena, I would here like to dwell for a while on Hiatt's (1971) interpretation of 'secret pseudo-procreation rites',[30] particularly his distinction between phallic and uterine rites (p.80).

I do not doubt the evidence of phallic and uterine symbols in the six Nunggubuyu myths, and, on the analogy of Hiatt's comparative data, find no difficulty in considering, for example, Thundering Gecko's stone (stories A and B), stone axe (E), tree (A), torch (A, B) and Brolga's grinding stone and stick (D) as indisputably phallic attributes. Nor would it be hard to consider Emu's basket for catching tadpoles (A, B), Old Woman's pandanus drag (C, E; a womb?) and Woman's stringybark canoe and paperbark cover (F) as uterine elements. Consequently, it would be only one step further to translate the distinction I made between a vertical (concentric) and horizontal (diametrical) notion as a phallic and a uterine notion (or rite) respectively. In sexological terms, then, the Thundering Gecko and Emu theme (or the mythological structuring of the moieties) may be seen to result from the *combination* of, or *interplay* between, phallic and uterine elements.

I emphasise the words 'combination' and 'interplay', for these indicate the primary condition for a correct 'sexological translation' of my structural conclusions. On the analogy of my interpretation, particularly of the mediatory functions of the main characters, this requires considering sexual union (and its consequences) rather than the indication of separate phallic and uterine categories as the principal sexual implication of the stories. Thus, Thundering Gecko's actions symbolise sexual union from a 'phallic viewpoint', naturally, when he lowers his stone (and Little Boy) through a narrow hole. Emu's alternatively capturing and loosing of Little Boy, and her swallowing and dropping (regurgitating?) a grinding stone, represent her uterine reactions to the coital situation. The symbolism of sexual union reaches its climax in the fire symbolism of the confrontation between Thundering Gecko and Emu, when the former burns the latter with his torch. This adds another dimension, incidentally, to the final separation of these characters (and the disjunction of the moieties) and perhaps also to Little Boy's partial separation upon his home-coming.

Anticipating this aspect in his 'Secret Pseudo-Procreation Rites among the Australian Aborigines' by considering this distinction mainly as a matter of stress rather than of 'the exclusive presence of one type of symbolism or the other' (1971:88), Hiatt gives full weight to the coition symbolism, and to the bisexuality of Rainbow Serpent, in his 'Introduction' to, and 'Swallowing and Regurgitation in Australian Myth and Rite' paper in, the present volume.[31] Since Róheim[32] seems to have been the first to recognise Rainbow Serpent's bisexual implications, this totemic concept offers a splendid example of the possibility for combining structuralistic and psychological analysis. 'Bisexuality' would indeed seem to be the correct sexological translation of the structural 'ambivalence' I ascribed to Rainbow Serpent and his representatives, whose main task seems to consist in connecting opposite dualistic notions. From this viewpoint, too, one should therefore not expect them to be sexologically either fully phallic or uterine, but to stand in the middle, to be bisexual and/or symbolise sexual union as such. Also structuralistically speaking, Rainbow Serpent strikes one as the logical extension of all other symbols relating to contacts between males and females; to be both male and female (mythological snakes of both sexes occurring side by side and in combination with one another); to be associated with both fire and water; to be supposed to live in water-holes; known to be dangerous and therefore to be avoided; to combine an 'inner truth' (men's secret) with an outer (natural) appearance; lastly, to be both benignant and malicious.

To return to, and finalise, my conclusions about the Nunggubuyu myths it is necessary to summarise the most important details in the following manner. To start with the Rainbow Serpent concept, it has been found to crystallise diadically into the principal characters of the hero and the trickster and, in a further 'centrifugal' stage, into a triadic relation with Little Boy as their mutual product or synthesis. The discontinuous and asymmetrical implications of their primary function — moving about between opposites, cannot be understood in terms of rigidly institutionalised categories but culminate in the intersection of two dualistic principles or transformational views (Figure 7). The dynamics of this process, the limits of reduction and transformation, have been seen to depend on clan and moiety organisation, and to be actualised by the narrator's engagement in Gumi's story A which started the ball rolling for the others.

The principal characters lend themselves to their tasks because of their ambivalent nature and partial interchangeability. They are not distinguishable in any clear-cut way, nor do they fit into fixed moral categories. The hero has been seen to be also deceiving and the trickster to do good. All of them share in the Rainbow Serpent's central force. For instance, the swallowing (and regurgitating) Emu transformed easily into Old Woman (C) and in this respect is strongly reminiscent of the pronounced Rainbow Serpent symbolism of the Gunabibi cult (R.M. Berndt 1951:12; R.M. and C.H. Berndt 1964:213; C.H. Berndt 1970:1323). Her maternal engagement in her children (whom she feeds with tadpoles) and particularly also in Little Boy gives her a touch of the All-Mother (or Fertility-Mother). This northern Australian concept 'tends to coalesce' (Elkin 1964:255) with the Rainbow Serpent concept, the Fertility-Mother in some versions of the Ngurlmak cult even 'becoming identified with the female Rainbow Serpent' (p.255). As with Rainbow Serpent and All-Mother (Stanner 1959–63:4–5), Emu can be frightening and destructive, or creative.

Little Boy is the most ambivalent[33] of the principal characters. As the product of the two others, particularly of Thundering Gecko, he replaces them (rather, him) whenever he makes his independent appearance (A/7, C) and, if absent, is replaced himself by either Woman (F), Thundering Gecko (E) or Brolga (D). Actually he is not only their product but also the principal object (mostly in a symbolical way) of all of their actions. This is explicit in stories A and B and clearly implicit in all other stories. During the analysis, particularly of story E, I have dealt extensively with Little Boy symbolism of Thundering Gecko and Emu's (and their replacers') activities. Suffice to recall that Little Boy's centralised qualities and close affinity to Rainbow Serpent are highlighted particularly in his own independent actions which show him passing through territories of all four sub-moieties on his return journey to Windangain (A), deceiving as expertly as Emu (C) and associating himself with various elements to avoid, or settle with, his opponent.

His interest in shooting gooseberries (A) remains a sort of a puzzle as yet, but again has probably something to do with his Rainbow Serpent background. This applies further to Woman's analogical and parallel action of wallaby hunting (F) which may offer a better clue in so far as it ends in the cooking scene. The transformation from raw into cooked wallaby meat, unnecessary of course in the case of the gooseberries but obviously comparable to the roasting of pandanus roots in story D, may perhaps be regarded in a Lévi-Straussian manner as marking off the passage from a natural to a cultural state. From this viewpoint, too, it is not surprising to find the stories referred to by Nunggubuyu as explaining a most important socio-ritual phenomenon — the structuring of their moieties. Perhaps superfluously, it is clear that the fighting and separation scenes, and the manipulations with fire (the act of sexual union, to repeat a former sexological consideration) conveys the same basic theme in the other stories.

In attempting to delineate the basic philosophy which is expressed through our principal characters and which makes 'cosmos and society correlative' (Stanner 1959-63:137), it is necessary to point out first of all that the myths do not function primarily as a system of moral codes. I have no concrete information about moral conclusions, if any, that the Nunggubuyu actually draw from the Thundering Gecko and Emu theme for their ordinary life. In deviation from R.M. Berndt's suggestion (1970:244) concerning the Dingari mytho-ritual complex from the Western Desert, such moral features here can only be secondary,[34] the mythological operations reflecting, as I have said, a high degree of ambivalence which allows of no categorisation into either 'good' or 'bad'. Rather, in most stories the asymmetrical hero — trickster relation is balanced by a symmetrical notion suggesting a deep appreciation and positive evaluation of all characters and operations involved. On a ritual level, and in spite of (or even due to) their contradictory functions, these represent without exception the essential values and conditions of life.

To be concrete, the Thundering Gecko and Emu theme aims primarily at keeping in balance forces with life and death as their most radical respective expressions.[35] To start with the latter aspect, it is represented by either females in the flesh (Emu, Old Woman) or by roaming spiritual beings. Characteristically, all of them respond in quite an immediate and emotional fashion to chance situations and meetings, and are obsessed by feelings of egoism and jealousy. They approach their prey surreptitiously or take it by surprise. They are unfamiliar with water and fire, and whenever relevant eat raw food only. Principally, all tricksters are terrestrial beings, females in the flesh combining this with coastal associations.

However, I have in general avoided considering these characters as symbols of particular categories, for example, death. Figures 4 and 7 show that the tricksters move and act freely under differently shaded territorial and mental circumstances. Keeping this 'diminishing opposition' effect in mind, the positive contribution of the tricksters may be redefined in more general terms as indicating the significance of experimental behaviour and the resulting changes (but also dangers) for maintaining human life.

On the opposite pan of the balance both males (Thundering Gecko, Little Boy) and females in the flesh (Brolga, Woman) have been seen to act as the true protectors of life. Unlike their opponents, particularly the males stand out because of their reasoned responses to situations of instability, and of their secret use of specialised techniques to obtain their goals. They appear to be intimately acquainted with water and fire. With the (not wholly convincing) exception of Little Boy, male and female heroes share an inland affiliation. The females, moreover, extend their secret actions outside places of comparatively residential permanence and combine this with a habit of collecting and hunting game. Strikingly, the females make fire and use hot ashes for cooking.

Generalising their ideological background as has been done before for the tricksters, we may say that hero activity in the six stories seems to express, in esoteric terms, the need for stability and setting of conflicts, thereby counter-balancing the experimental behaviour of their opponents.

Considering the explicit reference of these myths to the structuring of the Nunggubuyu moieties, the significance of these generalisations may appear particularly from their connection with the asymmetrical totemistic acceptance by the moieties of phenomena of foreign origin. I am here referring to the Macassan fishermen who visited the coasts of northern Australia with their sailing boats until 1907 (R.M. and C.H. Berndt 1954:70); to several types of European boats and ships, including historical ones like the *Curtiss* which played a role during the opening of the C.M.S. mission station at Rose River in 1952; and last but not least to such important modern means of transportation as aeroplanes, tractors and trailers. Characteristically, these phenomena have become totemic symbols of clans of the Yiridja moiety only, the Dua clans keeping to traditional items.

For several reasons this should, in my opinion, not be considered as a coincidence but rather as a structural regularity. For one thing, the emphasis on mechanical devices for transportation reminds us of such mythological details as the paddling of a boat across a river by the hero in the Yiridja story F. Comparable indications have not been found in the Dua stories. For another thing, the same asymmetrical implication characterises moiety organisation in other parts of Arnhem Land, notably in its north-eastern corner (Warner 1964:30–1; R.M. Berndt 1962:36; R.M. and C.H. Berndt 1954:62; Macknight 1972:303, 312, 314), the Yiridja clans always and exclusively appropriating new elements as totems. Worsley's analysis of the Wanindilyaugwa totemic system (1954:90, 107–8) relates the process of acceptance as an example to the imagination of one song-man from the Ship totem clan only, but this example is wholly consistent with the situation on the continental side of eastern Arnhem Land. Alice Moyle (1964:17–8) supplies further information concerning the Yiridja (East Wind moiety) association at Groote Eylandt with 'foreign' totems.[36]

In view of this structural regularity we may consider Yiridja clans to be more ready than Dua clans to accept ritually the mysteries and uncertainties of European culture because of the inferred experimental philosophy of their moiety heritage. This is the heritage of Emu's diametric view of life and receptiveness to new impressions and to change. The nature of the objects concerned admittedly is important, as the possibilities of modern means of transportation are the logical extension of the traditional and deep-seated nomadic pattern of life. As an additional circumstance Yiridja clans, owners from old of the boat dreaming, may not find it difficult to appropriate its modern equivalents as part of their ancestral heritage. Dua clans, on the other hand, lack this opportunity because of the heritage of their Thundering Gecko's concentric view, dynamic only in its esoteric stabilising influence on Emu's experimental ventures.

A final caution should go with these deductions. Apart from possible influences of historical and other additional factors, my conclusions about the asymmetry in moiety acceptance of foreign items most emphatically should not be taken to discriminate between everyday personal activities, attitudes and opinions of Dua versus Yiridja people. On the statistical level their lives are influenced at least as strongly by other (socio-psychological) forces, Dua people among themselves differing as much in appreciation of traditional versus modern cultural elements as Yiridja people do. The conclusions concern a philosophical abstraction on a mytho-ritual level, the moiety organisation presenting itself characteristically as a ritual form of organisation. On this level, too, it is possible to consider 'the dynamics of a developing religion' (Stanner 1959–63:165), that is, of a religion with built-in possibilities for internal change and external adjustment. Just as in pre-European days, so in modern time this structural mechanism may be seen to control the incorporation of new elements by virtue of its own rules and selective limits. In the last analysis, the asymmetrical orientation of the Nunggubuyu moieties towards foreign phenomena confirms that Aboriginal people in south-eastern Arnhem Land take a basically ritualistic view of their external contacts including those with Europeans. This asymmetry demonstrates the pliability of the mytho-ritual system, but also the limits to its adaptibility to rapidly changing cultural conditions.

Notes

1. I have carried out fieldwork at the C.M.S. Rose River Mission in 1964–1965 under the auspices of the Netherlands Organization for the Advancement of Pure Research (Z.W.O.) and the Australian Institute of Aboriginal Studies, and with the permission of the Welfare Branch of the Northern Territory Administration as well as of the Church Missionary Society. I am greatly indebted to L.R. Hiatt and K.J. Maddock for reading, correcting, and commenting on, the manuscript. Hiatt's editorial advice has been invaluable for simplifying the first draft. My study shows obvious points of contact with Maddock's study of 'The Emu Anomaly' elsewhere in this volume. I further owe my gratitude to A.P. Borsboom, himself now engaged in religious anthropological research at Maningrida, for his much appreciated assistance in analysing and interpreting the Nunggubuyu mythological texts before he left the Netherlands for Australia. A fellowship from the Netherlands Institute for Advanced Study in the Humanities and Social Sciences (1972–1973) made it possible for me to continue this work.

2. For the history of Dutch structuralism I refer to P.E. de Josselin de Jong (1960; 1972). Here, only authors are cited who have dealt with subjects closely related to the Nunggubuyu Thundering Gecko and Emu theme. Ouwehand analysed the dualistic relation between Catfish and Thunder God in Japanese folk culture. Locher considered the North American Indian mythological Thunderbird (Eagle) — Serpent theme, to which he applied J.P.B. de Josselin de Jong's theoretical views on the monistic and dualistic aspects of the triad of divine creator, culture hero and trickster. The latter developed these views by comparing structural characteristics of Hermes, the godly deceiver in the

classic Grecian pantheon, with those of heroes and tricksters in North American, Melanesian and African mythologies. At the time of his writing, in 1929, information about Australian Aboriginal mythology, especially trickster myths, was still scanty. The present essay may be considered as a continuation of De Josselin de Jong's study in so far as it applies his views to Nunggubuyu myths in which diadic and triadic features are manifest.

3. In a forthcoming publication I hope to deal extensively with Nunggubuyu social structure.

4. This does not seem to apply to people of Nunggubuyu origin living rather permanently at places such as Borroloola and Roper River where they appear to have adopted the current semi-moiety and subsection systems (Elkin 1971).

5. I owe this way of simplifying my presentation to L.R. Hiatt. Also on his editorial advice, a copy with full vernacular and esoteric particulars has been lodged with the Australian Institute of Aboriginal Studies under reference No. 8640.

6. The Reverend Earl Hughes of the Church Missionary Society at Rose River, who is preparing for publication the results of his Nunggubuyu language study, maintains the word Ru:l to be an English derivation (personal communication). I am myself not certain about this, as I found it very consistently used whenever the ritual complex was referred to. Moreover, unsuspected Nunggubuyu words such as *rulgulh*, 'making a shade', and *ruluid*, 'shade' (Hughes 1971:219), all refer to a concept, *viz.* 'shade' or 'hut', which is of essential importance to the Ru:l cult. In a wider region of eastern Arnhem Land Ru:l is better known by its Endhilhjaugwa (Groote Eylandt) name Amunduwuraria (Worsley 1954:139).

7. I borrow these terms from Maddock (1972:36–42). As other Arnhem Land people, Nunggubuyu use the English word 'boss', e.g. *warawa wadjudjunggai*, 'those-people boss-because-mother'. Ritual owner-manager relations seem to be general in Australia. Maddock explicates them in relation to the Dalabon as a special type of 'mutual dependency in religion' (p. 36). The owners of totemic sites and religious cults, particularly moiety cults, are dependent on their managers' permission for wearing totemic designs and performing dances. The manager 'decides upon the place [symbolically speaking, vdL], selects a design and paints its outline on the owner's body, and stipulates the dance to be executed, if need be instructing the owner in the steps'. 'The authority exercised by managers have not given rise to a social hierarchy, because every man is an owner in some contexts and a manager in others' (p. 36). Although the relation does not show everywhere the same kinship pattern (p. 42), a man always traces his managerial claims over his mother. See also p. 63 in this essay.

8 For vernacular and further religious details of the four religious traditions I refer to A.I.A.S. document (Van der Leeden 1973:3–5, Figure 1).

9. Meggitt (1966:88) after suggesting a basic similarity underlying the ceremonies of the northern Gunabibi [with the Mandabari complex, vdL] and those of the southern Ingkura, goes on to say: '. . . but it seems to me . . . that the quality of each configuration is different. In the north the Mother as a sexual and fertility object is in effect freely accessible to all without such fierce competition between old and young men . . . In the south, however, the bitter contest to possess the Mother is suppressed at the conscious level and can emerge only in the disguise of the ritual symbolism'. It would be interesting to investigate what significance may in this connection be attached to the massacre of all Muru people (women included) on the northern bank of the Roper River except for the two men who according to my mythological information brought Gunabibi across the Roper River into Djingili country, the border area between north and central Australia.

10. For full details see Van der Leeden, 1973:3–6, Figure 1.

11. Members of another Warndarang Dua clan represent a third Gunabibi tradition, *viz.* Gudanggidji. This is also Mara. As Murungun, it relates the journey of a crowd of mythological persons who travelled from Marumaru (near the mouth of the Roper River) southwards along the Neirindji or Baramandi Creek to end up at a place called Warlbundji. Besides the notion of a crowd of people, their parallel travelling routes suggests a close connection with Murungun. However, further investigation on this point is necessary.

12. Here, the stories are rendered in English translation following the Nunggubuyu texts as closely as possible, but sufficiently free to include relevant though unmentioned information. For original texts and registration numbers of tape recordings I refer to Van der Leeden, 1973.

13. I am not quite sure how to interpret the text word *unadadagwaba*, which my assistants translated as 'she [the mother, vdL] covered him with grass'. However, a misunderstanding seems to be involved, the prefix [*una-*] clearly indicating a plural subject. Furthermore, the expression may also refer to *ana-marda* grass bracelets with which newly initiated boys are decorated upon returning to the ordinary pattern of daily camp life.

14. The expression 'I might sing (call) out for the sky', to which should be added: 'so it might cover us up' (compare story B) should probably be taken as a curse.

15. Nunggubuyu is a so-called noun classifying language. Although still imperfectly understood, its five general grammatical noun-classes probably have mythological significance. They are frequently indicated by special noun-prefixes. As also indicated by Hughes and Healy (1971:60), the [*na-*] noun class (here conveniently though not quite correctly indicated as 'male') consists of two sub-classes, one for human beings and the other for animals which fall into the same general class.

16. Particulars relating to the [*na-*] noun class also hold for the [*ngara-*] class of 'females'.

17. L.R. Hiatt reminded me of other 'kidnapping' cases in Australian myths where the 'mother' is malevolent, e.g. that of Mutjingga, the Old Woman in the myth central to the Murinbata ceremony of Punj (Stanner 1959–63:40–3).

18. I here refer to mutually different totemic Ru:l attributes and decorative patterns of different Yiridja clans.

19. L.R. Hiatt reminded me of this similarity in personal communication. It refers particularly to managerial functions of the ZS group in Gidjingali mortuary rites and in Gunabibi.

20. According to Lévi-Strauss, symmetrical oppositions like summer and winter, earth and sky, and upper and lower, are continuous or homogeneous. Discontinuous or heterogeneous, for apparently asymmetrical, are oppositions such as state and process, stability and change, but also cooked food and raw food, and marriage and celibacy. The contrast between continuous and discontinuous oppositions is itself discontinuous, for Lévi-Strauss demonstrates the interplay between their respective diadic and triadic implications.

21. It may be more than a coincidence that the 'triangular dance ground of the snake's body' (Warner 1964:254–5) during Djungguan performances in north-eastern Arnhem Land exhibits notably similar triadic implications, the top of the triangle representing the 'totem well of the python' (p. 255), and the adjacent sides 'the side of the snake' and more in particular the Yiridja and Dua moiety respectively (pp. 255–6).

22. Lévi-Strauss pays much attention to natural qualities of animal species in his *Mythologiques* studies. I refer also to Leach (1972) theory of taboo and ritual value regarding amorphous animal categories. It does not seem a coincidence that reptiles and 'birds' like emus and cassowaries generally occur as mythological mediators.

23. Nunggubuyu Aborigines were familiar with Christianity long before 1952 when the C.M.S. Rose River Mission was opened. The Church Missionary Society has been active in eastern Arnhem Land since 1907 at Roper River (R.M. and C.H. Berndt 1954:108) and since 1921 at Groote Eylandt (Worsley 1954:2).

24. Unpublished text of a recording by the Reverend Earl Hughes at the Rose River Mission Station (1963).

25. I am not sure whether this is a correct English tree 'name'.

26. K.J. Maddock has drawn my attention to the earliest allusions he knows to the Rainbow Serpent in the north of the Northern Territory. They are made by the naturalist Dahl (1926:21, 67), whose book originally was published in Norwegian in 1898. Maddock finds other allusions in Spencer (1914:290–305). In the present volume (in his 'Swallowing and Regurgitation in Australian Myth and Rite' p. 147), Hiatt takes up Warner's Murngin evidence on Rainbow Serpent's thunder and lightning qualities.

27. Arnbali singers use alternate songwords referring to her aerial view of earth and human society with songwords relating her habit of standing on the ground and eating her favourite roots. Mabu's rendering of Brolga's evocations (cf. D/11) is consistent with, and contains songwords from, Arnbali brolga songs.

28. The linguistic evidence (cf. Van der Leeden 1973: footnote 26) points almost certainly to a rest of Spirit itself, but I have not made sure whether the text does not also refer to the roasted piece of wallaby offered to it by Woman. Although tempting, lack of information does not permit us to relate this operation to the sacrificial offering of ceremonial dugong meat to Thundering Gecko in B/6.

29. Nor do any extralinguistic references to an animal being of the female [ngara-] noun class exist.

30. Hiatt (1971) supplies the best starting point for this discussion, but it is important to draw attention to his contributions in the present volume as a further deepening (and, partly, revision) of his 1971 views.

31. See particularly his discussion of Róheim's views of the waninga and the Milky Way (Introduction, pp. 8–9; referring to Róheim's The Riddle of the Sphinx, 1934) and of Rainbow Serpent's role concerning separation anxiety ('Swallowing and Regurgitation', p. 155, referring to The Eternal Ones of the Dream, 1945). From Hiatt's present analysis one may probably infer that he would no longer hold to his former (1971:82) and principally phallic interpretation of the Wondjina or Rainbow Serpent figures from the Kimberleys. In a footnote (p. 82) he explains that 'the problem demands a much more detailed analysis than I have given here'.

32. Róheim, The Eternal Ones of the Dream (1945:178–99), as quoted by Hiatt (present volume, 'Swallowing and Regurgitation', p. 155).

33. Little Boy is as 'baffling and mysterious' as Kukpi or Black-Snake Woman, the figure in Murinbata mythology that 'moves in and out of focus almost, though not quite, as much as that of Kunmanggur' (Stanner 1959–63:126), the Murinbata Rainbow Serpent.

34. This need not apply to all mytho-ritual systems. Without suggesting a primary moral function for any Nunggubuyu cult, I obtained explicit information about moral aspects of the Ru:l cult, both on a ritual level and as part of ordinary life.

35. My formulation of the myth's philosophical message serves obviously a practical purpose. Essentially it would seem to be consistent with Stanner's (1959–63) generalisations about the 'ontology of life' in Australian Aboriginal religion. Compare Hiatt's Introduction to the present volume, pp. 10–12.

36. Alice Moyle (1964:17), who drew my attention to the wide distribution of this phenomenon, criticises Worsley (1954) for reversing the totemic moiety

orientation by ascribing Bara, Westwind, to Yiridja (actually, Groote
Eylandt moieties do not bear proper names), and Mamariga, Eastwind, to
Dua. I confirm that the Nunggubuyu interpretation of the wind directions
tallies with Alice Moyle's information.

References

BANKS, J. 1971 *His diary, manuscripts and collections*, (ed.) A.M. Lysaght.
London, Faber & Faber.

BERNDT, C.H. 1970 Monsoon and honey-wind. In *Échanges et communications*,
(eds.) J. Pouillon *and* P. Maranda, pp. 1306–26. The Hague, Mouton.

BERNDT, R.M. 1951 *Kunapipi: a study of an Australian Aboriginal religious cult.*
Melbourne, Cheshire.

—— 1952 *Djanggawul: an Aboriginal religious cult of north-eastern Arnhem
Land.* London, Routledge & Kegan Paul.

—— 1962 *An adjustment movement in Arnhem Land, Northern Territory of
Australia.* The Hague, Mouton.

—— 1970 Traditional morality as expressed through the medium of an
Australian Aboriginal religion. In his *Australian Aboriginal anthropology*,
pp. 216–47. Australian Institute of Aboriginal Studies. Nedlands, University
of Western Australia Press.

BERNDT, R.M. *and* C.H. BERNDT 1954 *Arnhem Land: its history and its people.*
Melbourne, Cheshire.

—— *and* —— 1964 *The world of the first Australians.* Sydney, Ure Smith.

CAPELL, A. 1960 Myths and tales of the Nunggubuyu, S.E. Arnhem Land.
Oceania, 31(1):31–62.

CAYLEY, N.W. 1959 *What bird is that?: a guide to the birds of Australia.* 3rd ed.
Sydney, Angus and Robertson.

DAHL, K. 1926 *In savage Australia: an account of a hunting and collecting
expedition to Arnhem Land and Dampier Land.* London, Allen.

ELKIN, A.P. 1964 *The Australian Aborigines: how to understand them.* 4th ed.
Sydney, Angus and Robertson.

—— 1971 Yabuduruwa at Roper River Mission, 1965. *Oceania*, 42(2):110–64.

GUIART, J. 1972 Multiple levels of meaning in myth. In *Mythology, selected
readings*, (ed.) P. Maranda, pp. 111–26. Middlesex, Penguin Books.

HIATT, L.R. 1965 *Kinship and conflict: a study of an Aboriginal community in
northern Arnhem Land.* Canberra, A.N.U. Press.

—— 1971 Secret pseudo-procreation rites among the Australian Aborigines.
In *Anthropology in Oceania: essays presented to Ian Hogbin*, (eds) L.R. Hiatt
and C. Jayawardena, pp. 77–88. Sydney, Angus and Robertson.

HUGHES, E.J. 1971 Nunggubuyu - English dictionary. Sydney (Oceania linguistics monograph no. 14), University of Sydney.

HUGHES, E.J. *and* A. HEALY 1971 The Nunggubuyu language: part 1, the
Nunggubuyu verb. In *Papers on the languages of Australian Aboriginals*,
pp. 46–58. Canberra, Australian Institute of Aboriginal Studies.

JOSSELIN DE JONG, J.P.B. DE 1929 De oorsprong van den goddelijken bedrieger.
In *Mededelingen der Koninklijke Akademie van Wetenschappen*, Afdeeling
Letterkunde, 68 B, 1:1–29.

JOSSELIN DE JONG, P.E. DE 1960 Cultural anthropology in the Netherlands.
Higher Education and Research in the Netherlands, 4(4).

—— 1972 Marcel Mauss et les origines de l'anthropologie structurale
hollandaise, *L'Homme*, 12(4):62–84.

LEACH, E. 1972 Anthropological aspects of language: animal categories and
verbal abuse. In *Mytholoyy, selected readings*, (ed.) P. Maranda, pp. 39–67.
Middlesex, Penguin Books.

LEEDEN, A.C. VAN DER 1973 The thundering gecko and emu theme: mythological
structuring of the Nunggubuju patrilineal moieties in southeastern Arnhem
Land. [Canberra, Australian Institute of Aboriginal Studies.] Unpublished
report (Doc. no. 73/1403).

LÉVI-STRAUSS, C. 1956 Les organisations dualistes existent-elles? *Bijdragen tot de Taal-, Land- en Volkenkunde*, 112:99–129.

―――― 1958 La structure des mythes. In his *Anthropologie structurale*, pp. 227–55. London, The Penguin Press.

LOCHER, G.W. 1932 *The serpent in Kwakiutl religion*. Leiden, Brill.

MACKNIGHT, C.C. 1972 Macassans and Aborigines. *Oceania*, 42(4):283–321.

MADDOCK, K.J. 1970a Imagery and social structure at two Dalabon rock art sites. *Anthropological Forum*, 2(4):444–63.

―――― 1970b Myths of the acquisition of fire in northern and eastern Australia. In *Australian Aboriginal anthropology*, (ed.) R.M. Berndt, pp. 174–99. Australian Institute of Aboriginal Studies. Nedlands, University of Western Australia.

―――― 1972 *The Australian Aborigines: a portrait of their society*. London, Allen Lane.

MEGGITT, M.J. 1966 *Gadjari among the Walbiri Aborigines of central Australia*. Sydney (Oceania monograph no. 14), University of Sydney.

MOUNTFORD, C.P. *and* A. ROBERTS 1969 *The dawn of time: Australian Aboriginal myths*. Adelaide, Rigby.

MOYLE, A.M. 1964 Bara and Mamariga songs on Groote Eylandt. *Musicology*, 1:15–24.

OUWEHAND, C. 1964 *Namazu-e and their themes: an interpretative approach to some aspects of Japanese folk religion*. Leiden, Brill.

RADCLIFFE-BROWN, A.R. 1926 The rainbow-serpent myth of Australia. In *Royal Anthropylogical Institute, Journal*, 56:19–25.

―――― 1930 The rainbow-serpent myth in south-east Australia. *Oceania*, 1(3):342–47.

―――― 1930–1931 The social organization of Australian tribes. *Oceania*, 1(1):34–63; (2):206–46; (3):322–41; (4):426–56.

RÓHEIM, G. 1934 The riddle of the sphinx or human origins. London, Woolf.

―――― 1945 *The eternal ones of the dream*. New York, International Universities Press.

SPENCER, Sir W.B. 1914 *Native tribes of the Northern Territory of Australia*. London, Macmillan.

STANNER, W.E.H. 1959–63 *On Aboriginal religion*. Sydney (Oceania monograph no. 11), University of Sydney.

WARNER, W.H. 1964 *A black civilization: a study of an Australian tribe*. Rev. and shortened ed. New York, Harper.

WORRELL, E. 1970 *Reptiles of Australia*. 2nd ed. Sydney, Angus and Robertson.

WORSLEY, P.M. 1954 The changing social structure of the Wanindiljaugwa. unpublished Ph.D. thesis, Australian National University.

WOUDEN, F.A.E. van 1935 *Sociale structuurtypen in de Groote Oost*. Leiden, Ginsberg.

The Emu Anomaly

Kenneth Maddock

The thesis to be defended in this paper[1] is that emus, the commonest and perhaps the only flightless birds in southern Arnhem Land,[2] pose a difficulty for Dalabon thought about nature, and that a myth, in which an emu's relation to other birds is recounted, offers a resolution. The difficulty takes two forms. On the one hand there is the special difficulty that emus are out of place in Dalabon taxonomy. On the other hand there is the general difficulty that what we, in English, call flightless birds are bound to be puzzling because they pair inability to fly with numerous striking resemblances to birds that fly. The first difficulty is contingent upon the logic or rationale of the local taxonomy, and would not arise in cultures in which flightless birds are placed concordantly with the local taxonomic logic. The second difficulty may be presumed to be inescapable no matter what taxonomic position is accorded to flightless birds.

My paper falls into five parts. First, I explicate Dalabon taxonomy; secondly, I discuss a Dalabon emu myth; thirdly, I analyse it to show how it treats the anomaly; fourthly, I discuss some other emu myths in order to show that the Dalabon is one of a group, each member of which is related to others by a number of permutations; and finally, I consider what wider significance the emu studies may be taken to possess.

Dalabon Taxonomy

Dalabon recognise expressly two kinds of taxa.[3] The more inclusive will here be called genera and the less inclusive species. The various species of tree are put together as *dul*, of fish as *djenj* and of large marsupial as *gunj*. Birds, dingos, insects, lizards, small marsupials and snakes are *manj*. Humans are *biji*. I did not discover that plants, excepting trees, are grouped into genera, but whether none exist is doubtful, for my taxonomic inquiries were conducted incidentally to what seemed then to be more pressing concerns and were not at all systematic.[4] However, I do not see that plant taxonomy could prove critical in the case before us.

Relations between genera are defined genetically. The Dalabon posit that most non-humans are descended from, or once were, *biji*, and that they owe their form to metamorphoses modelled on, and provoked or inspired by, world-creative powers during The Dreaming. Humans themselves are descended from those *biji* who did not turn into other forms of life. Some contemporary members of some species, and more particularly certain trees, are said to have once been powers or objects used by powers.

The question must now be raised of the rational basis, if any, of the generic grouping of non-human species, for anomalies presuppose rationality. In the course of attempting to account as economically as possible for the

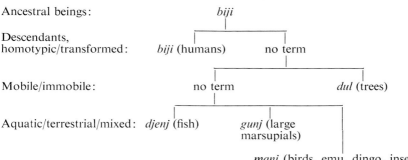

DIAGRAM 1

Dalabon Taxonomy

Ancestral beings: *biji*

Descendants,
homotypic/transformed: *biji* (humans)   no term

Mobile/immobile: no term   *dul* (trees)

Aquatic/terrestrial/mixed: *djenj* (fish)   *gunj* (large marsupials)

manj (birds, emu, dingo, insects, lizards, small marsupials, snakes)

ordering of species, I succeeded in formulating two criteria which, between them, come close to answering my purpose. The first asks whether the members of a species enjoy the power of movement. The second, which depends upon an affirmative reply to the first, asks in what elements do the members of a species habitually exercise their power to move (see Diagram 1). What results are furnished by these criteria?

Members of *dul* species are unable to move independently. This genus may accordingly be distinguished from the others, since all their members are able to move. *Gunj* and *djenj* species move habitually in one element only, but these genera may be distinguished from each other by the nature of their element, which is terrestrial for the one and aquatic for the other. As for *manj* species, it is typical for them habitually to move in more than one element. Thus crows fly and walk (aerial and terrestrial), possums climb trees and walk (arboreal and terrestrial), water goannas swim and walk (aquatic and terrestrial) and certain honeybees fly, walk and go into the earth (aerial, terrestrial and subterranean).

A taxonomic logic like this may seem decidedly odd, and yet really it is not, for the Dalabon used to live by hunting and gathering, a mode of life whose practitioners may be presumed to be vitally interested in the whereabouts of the various species and in their capacity to move. *Gunj* and *djenj* species are confined to a single element, but members of the *manj* genus, seemingly a ragbag of species, switch from one element to another, and often do so if alarmed.

The criteria presented here fail to account for the generic classification of all species. The exception that concerns us in this paper is the emu. Emus move habitually only in one element, the terrestrial, and should, on my criteria, be *gunj*. They are out of place as a *manj* species. Dalabon thought could either ignore the emu anomaly or maintain that, despite appearances, emus really are in the right place. The latter is the solution adopted, and it is communicated mythically.

It is possible that there are other exceptions, such as certain species of small wallaby generically classed as *manj*, but of which I have never sighted

103

a specimen. Until recently I had considered them to be habitually terrestrial, and hence properly *gunj* on my criteria, but information recorded by the Norwegian naturalist Dahl (1926:208–9), who spent two years in Arnhem Land during the 1890s, raises a serious doubt as to this. He describes a rock wallaby (*Petrogale concinna*) that sleeps by day in deep chambers and crannies within rock formations, and another (*Petrogale brachyotis*) that also is to be found lurking within rock formations. Aborigines he met around the headwaters of the Mary River called these species *balwak* and *doria* respectively, which may well be the species recorded by me under the names *balgidj* and *dorija*. Animals like these, being terrestrial and subterranean, satisfy the criteria of *manj* membership. Be that as it may, the possibility of exceptions other than the emu does not, I think, affect the argument of the present paper, since there could well be more anomalies than one in a system of classification. Whether these other anomalies, assuming them to exist, are resolved mythically is a question of fact calling for investigation separately.

When I asked Aborigines whether these small wallabies were *gunj* I was told that they were 'too small' for this genus. But it would be erroneous to conclude that *gunj* is properly the genus to which large species belong, for if it were, emus, pythons and saltwater crocodiles should be assigned to it instead of to *manj*. Size, then, is not applied systematically to produce genera of species, though it may be used occasionally to rationalise the *manj* membership of creatures felt to be *gunj*-like. That is to say, size is perhaps to be regarded as pertaining to a native model of classification. The explanatory power of this criterion is slight, and I do not remember ever having heard other criteria used. My criteria, by contrast, do produce, with one or a few exceptions, the Dalabon genera of species. Should there turn out to be a comprehensive native model (that is, a consciously entertained model) it would compete with mine, unless they happened to be identical, and they would have to be compared for adequacy like any other competing models or theories.[5]

It might of course be urged against me that, even if emus are misplaced in their genus, it is factitious to suppose that native thought sees an anomaly to be resolved. To answer this hypothetical objection it is necessary to fall back on the distinction made at the outset between the special difficulty emus pose for Dalabon thought (given their taxonomy) and the general difficulty posed by flightless birds (not all of which are emus). It seems indubitable that flightless birds pose a very real puzzle for native classifiers, who sometimes meet it radically by denying that 'flightless birds' are 'birds'. Thus in New Guinea both the Melpa and Kyaka classify cassowaries as birds, but the Karam and Fore (Bulmer 1967:10, 23) and the Marind (van Baal 1967:192) do not. The myths to be considered in my fourth section are significant in this respect, as will presently appear. Where the special and general difficulties both are present it is hard to see how their repercussions could be disentangled: it is rather the case that the special difficulty exacerbates the general. Whether the analytic distinction between these two difficulties always is relevant in Australia is obscure because our knowledge of Aboriginal taxonomies is slight. Clearly much work remains to be done on problems of classification, and in the meantime I prefer to keep sight of the distinction between special and general difficulties.

A Dalabon Emu Myth

The emu figures prominently in a Dalabon myth which I heard several times. The versions differed in length, but were pretty consistent as to their detail. Here is one of the versions I obtained:

> M_1.   The emu *(ngurudu)* used to eat all the food brought back to camp by her followers. She would ignore their hungry appeals for something to eat. One day the jabiru *(gandji)* and brolga *(bonarong* or *godo)* spotted a male plains kangaroo *(gudubu)* eating fresh grass. After creeping close to look, they returned to camp to tell of their discovery.
>
> The cuckoo-shrike *(wiriwirijag)* was lying in camp, but when they asked him to hunt the kangaroo he replied that his foot was too sore. So they bound it up with paperbark and string, after which he went out and speared the kangaroo. Its tail was as large as a petrol drum.
>
> The birds roasted the kangaroo by a creek. The emu was dispatched to fetch the soft grass *(djiri)* used for sopping up gravy from a roasted kangaroo's stomach cavity. She went some distance away before asking whether she was in the right place for that kind of grass. 'No, not there!' the birds called, 'We urinated there! You can't pick that grass!'
>
> The emu went further away. 'What about here?'
>
> 'No!'
>
> 'Here?'
>
> 'No! Look at Bodombod, Ju:lwon, Gamarung, Djelbei' (all of them far away places).
>
> While the emu was absent the birds cut up the kangaroo and flew into the sky with the pieces. Only the tail was left behind, and this was with the grass pigeon *(djiridi)*. When the emu returned she found her followers gone. Only blowflies were to be seen. She looked in the grass and bushes for meat, but there was none. She cursed. Again she looked. This time she spotted the grass pigeon, who had been in hiding, but when she made to catch him he flew up with the tail. All the birds laughed, saying 'We don't want that old woman!' She had had many followers, but now had lost them by her refusal to share food.
>
> The emu now swallowed a stone (of the kind called *ngalwad),* which is why emus lay eggs. She made her neck and tail from two sharp yamsticks *(woradji)* and her hair from vine (of the kind called *buda).*

This story is set at Gumberin, east of the Wilton River, and probably near Baidjalubur and Bajaramerei, two mythically important places. Once I was given Ju:lwon as the setting, but this is the only discrepancy I noticed in the different tellings. According to Robinson (1966:164–9), who gives a Djauan myth so like the Dalabon that I shall denominate his as M_{1a}, the emu went to Gumberin after losing her followers.

The birds were moved to rebellion by hunger, which sprang, not from a dearth of food, but from their leader's refusal to share what they gathered and brought back to camp. One man enumerated *buda, bulgalu, gundjilk, ma:gunbu* and *ngadjo*, all bush vegetables, as the foods collected. Thus the emu denied her followers plant food, and they denied her animal food. She deprived them to their faces, whereas they deprived her by trickery.

M_1 does not account for the emu's flightlessness as such, but addresses itself rather to her separation from all other birds. She is the one who was left behind when they took to flight: they flew from her. But the myth does explain emus in part, for incorporated natural things (stone, vine) and artefacts (yamsticks) were transmuted into anatomical or physiological things (eggs, feathers, neck and tail). M_{1a} has it that the emu missed her aim when she threw a pointed stick up at the grass pigeon (Jirritt-jee in Robinson's rendering) and the stick, returning to earth, stuck in her forehead. She decided then to become an emu. I recorded another Djauan version (M_{1b}), according to which the emu was knocked down for a long time by a blow on the throat from a yamstick dropped (deliberately?) by a bird flying overhead. M_{1b} agrees with M_1 that the emu set out to fetch a soft grass (*munmun* in Djauan), but M_{1a} has it that she went for water. M_{1a} agrees with M_1 that the birds tricked her into going further and further away by telling her that the water or grass was dirty, but M_{1b} omits this motif.

On another telling of the Dalabon myth a great stress was put on the other birds' enlarged capacity for movement. The kangaroo's tail proved by its size ('not like kangaroo tails now') to be too heavy for any bird save the grass pigeon to carry right up into the sky:

> They tried to lift it into the sky. They went up halfway and came down; they went up halfway and came down; they went up and came down. The jabiru took it but only halfway. The crow *(wa:gwa:g)*, the brolga, the cuckoo-shrike, all kinds of bird, tried. The grass pigeon tried. He took the tail halfway and came down. He tried again, went right up, came down again, went up again. The others said to him, 'Take the tail when the emu returns.'
> They laughed from above. The emu came back, came back, came back. She looked around, looked around, looked around. She saw nothing, because the grass pigeon was hiding in the grass. She looked around, put down her foot, took away the grass and reached down for the meat, but the grass pigeon shot up. They all called out to the emu, 'We're leaving you by yourself now!'

Aborigines undoubtedly are amused by the thought of the emu standing empty-handed on the ground while her erstwhile followers, loaded with meat, fly about in the sky. But the mythical events are more than diverting; they are instructive. For example, on one occasion this exchange was related as having occurred:

> 'What do we follow you for? You don't give us food.' They were close to fighting her.
> 'You can't fight me. This is my food.'
> 'We work for you, we follow you.' They'd been working for her for nothing. She hadn't given them food. She was too mean.

And on another occasion it was commented that 'The emu hadn't been giving food to the birds. We had been going to give nothing to our family, let them starve, but they (the birds) punished her.' Had the birds remained quiescent, the emu's 'law' would have been observed to this day. I am glad to be able to say that one of the Aborigines contrasted my relation to them with the emu's relation to the other birds: unlike her, I fed my followers well.

All the Dalabon versions I heard passed quickly over the motif of the cuckoo-shrike's sore foot, but M_{1a} treats it more fully. The cuckoo-shrike refused to hunt the kangaroo of which the crow and brown pigeon brought news, because he had a stake embedded in his foot. The crow offered to remove the stake, but so sore was the cuckoo-shrike's foot that he would not at first submit to an operation. Finally he agreed, only to cry out to the crow and brown pigeon to stop because they were causing him pain. But they continued to operate until the swelling in his foot burst, spattering them with a white stuff (pus?), which is why these birds are marked now as they are. The cuckoo-shrike thereupon declared himself fit to hunt.

Resolution of the Anomaly

A structural analysis of a myth always leaves the impression that a different analysis could have been made, that is to say, it does not seem possible to make *the* structural analysis, and indeed, it may be doubted that this ever will be done. The hope that *the* analysis might be made is held out, or so it seems, by Lévi-Strauss in his paper on 'La structure des mythes' (1958a: 227-55), in which he convicts earlier approaches to mythology of platitude, sophism, banality and confusion, offers and illustrates a new approach, inspired in part by linguistic precedents, and uses expressions like 'la structure du mythe' and 'la structure synchronique qui caracterise le mythe'. As de Meijer (1970:156) puts it in his comparison of Propp and Lévi-Strauss, after Lévi-Strauss 'One looks for *the* structure of *the* mythical tale, or of *the* tale in general' (emphasis in the original, KM).

Lévi-Strauss's Oedipus study has been emulated by other anthropologists using different bodies of mythology, for example Hebrew (Leach 1962; 1966), Maori (Jackson 1968) and Sinhalese (Robinson 1968), but these, interesting though they are, hardly escape the monolithic defect of their model. One may agree with Richard (1967:122) when he says that 'The application of the "principles which serve as a basis for structural analysis" does not seem absolutely to guarantee that the myth has not been solicited to respond to the *a priori* ideas of the analyst.' Burridge (1967:102-9) has expressed himself to similar effect. He admits his inability wholly to understand the Oedipus model; produces several different, but internally consistent, accounts of a short Tangu myth none of which is evidently closer than its rivals to the model; and observes in passing that 'if the method works the answer is predicated by the initial address'. Guépin (1973), Hiatt (1966), Nathorst (1970) and Turner (1969) have addressed themselves even more critically to the Oedipus model.

'La structure des mythes' belongs to an early stage in its author's thinking about mythology, and neither in his recent major works, the volumes of

107

the *Mythologiques* series, nor in that of admirers or disciples like Detienne (1972), de Heusch (1972), and Sebag (1971) is the Oedipus model central. It is rather to Lévi-Strauss's papers on Asdiwal (1958b), on Propp (1960) and on comparative religion (1968) that one must turn for a brief guide to the lines of inquiry he pursues in his *Mythologiques*.[6]

In the first *Mythologiques* volume, Lévi-Strauss (1964:11) draws an analogy between microscopic and myth analysis. What one sees on looking through a microscope is conditioned by the degree of magnification. It follows analogically that a myth is to be regarded as having an indefinite number of structures, none of which can be accepted as *the* structure. Each is *a* structure. But what are we then to make of the relation between different analyses of the same myth? He who uses a microscope can relate his observations to each other as a function of degree of magnification. It does not seem that any such precise means of stating relationships exists in myth analysis. The analyses which follow certainly do not solve this problem. They show simply that different analyses may be made of the same material, each of which makes its own selection of data and capitalises on features ignored or touched upon only lightly by the other.

A first analysis

M_1 relates that refusal to share food led to the dissolution of a primeval community. One of its members, an emu, remained behind on the ground, while all the others flew up into the sky. Social decomposition thus went along with a new power of movement (flying as well as walking or running), a new element in which to be at home (aerial as well as terrestrial) and a new spatial plane on which to move (vertical as well as horizontal). The problem of the flightlessness of emus, that is, of relations within a taxonomic system, gets mythically restated as a problem of sharing, that is, of relations within a social system, in the resolution of which all the other birds separated themselves from the emu. Aboriginal myths often have recourse to some such displacement of the issue. Thus in many fire myths the technical question of how to make fire is turned into the moral question of whether to share fire. By restatement and displacement a problem with which Aborigines can cope is substituted for one with which they cannot, given the state of their knowledge, and the solution of the first is passed off as a solution of the second.

However, to say that the emu used to live with all other birds hardly suffices to resolve the anomaly. This is accomplished by the organisation of the narrative into *opposed sets of characters*. Notice, first, that birds are contrasted with a kangaroo as collective to solitary, hunter to prey, killer to victim, cook to cooked, divider to divided. As the emu belongs to the community of birds until the end when she is tricked out of a share in the cooked meat, the bird/kangaroo opposition may be taken as asserting that an emu's place is with other birds (who happen to be *manj*) rather than with large marsupials (who happen to be *gunj*). But the difference between emus and other birds has also to be explained. This is the function of the second opposition. The emu is contrasted with other birds as leader to follower, refuser of food to asker of food, tricked to trickster, earthbound to airborne, solitary to collective. These first two oppositions (birds/kangaroo and emu/other birds), taken jointly, affirm that emus really are properly placed as *manj*, despite their failure to satisfy the criteria for inclusion in that genus, because the emu's union with and likeness to other birds, and her and their opposition to the kangaroo, antedated her unlikeness to other birds, and that it was only out of her and their opposition to the kangaroo that they separated from her. Emus and kangaroos, then, have it in common that they are unlike birds who fly, but mythically they stand in a different relation to flying birds. Originally the emu was at one with them and later came to be at odds, whereas the kangaroo always was an outsider.

The clarity of this message is improved by a third opposition, which sets up contrasts between the emu and kangaroo. She is female and he male. Her femaleness is stressed by the reference to eggs, which emus lay because she swallowed a stone, and yamsticks, typically feminine implements from which she made neck and tail. His maleness is stressed by the references to his tail, for *molo*, Dalabon for tail, is used also for penis. Furthermore, as noted, they differ in their relation to birds who fly. Between birds and kangaroo there is neither communication nor reciprocity. The kangaroo is a passive victim in whose transformation (killed, cooked, divided) is prefigured the transformation and dissolution (through withholding and trickery) of the bird community. Between birds and emu there is communication, albeit flawed, since they collect plant food for her and she sets off to fetch grass for use in eating cooked meat.

Each of these three oppositions has a distinctive character. That between birds and kangaroo is marked by activity on one side and passivity on the other; it may be described as a relation of victimisation. That between birds and emu is marked by activity on each side; it may be described as a relation of antagonism. That between emu and kangaroo is supplementary to the first two; it may be regarded as serving to accentuate the difference between being an antagonist to and a victim of birds who fly. The first occurs between a community and an outsider, the second within a community, and the third between a member of the community and the outsider.

It may in conclusion be suggested that by addressing oneself to the opposed sets of characters about whom M_1 is organised, one is enabled to disentangle the repercussions of the special and general difficulties defined earlier in the paper. If all that is at stake is the general difficulty, then the kangaroo, a member of a terrestrially limited genus, is superfluous. If, however, the special difficulty also is at stake, then it is right and proper to include a kangaroo among the myth's characters, for *gunj* is the alternative genus in which to place emus.

A second analysis

Although the first analysis indicates a resolution of the emu anomaly, it is far from exhausting the mythical material. More particularly, the first analysis makes its point by addressing itself to opposed sets of characters. A complementary analysis is suggested by Lévi-Strauss's Oedipus study, whose fertility is remarkable despite the critical objections to which it is open. This analysis addresses itself to *opposed sets of actions*.

One of the rules of method applied by Lévi-Strauss in that study is that mythical incidents should not be regarded in isolation, but should instead be grouped in bundles according to their themes. Thus in M_1 the cuckoo-shrike's sore foot, which he pleads as an excuse not to hunt, should be seen as manifesting the same theme as the kangaroo's death, by which he is immobilised, and the emu's abandonment on the ground, by which her inability to fly is emphasised. The bundle comprising these incidents may be characterised by the common feature of its constituent items, namely impeded movement. The sore-footed cuckoo-shrike is impeded relative to himself when cured; the dead kangaroo relative to himself when alive; the earthbound emu relative to her former followers flying in the sky; the other birds before they take to flight relative to themselves after taking to flight; birds carrying the kangaroo's tail relative to themselves when unencumbered by it; and the grass pigeon at his first attempt to fly up with the tail relative to his second attempt so to do. These relationships give us two bundles standing in opposition to each other. To the one belong such items as 'Cuckoo-shrike is unable to walk normally because of his sore foot', and to the other such items as 'Cuckoo-shrike, his foot cured, goes off to hunt'. The opposition is of impeded and free movement, each term being understood relative to the other. This pair of bundles accounts for much in the myth.

Much else is accounted for by another pair of bundles standing also in opposition. Consider the number of items having to do with cooperation. Plant foods are collected; intelligence as to the whereabouts of the kangaroo is communicated; a lame hunter consents to be, and is, operated upon; the kangaroo is hunted and the carcass brought back to camp to be cooked and divided; a conspiracy is organised against the emu; and the meat is carried up into the sky. To these instances of helping and sharing may be opposed withholdings of succour and aid. The emu refuses to share plant foods with the other birds, even though they are the providers; the cuckoo-shrike initially excuses himself from hunting; and the other birds keep cooked meat from the emu. This opposition could perhaps be summed up as one between acceptance and refusal of cooperation. The message of the two oppositions is that refusal of cooperation is to acceptance of it as impeded movement is to free. Instead of refusal or acceptance of cooperation one could speak of exclusion from or inclusion in the cooperative circle, but the difference seems immaterial, since the myth makes it plain that stubbornly to refuse to cooperate leads to exclusion from the circle.

This conclusion needs to be enlarged upon to account for the kangaroo. He finishes up with the most radical impediment of all, namely immobility, even though he does not ever refuse to cooperate. Now a refusal of co-operation is possible only within a system of social relations, and it is precisely to this that the kangaroo does not belong. The myth thus presents cooperation and movement in three ways. He who always is outside the cooperative circle becomes totally immobilised. Those who are within the circle and conduct themselves cooperatively become enhanced in their power to move. She who is within the circle but will not cooperate with its other members becomes excluded from it and, although absolutely unchanged in her power to move, relatively impeded. Once more, then, the emu and kangaroo are contrasted both with birds who fly and with each other.

The second analysis brings out more clearly than the first the relation between the primary issue, which is original and insoluble, and the secondary, which is derived and soluble, that earlier I referred to as displacement. The primary issue, the flightlessness of emus, is displaced but not replaced, and it is put in relation not only with what displaces it, namely moral conduct, but with what is like it, namely other handicaps to movement. But the secondary issue dominates the primary: movement is explicated by cooperation, not cooperation by movement.

The reading of the myth obtained by my second analysis might be thought to run into a difficulty. Is it not the case that the emu leaves the cooking place to fetch grass to use in eating the kangaroo? Is not this a cooperative gesture on her part? Now the myth leaves uncertain the emu's intention in setting off for grass. Perhaps she meant to share with the other birds; perhaps she meant to eat the entire meal herself. What we do know is that by the time she started out she had been excluded from the cooperative circle. Had she realised this she would doubtless have remained at the cooking place; the trick played on her was to feign cooperation in order to get her out of the way. The emu has to fall for the trick, if only because emus are flightless and other birds can fly.

Comparable inevitabilities are to be found in fire and death myths from Australia (Maddock 1970:177; 1972:158–61). In the former, characters who wish to withhold fire from all the world have to be worsted, and in the latter, characters who introduce death to the world have to commit, wittingly or unwittingly, their deed. The objective necessities of the situation constrain them with fateful inexorability. Lévi-Strauss (1958a:229) has pointed out that anything can happen in a myth, that the succession of events it portrays seems free from any rule of logic or continuity. Hence the paradox of mythology: the similarity, in widely separated localities, of seemingly arbitrary creations. But clearly one constraint present in many myths is that often a myth is a coming to terms with objective features of the world. No imagining, however bold, can deny the emu's inability to fly or the common possession of fire or the common subjection to death.

The Dalabon in Relation to other Emu Myths

Myths explaining the emu's inability to fly are reported from a number of Aboriginal societies. It is possible accordingly to supplement the foregoing analyses, in which M_1 was considered in its own light and in the light of practices or notions belonging to or represented in its own society, with an analysis in which it is considered in the light of myths from other places. Two myths from Arnhem Land and four from south-east Australia have been chosen for this purpose.

A reputed Nunggubuyu or Ngalagan man from Ngukurr (as it now is) gave me a long myth from which I have extracted an episode about an emu.

M$_2$. A woman was out in the middle of a plain with her daughter's daughter and the Milky Way. The younger woman said to the older, 'Lift the Milky Way so I can see it.' While this was happening the two women were watched by an emu, who thought to steal their fire, for he felt cold, and were seen also by a goanna, who was travelling with his wife, another goanna, towards Jamiri (Mt Roper). The goanna decided that the Milky Way should be lowered to the ground, so he went up to the women and said, 'Put it down! Leave it down!' The older woman had already expressed the opinion that it should be put down, because otherwise people would see it. The two women stayed out in the plain with the Milky Way, which can still be seen there as a white stone amidst scrub.

The emu was still thinking about fire. Up he came, took the women's fire and returned with it, hidden beneath his wings, to the river. In those days the emu had large wings and could fly.

Presently a chickenhawk and goanna arrived from Namiliwiri. The chickenhawk told his companion to travel on, adding, 'I can see somebody down there. I want to get the fire.' In the meantime, another chickenhawk, this time from Narwarwar (near Mt Moore) had been trying in vain to take the emu's fire. The Namiliwiri chickenhawk, seeing the emu making fire, flew down, snatched it and set alight the grass. The emu was burned in the blaze, which is why emus now have small wings and cannot fly.

Elkin (1971:129fn., 144) gives a fragmented version of this myth. According to his information chickenhawks three times tried to get the emu's fire. Smoke from the grass fire lit by sparks the thief dropped reached the sky to become the Milky Way. Elkin's version gives the emu once as male and once as female. The masculine pronoun was used by my informant, but as this is commonly employed by Aboriginal speakers of English for females as well as males one cannot be sure that a male emu was meant. The emu's sex in M$_2$ must accordingly be regarded as doubtful, in contrast to M$_1$, where certainly it is female.

These first two myths superficially are unlike, and yet in each an emu (gregarious and female or solitary and of uncertain sex) is discomforted (left behind on the ground without cooked meat or burnt) through the medium of something culinary (food or fire) of which the emu had been guilty of depriving others (birds or two women). In each myth the emu is in a relation of antagonism to birds who fly. In M$_1$ a gregarious emu is opposed to all species of flying bird; in M$_2$ a solitary emu is opposed to a single species of flying bird. Each myth is a play on movement on different planes in different elements by different modes of locomotion, and has its characters change relative to one another in their power to move. Some characters get immobilised (kangaroo or two women), some retain the same power throughout (emu or goannas and chickenhawks), and others are enhanced (birds who fly in M$_1$) or diminished (emu in M$_2$).

Our ignorance of the taxonomy of the people to whom M$_2$ belongs prevents us from asking whether their myth resolves a taxonomic anomaly, but certainly it accounts for the difference between emus and birds who fly. The emu used to be like other birds, but became diminished in power. M_1 makes the same point by inversion: other birds used to be like the emu, but became enhanced in power. That M_1 puts the matter positively (enhancement) and M_2 negatively (diminution) is to be connected with their different initial assumptions. In M_1 it is supposed that no birds could fly, and hence the problem is to differentiate birds who fly from emus. In M_2 it is supposed that emus could fly, and accordingly the problem becomes one of differentiating emus from birds who fly.

The next myth is from the Murngin area, for which we possess some taxonomic data. I am indebted to Nicolas Peterson for his advice that the emu is there included together with marsupials, lizards and snakes in a taxon named *warrakan* (within which snakes are distinguished as *bapi*). All birds, except emus, are *wayin*. Small birds that normally are not eaten can be spoken of as *djikai*, but Peterson inclines to the opinion that this is a segment of *wayin*. The Murngin taxonomy, by separating birds who fly from reptiles and marsupials as well as from the flightless emu, is spared the special difficulty with which the Dalabon are faced. One may presume that ability to fly is a criterion of Murngin ordering of species; if so, then emus are not obviously out of place. The general difficulty remains.

> M_3. The jabiru, the emu's sister's son and daughter's husband, went fishing by canoe with his wife. On their return he cooked and ate the fat, the choicest part, of the stingrays they had caught, keeping only lean meat for his mother's brother. When the emu, who had been looking forward to a good meal, learned what had happened, he upbraided his sister's son for being greedy and heartless and clubbed him across the buttocks. The jabiru retaliated by breaking his mother's brother's arms with a stick, which is why emus are unable to fly, and by throwing a stone at him, which entered the emu to become his[!] egg.
>
> Next the jabiru flew into the sky where he circled around while the emu lay almost lifeless on the ground. The emu revived, took a spear from his son, and threw it at the jabiru, piercing him in the buttocks. The jabiru plummeted to earth, landing in a saltwater swamp. There he decided to stay. The spear, which had passed through his mouth, became his bill. For his part, the emu left for the bush, resolving to keep away from the water

(Warner 1937:543–5).

The Berndts (1964:333–4) and Robinson (1966:161–3) give versions of this myth. As in Warner's version, the quarrel between the emu and jabiru arises out of the way in which the latter, who is depicted as a fisherman, shares cooked fish. The motif of injury to the emu is missing from Robinson's version.

M_3, like the first two, works itself out in terms of different modes of movement on different planes in different elements. But there is a shift in elemental stress. On the one hand, the aquatic element is emphasised by references to fishing, a canoe, stingrays and the wading habit of the jabiru. On the other hand, the emu and jabiru end up by being characterised as creatures of the dry bush and brackish swamp respectively. Thus whereas

M_1 and M_2 refer more especially to the aerial/terrestrial opposition, M_3 prefers the terrestrial/aquatic. This 'lowering' of the scene of action is very possibly a distinctive feature of coastal as against inland northern Arnhem Land myths. In fire myths, for example, as one proceeds from Dalabon to Gunwinggu and Murngin one finds a closing of distances between the opponents brought about by the 'higher' term coming nearer to the 'lower' (Maddock 1970:182–3). The Dalabon pair the crocodile with the rainbow bird, which spends much of its time fluttering about in the air or in treetops; the Gunwinggu with the plover, a bird which spends much of its time on the ground; and the Murngin with an arboreal lizard. This downward trend in the fire myths invites comparison with the trend in the emu myths by which the Dalabon oppose the emu to birds generally and the Murngin to a bird which spends much of its time wading. An evident geographical correlate of these differences is that the coastal Arnhem Land peoples are in touch with the sea and use the flats along the shore, whereas their inland neighbours are habituated to the so-called Stony Country, a broken sandstone plateau.

Another difference is in the morality of the antagonists. The first two myths depict the emu as one who takes from others without making any return. Eventually the emu suffers a loss, either at the hands of those she has deprived (M_1) or at the hands of a newly introduced character (M_2). But in M_3 it is the emu's antagonist who is depicted as a taker. He has obtained the emu's daughter as wife, and now he keeps the choicest food. The emu, like the other birds in M_1, is moved to antagonistic action by a partner's failure to render what is due. Between them the first three myths present as many variations on the relation between taker and deprived:

M_1 The taker is deprived by those she had deprived.

M_2 The taker is deprived by another taker.

M_3 The taker takes again.

In each case, however, the emu loses in the end to his or her antagonist; the variation accordingly is in preliminaries. Indeed, the emu must lose, for after all emus cannot fly, and the point of these myths is that inability to fly, however brought about, is a lack comparable to lack of success in relationships with others.[7]

In some other respects M_3 is intermediary between the first two or combines elements from each. As in M_1 the emu is flightless throughout, but as in M_2 he suffers a crippling injury to the organs of flight. As in M_1 the emu belongs to a community, but as this comprises only the families of the emu and jabiru M_3 has moved in the direction of M_2, in which the emu is throughout a solitary. Whereas M_1 has it that the emu's antagonists became enhanced while the emu remained the same, and M_2 that the emu became diminished while his (or her) antagonists remained the same, M_3 relates an enhancement of the emu's antagonist and a diminution of the emu. The jabiru takes to flight and the emu is crippled.

That the emu in M_1 does not suffer any diminution raises a problem. Why, it might be asked, does she not take to flight like her former followers? It is true that she was tricked into leaving the cooking place, the site of transformation, but in other myths the emu suffers an injury sufficient to explain flightlessness. Some Arnhem Land fire myths also exhibit the peculiarity of solving one problem only to raise another, for they show a character in possession of fire or of the knowledge of it, but do not explain how he came to have or know fire. In analysing those myths, I argued (1970:181–6) that they may be regarded as links in a super-myth, a chain of narratives from different areas that hold together in such a way that each has its unsolved problem answered in the myth before it, until at last we arrive at a logically prior myth explaining the first origin of fire. Could the emu myths also be seen as links in a chain? The unsolved problem of M_1, which impels us to seek a prior myth, is that the emu remained on the ground. M_2 and M_3 offer an answer: the emu stayed behind because crippled. In short, if we take M_1 on its own, the emu's inability must be seen as connected with culinary transformation, but if we widen the inquiry to take in other myths, the emu's inability can alternatively be seen as connected with the history of birds of this species.

M_{1-3} are from Arnhem Land, an area included in the part of Australia from which I drew my northern group of fire myths (1970:196). The next two emu myths are from the area of my central group of fire myths. Each belongs to the Kamilaroi or Euahlayi of north-east New South Wales, but they will here be treated as separate, for not only do they differ interestingly in content, but Parker worked among these people more than half a century before Robinson.

> M_4.   The bustard, envious of the emu's unsurpassed powers of flight, induced her to amputate her wings by appealing to her wish to be outstanding among the birds. When the emu realised the trick played on her, she obtained revenge by inducing the bustard to kill all save two of her young in order that she might have young of outstanding size
>
> (Parker 1896:1–5.)

> M_5.   The emu induced the brolga to kill all save two of her young by appealing to her wish to have something good to eat. When the brolga realised the trick played on her, she obtained revenge by inducing the emu to amputate her wings in order that she, too, might have something good to eat.
>
> (Robinson 1966:196–7.)

A double injury occurs in each of the central myths. The character who first is injured turns the tables by bringing about an injury to the other. In each myth one injury takes the form of mutilation and the other of infanticide, but in M_4 amputation occurs first and in M_5 infanticide. In each myth the characters injure themselves thanks to their credulity when a tricky suggestion is made, but in M_4 it is vanity that is played upon and in M_5 greed for food.

Comparing these central with the northern myths we find that two features are exclusive to the former. One is the motif of self-inflicted injury, with the emu mutilating herself and the emu's antagonist destroying most of her own offspring (if it is thought that to injure one's offspring is not really

115

to be considered as a self-inflicted injury, then the characterisation could be amended to make it refer to the fact that injuries are inflicted and received within the species). The other is a reduction to two of the number of species from which the characters are drawn. In the north at least three species appear on the scene, and injuries are inflicted by a member of one species on a member of another. Furthermore, the northern myths contain the motif of the passive victim (kangaroo, two women, stingrays) belonging to a species different from that of the antagonists (emu/birds who fly, emu/chickenhawks, emu/jabiru). It is true that the central myths contain passive victims under the form of the offspring of one of the antagonists, but as killer and killed are of the same species the inclusion of this motif serves no longer to make species contrasts.

In other respects the myths of the central group can be seen as nearer now to one and now to another of the northern group. They are nearer to M_1 in that their emus are female and that each antagonist engineers a loss for the other. They are nearer to M_{2-3} in that their emus get crippled. They are nearer to M_2 in that they recount diminution but not enhancement in power to move, and nearer to M_3 in that offspring are mentioned. They are nearer to $M_{1,3}$ in that death occurs.

If the central myths are compared with each other, M_5 is seen as somewhat more akin to the northern group, for on the one hand M_5 contains the culinary motif present in all of the northern myths, and on the other it opposes the brolga, a bird figuring in M_1, to the emu. The brolga occurs also in another northern myth as an antagonist to the emu. This is a Wikmunkan tale (McConnel 1957:91–4) according to which two emus, husband and wife, out of envy hid children entrusted to them by two brolgas, also husband and wife. But the Wikmunkan myth falls outside our terms of reference, because it fails to account for the flightlessness of emus. Its interest here is merely that, like $M_{1,5}$, it depicts an antagonism between the emu and brolga, and, like M_{4-5}, depicts the emu as an enemy of the young. Even allowing for these differences, it is evident that M_{4-5} have more in common with each other than either has with any myths of the northern group.

That it is good to think of brolgas in opposition to emus is brought out when two myths from the area of my southern group of fire myths are added to those already considered. One is from the Murray River Aborigines.

M_6.   The emu used to live in the sky until the brolga induced her to have her wings amputated in order that she might live on earth like other birds. Next the brolga induced the emu to break all save one of her eggs in order that she might be free of a numerous brood. The brolga was punished for these tricks by the All-Father's son, who bent and wrinkled her neck, reduced to one or two the number of eggs she lays, and changed her voice from sweet to harsh.

Afterwards the brolga insulted the emu and, taking advantage of her impetuous rush forward, leapt over her back and smashed all her eggs save one. The brolga escaped into the air with the surviving egg, which she threw at a heap of wood in the hope of

smashing it, but the force of impact caused a fire by which the
world was illumined. The light so impressed the All-Father
that he resolved to kindle a fire each day.

(Massola 1968:99–102.)

This myth is repetitive, since the brolga twice smashes all except one
of the emu's eggs, and the repetition is unnecessary to account for the
emu's peculiarities, or even for the brolga's, because that has been accomplished in the first half of the narrative. But the incidents related, apart from
intervention by the All-Father and his son, would not be out of place in
M_{1-5}. More particularly, by casting the emu as a repeated loser, M_6 calls
M_3 to mind, even though, in the Murngin tale, the emu's first loss is implied
rather than expressed. The other southern myth, from the Wotjobaluk, is
reminiscent of $M_{1,4-5}$ in that the emu and her antagonist are portrayed
as each bringing about a loss for the other.

M_7.   Despite their jealousy of each other, the emu and brolga
were friends. One day they set out to collect xipha roots.
Afterwards they lit a fire to cook the roots. Because the brolga
would not lend her yamstick, the emu had to push roots into the
fire with her feet, wings and bill in that order, with the result that
she was scorched and her wings made useless for flight.
  When next the pair went collecting roots the emu induced
the brolga to kill all except two of her young by saying that
she had done the same with hers and then cooked and eaten them,
their flesh being better than roots.

(Massola 1968:36–7.)

The southern group is in some ways closely akin to the central. The emu
and her antagonist are female, losses are suffered by trickery, diminution
occurs without enhancement, offspring of one of the antagonists are destroyed, and either the emu cripples herself or she acquiesces in the action
by which another cripples her. The first, fourth and fifth of these motifs
are missing from the myths of the northern group, and the second and
third each occur only in one of them.

In one way, however, the southern group is akin to the northern, but
distinct from the central. This is in the presence of a species additional to
that of the antagonists. But the motif of the extra species is worked out
differently in the two areas, for in the north its representatives are immobilised, whereas in the south they are neither diminished nor enhanced.
It may be noted in this connection that M_7 is closer than M_6 to the northern
myths, since the xipha roots, like the kangaroo, two women and stingrays,
figure passively, whereas the All-Father and his son are active. The central
and southern myths do not omit passivity, but their tendency is to identify
the species of antagonist with that of victim (hence the destruction of offspring in the form of eggs or young of one of the antagonists in M_{4-7})
in contrast to the northern myths, which make a species separation of
antagonist and victim. M_7 is accordingly of double interest, for it has
passive victims of the species of one of the antagonists and others of an
additional species.

117

We have seen that in certain respects the southern group is fully comparable now to the central and now to the northern group. As those features in which southern compares to central are more numerous than those in which southern compares to northern, and as there are no respects in which central and northern are fully comparable, we are surely justified in regarding the central and southern groups as falling together in opposition to the northern. This finding leads us in turn to consider the connection, if any, between emu and other myths. Here reference may be made to fire myths.

My study of the fire myths arrived at the conclusion that wherever the possession of fire is disputed, the loser and winner are placed differently in the vertical register, but that this rule manifests itself differently in north and south. The northern rule is that lower loses to higher, for example a crocodile to a bird, and the southern that higher loses to lower, for example a star to a bird. The central rule follows the northern rather than the southern, except that the distance separating higher and winner from lower and loser is reduced, which may be taken as presaging the inversion that occurs as one moves further to the south.

These rules, and their relation of inversion, cannot entirely be matched in the emu myths. It is true that the central and southern myths convey the suggestion that the emu could fly better than any other bird, which accounts for her antagonist's enmity. The conclusion, that higher loses to or is defeated by lower, is like the rule in the southern fire myths. In the central and southern emu myths, however, the emu, except in M_6, scores a victory of another kind over her antagonist, so that she cannot be represented in an unqualified sense as a loser. Furthermore, the northern emu myths suggest that the antagonists were originally on the same level ($M_{1,3}$) or leaves their relative positioning in the vertical register obscure (M_2).

Two inversions can be established between the northern and southern emu myths, with the central myths akin to the southern (in contrast to the situation with the fire myths, where the central group is akin to the northern). In the south and centre if the emu and her antagonist are of the same sex they both are female. In the north if of the same sex they both are male. They are of the same sex in all of the central and southern myths, but in the north this is certainly the case only for M_3.[8] It is interesting to reflect that the emu myths contain a feminine emphasis precisely in those areas where the All-Father, a male transcendental power, was especially significant in Aboriginal cosmology and ritual, and a masculine emphasis (weaker, it must be admitted, than the corresponding emphasis to the south) in areas where the All-Mother, a female transcendental power, is significant.

The other inversion concerns not sexuality but the mood or spirit in which the antagonists respond to each other. In the south and centre they are remarkable for their acquiescence: an injurious proposal has only to be put to the emu or her antagonist for it to be accepted and acted upon. And when, in M_7, the brolga refuses the use of her yamstick, the emu accepts the denial without demur and, using her wings instead, proceeds to cripple herself. The mood of acquiescence in injury to oneself usually is succeeded by a determination to obtain revenge when the trick is appreciated: the original victim then finds her antagonist as acquiescent as she herself had been. The spirit is different in the north. There one inflicts an injury or loss in the course of a deliberate and conscious antagonism or as an outcome of it. The southern rule, valid for the central as well as the southern myths, is then that the emu consents to her own diminution. The northern rule is that the emu does not so consent, and that diminution, if it occurs, has to be inflicted upon him (or her). It would be tempting to infer that these rules are connected with real or putative differences in sexual psychology, female characters being depicted as devious, credulous and acquiescent, male as forceful and obstreperous. But such a female character scarcely fits the brolga in M_6, and in M_2 the emu's sex is uncertain.

But when all differences between myths and groups of myths are acknowledged, a striking similarity remains. This is that the relation of antagonism, an outcome of which is differentiation in capacity to move, always is between the emu and *a flying bird or birds*. The implication is that, whatever taxonomy may say, emus are associated more closely with birds who fly than with other creatures. It looks as though the myths are hinting that what we in English call flying and flightless birds belong to the same family and that differences amongst them are like differences within a family. Following on from this it is interesting that differentiation usually is brought about by the emu's diminution. Logically, other birds could be enhanced, as in M_1, but this alternative requires all members save one of the family to change in capacity to move, whereas diminution of the one who is the family's problem member achieves the same end more economically.

Theoretical Significance of the Emu Studies

Is anything of theoretical significance to be gathered from this succession of approaches to a single Dalabon myth? Two points do, I think, stand out prominently. One has to do with relevance, the other with depth.

As to the first, it is clear to me that a criterion of relevance is essential if analysis is to be sound. Analysis without relevance is like evidence without a theory, which is why the Oedipus model ought not to be used unless one has already some notion of a contradiction at the heart of the myth. A criterion of relevance has been furnished in this paper by a difficulty supposed to be raised by flightless birds. This anomaly or puzzle accounts for much in M_{1-7}, but not for all. Consider, for example, the frequency with which emus are set against brolgas. What is the reason for this, and why does another bird sometimes appear as the emu's antagonist? Personally I think that an answer could be found by applying the principle of the union of contraries as worked out by Radcliffe-Brown (1951), and before him by Thomas (1906:53-4) and by Durkheim and Mauss (1903:26). The shift from a brolga to a jabiru or chickenhawk could then be explained along lines suggested by Lévi-Strauss (1960:25-6) as a series of substitutions indicating that the pertinent opposition is not so much between *this* bird and *that*, as between flight and flightlessness or sky and earth or whatever it might be. But to argue in that way would require acceptance of a criterion of relevance differing from the one I have chosen. The conclusion must be drawn that analysis is relative to a criterion, and accordingly that to change the criterion changes the analysis.

The second point to be made here concerns depth. While it is hardly possible to relate different myth analyses to one another in the precise way that different microscopic analyses can be related to one another, an indication of depth is given by the range of material appropriated in analysis. Thus an analysis confined to mythology alone might be thought to be shallower than one inclusive of ritual as well. The trouble here is that analyses can be 'deep', if one may say so, in different ways. An analysis which shows that a myth evinces structures like those of ritual and an analysis which shows that a number of myths are similarly structured can each claim to be deep — but which is the deeper? And depth might be pursued, as by Lévi-Strauss in his Asdiwal study, by relating a myth to a number of practices established in the same society, or, as by the same author in his *Mythologiques*, by showing connections amongst many myths from many societies. Some other conception of depth might of course be proffered, but it may be doubted if it would be more than just another deep analysis, supplementing rather than superseding those already in use.

Notes

1. Earlier versions of parts of this paper were presented at the Canberra conference of the Australian Institute of Aboriginal Studies in May 1972, and at Professor Meyer Fortes's seminar in King's College, Cambridge, in January 1973. The Institute had earlier supported the fieldwork during which I gathered my Dalabon material. Some of the data appearing herein have been discussed with A.C. van der Leeden and members of the Australian Working Group at Nijmegen University and with Sheila Mackay and L.R. Hiatt. The paper as a whole has been revised and completed at Wassenaar during my tenure of a fellowship from the Netherlands Institute for Advanced Study in the Humanities and Social Sciences. I am indebted to all these persons and institutions for the different kinds of assistance they have rendered to me.

2. At the Canberra conference N.B. Tindale and John Calaby drew my attention to reports of cassowaries in this area. The evidence is exiguous, and seems not to justify a conclusion one way or the other. If cassowaries are to be found in southern Arnhem Land, they must surely be rare, for otherwise one would expect them to be as well known as are emus. It may be worth mentioning that the Dalabon distinguish two species of emu but, if asked for their name for emus, seem always to give *ngurudu*, which is the name of the emu in my myth. The other kind is called *gulbanban*. Conceivably it is a cassowary. Or perhaps the Aborigines, now that English is their *lingua franca* and the only tongue spoken by them all, use the word 'emu' for two birds between whom no nominal connection was made in earlier times. In the latter connection it is noteworthy that the Aborigines sometimes speak of the grass pigeon, the emu's leading antagonist in my myth, as 'little emu'. Aborigines told me that *gulbanban* and *ngurudu* are the same, but that the former is black-faced and belongs to the *Dua* moiety, whereas the latter is *Yiridja*. *Gulban* and *gulbanda* occurs as names of *ngurudu* in songs of the Gunabibi cult.

3. The taxonomy conveyed through the *lingua franca*, Aboriginal English, differs from that discussed here without, however, being the same as the taxonomy popular among white Australians. I assume that my Dalabon myth antedates the Aboriginal English taxonomy. Another classification is made by imposing upon nature the clans and classes of the human social order. This classification will here be ignored. I have discussed elsewhere

(1972:95–108) some characteristics and interrelationships of these two ways — the taxonomic and the human social — of ordering nature.

4. Biologists have, I understand, yet to work out a taxonomy of their own for Arnhem Land flora and fauna. Another difficulty facing the student of Aboriginal taxonomy, at least in many parts of Australia, is that it is usual for contemporary Aborigines to live outside the areas to which their taxonomies primarily refer. This is the case with the Dalabon, who live now at places like Bamyili on the Beswick Reserve, but lived formerly around the Wilton River in country that now is deserted because of emigration.

5. The adequacy of these, or any rival, criteria could easily be tested. One would write the name of each species on a separate card and create as many boxes as there are genera. Cards would then be put in boxes according to what one supposed the logic of the taxonomy to be. The best criteria would be those that enabled one to come closest to the actual distribution of species in genera. A control test could be made by putting cards randomly in boxes.

6. My opinion here departs from that of Lévi-Strauss himself (1964:10) and one of his most eminent commentators, de Josselin de Jong (1973), both of whom stress the continuity of Lévi-Strauss's myth studies.

7. It is interesting to find that the Karam myth explaining the cassowary (Bulmer 1967:17–8) treats the cassowary as a loser, even though no reference is made to its inability to fly. The first cassowary was a woman who exchanged gifts disadvantageously with her brother. She gave green snail shells, axes 'and other good gifts', and received in return 'very poor things'. Next she fell into a trap her brother had concealed. He knew she was coming that way. While in the trap she turned into a cassowary. Later she followed two girls back to their settlement, only to be espied by the residents, who pursued and killed her. From the other hemisphere comes a Flemish tale of the hen and dove (de Cock 1911:45), according to which the dove was pursued and mistreated by her opponent until one day Our Dear Lord intervened to decree that henceforward the hen would be unable to fly more than a step or two.

8. It is hard not to suspect significance in the frequency with which the emu is characterised as female, setting aside for the moment the sex of her antagonist(s). In $M_{1,4-7}$ the emu is female, in M_2 sex is uncertain and in M_3 the emu is ambiguous, being depicted as a mother's brother into whom a stone entered to become an egg. The Karam have it that the first cassowary was female and, according to Burridge (1969:253 fn.2), the Tangu, another New Guinea people, think that 'a cassowary in itself is female rather than male'. The predominance of females among mythical flightless birds perhaps is best explained by invoking a ritual analogy, viz. that birds who fly are to birds who cannot as humans who pass are to humans excluded from passage (flying birds:flightless birds::men:women). But why, in that case, are female emus so often opposed to female birds of other species?

References

BAAL, J. VAN 1967 *Dema: description and analysis of Marind-Anim culture (south New Guinea)*. The Hague, Nijhoff.

BERNDT, R.M. *and* C.H. BERNDT 1964 *The world of the first Australians: an introduction to the traditional life of the Australian Aborigines*. Sydney, Ure Smith.

BULMER, R. 1967 Why is the cassowary not a bird? A problem of zoological taxonomy among the Karam of the New Guinea highlands. *Man*, 2(1):5–25.

BURRIDGE, K.O.L. 1967 Lévi-Strauss and myth. In *The structural study of myth and totemism*, (ed.) E.R. Leach, pp. 91–115. London, Tavistock Publications.

———— 1969 *Tangu traditions*. Oxford, Clarendon Press.

COCK, A. DE 1911 *Natuurverklarende sprookjes*. Gent, Hoste.

DAHL, K. 1926 *In savage Australia: an account of a hunting and collecting expedition to Arnhem Land and Dampier Land*. London, Allan.

DETIENNE, M.   1972   *Les jardins d'Adonis*. Paris, Gallimard.

DURKHEIM, E. *and* M. MAUSS   1903   De quelques formes primitives de classification. *L'Année sociologique*, 6, 1901–02:1–72.

ELKIN, A.P.   1971   Yabuduruwa at Roper River Mission, 1965. *Oceania*, 42(2):110–64.

GUÉPIN, J.P.   1973   Propp kan niet en waarom (II). *Forum der Letteren*, 14:30–51.

HEUSCH, L. DE   1972   *Le roi ivre ou l'origine de l'état*. Paris, Gallimard.

HIATT, L.R.   1966   Lévi-Strauss and Oedipus Rex. Unpublished paper, Department of Anthropology, University of Sydney.

JACKSON, M.   1968   Some structural considerations of Maori myth. In *Polynesian Society, Journal*, 77:147–62.

JOSSELIN DE JONG, P.E. DE   1973   Voltooide symphonie: de 'Mythologiques' van Claude Lévi-Strauss. *Forum der Letteren*, 14:95–120.

LEACH, E.R.   1962   Genesis as myth. *Discovery*, 23:30–35.

———   1966   The legitimacy of Solomon: some structural aspects of Old Testament history. *European Journal of Sociology*, 7:58–101.

LÉVI-STRAUSS, C.   1958a   *Anthropologie structurale*. Paris, Plon.

———   1958b   La geste d'Asdiwal. In *École Pratique des Hautes Études, Section des Sciences Religieuses*. Annuaire (1958–9):3–43.

———   1960   La structure et la forme: réflexions sur un ouvrage de Vladimir Propp. *Cahiers de l'Institut de Science Économique Appliqué*, 99:3–36.

———   1964   *Mythologiques: le cru et le cuit*. Paris, Plon.

———   1968   Religions comparées des peuples sans écriture. In *Problèmes et méthodes d'histoire des religions: melanges publiées par la section des sciences religieuses à l'occasion du centenaire de l'école pratique des hautes études*. Paris, Presses Universitaires de France.

MCCONNEL, U.H.   1957   *Myths of the Mungkan*. Melbourne, Melbourne University Press.

MADDOCK, K.   1970   Myths of the acquisition of fire in northern and eastern Australia. In *Australian Aboriginal anthropology: modern studies in the social anthropology of the Australian Aborigines*, (ed.) R.M. Berndt, pp. 174–99. Nedlands, University of Western Australia Press.

———   1972   *The Australian Aborigines: a portrait of their society*. London, Allen Lane, the Penguin Press.

MASSOLA, A.   1968   *Bunjil's cave: myths, legends and superstitions of the Aborigines of south-east Australia*. Melbourne, Lansdowne Press.

MEIJER, P.W.M. DE   1970   Eenvoudige vertelstructuren: Propp en Lévi-Strauss. *Forum der Letteren*, 11:145–59.

NATHORST, B.   1970   *Formal or structural studies of traditional tales*. Stockholm, Almqvist & Wiksell.

PARKER, LANGLOH K.   1896   *Australian legendary tales: folk-lore of the Noongahburrahs as told to the piccaninnies*. London, Nutt.

RADCLIFFE-BROWN, A.R.   1951   The comparative method in social anthropology. In *Royal Anthropological Institute, Journal*, 81:15–22.

RICHARD, P.   1967   Analyse des mythologiques de Claude Lévi-Strauss. *L'Homme et la Société*, 4:109–33.

ROBINSON, M.S.   1968   'The house of the mighty hero' or 'The house of enough paddy?' Some implications of a Sinhalese myth. In *Dialectic in practical religion*, (ed.) E.R. Leach, pp. 122–52. London, Cambridge University Press.

ROBINSON, R.   1966   *Aboriginal myths and legends*. Melbourne, Sun Books.

SEBAG, L.   1971   *L'invention du monde chez les indiens Pueblos*. Paris, Maspero.

THOMAS, N.W.   1906   *Kinship organisations and group marriage in Australia*. Cambridge, Cambridge University Press.

TURNER, T.S.   1969   Oedipus: time and structure in narrative form. In *Forms of symbolic action*, (ed.) R.F. Spencer, pp. 26–68. Seattle and London, University of Washington Press.

WARNER, W.L.   1937   *A black civilization: a social study of an Australian tribe*. New York, Harper.

Sexual Conquest and Submission in the Myths of Central Australia

Isobel M. White

In this paper I examine Central Australian Aboriginal myths and the relationships they depict between men and women, especially the sexual relationship. I find that most often the myths symbolise 'antagonism between the sexes', as R.M. Berndt suggested in an article (1970:235). In the myths men and women live apart from each other, sometimes as single individuals, sometimes in all-male or all-female groups. Instances are rare of the nuclear family living and travelling as a unit. Male and female come together only for sexual intercourse, but seldom by mutual agreement and in a relationship approved by the strict kinship rules. Women flee from men's advances and rape is frequent. As a contrast, in some myths women are represented as threatening and dangerous.

I interpret the myths as symbolising the values of a male-dominated society, where women are seen by men primarily as sexual objects, rather than as companions and equal partners, even in marriage, while men are seen by women as sexual conquerors, to whom submission must finally be made, but not without a show of resistance. I then compare the mythical picture of sexual relationships with the available accounts and records of traditional Aboriginal society and with my own observations of Western Desert people living in changed conditions after half a century of contact with Europeans.

I studied the literature on Aboriginal myths, mostly collected from male informants, and examined my own transcriptions and observations of the women's myths and ceremonies. Since my own fieldwork[1] has been confined to South Australia (mainly with Western Desert, but also with Simpson Desert and Flinders Ranges, people) I have limited my study to Central Australia, with only brief reference to other areas. My chief literary sources were R.M. and C.H. Berndt and N.B. Tindale for the Western Desert, M.J. Meggitt for Walbiri, B. Spencer and F. Gillen and T.G.H. Strehlow for Aranda.

The more myths I studied the more evident it became that sexual relations in myths are not typical of those in traditional Aboriginal society. Myths record almost no cases of licit sexual intercourse with mutual agreement of both parties; where there is mutual agreement then the relationship is usually illicit, either incestuous or adulterous or during a period of sexual taboo for one or other party; or if it is licit, it consists of rape, or it takes place after a long chase and difficult subjugation of the female.

It is necessary here to explain the terms licit and illicit. Illicit sexual relationships can be of three types. First there are those unions regarded

123

as incestuous because of the kinship status of the partners. From the point of view of an individual all members of his society are grouped into certain kinship categories and a man must take his wife, and indeed any sexual partner, from one, or possibly two, of the female kin categories. All other unions are incestuous and subject to punishment. Secondly, adultery is illicit unless permitted or condoned by the non-participating partners. Thirdly, during certain times one or other partner may be under a ban, for example, a boy segregated for initiation or a woman who has recently given birth. Licit sexual intercourse means a union between partners (not necessarily husband and wife) to whom none of these interdicts apply.

The discussion in this paper will deal with the violence of mythical sexual relations rather than with their frequently illicit nature. It is therefore important to examine the meaning of the term rape as it is used in the literature. In English it can suggest for example several males holding down a woman while another has intercourse with her, one male holding down a weaker female by force, or one male using threats of violence or blackmail to compel submission. Unfortunately, I do not know what the Aboriginal male informants themselves implied by the term which has been translated as rape. The women use one of the normal terms for copulation in telling their myths, and qualify it to suggest force. The question of what is implied by rape is made more tantalising by the fact that Aborigines normally use the oceanic position for sexual intercourse, a position requiring co-operation of the female and quite impossible for violent rape. The final submission of the female, which I have witnessed enacted in the women's ceremonies, takes place usually in the oceanic position, less frequently in a horizontal (but not missionary) position. I suspect that the women's myths reflect an attitude on the part of the woman best summed up in the old proverb, 'If rape is inevitable, relax and enjoy it.' But in at least one Western Desert men's myth, rape is described as extremely cruel and violent. Mr N.M. Wallace (personal communication) was shown a site in the Mann Range where a Goanna Man (not one of the Two Men, whose exploits are discussed later) battered and raped a woman, and seriously injured her. There are red marks on the rocks representing her blood.

The mythical stories of the extensible or detachable penis must be interpreted as fantasies reflecting sexual ambition on the part of the men and sexual fear on the part of the women.

The ethnographic literature, the evidence I have gathered myself, and verbal information from colleagues, all lead to the conclusion that rape carried out by brute strength was, and is, rare in Aboriginal society. But there is some evidence of rape occurring under threat. P.M. Kaberry (1939:229) tells of a Wolmeri man who forced a classificatory mother-in-law to copulate with him by showing her a sacred object which women are forbidden to see and threatening to kill her for seeing it if she did not submit. Kaberry adds that the Djaru admitted that men sometimes used this stratagem to compel women to have intercourse with them. Meggitt (1964: 72), discussing the power of the medicine men, suggests that they might use the threat of sorcery to compel women to submit to them, but that this tactic was most unfavourably regarded. Women in most Aboriginal societies could expiate a crime of sacrilege by submitting to all the initiated men of the offended group, another example of rape under duress, since the alternative was for the women to be killed (R.M. Berndt 1965:192; Spencer and Gillen 1927: vol. 1, 168; Meggitt 1962:53).

My reaction to the violent nature of sexual relations in recorded myths and to the absence of the nuclear family was that perhaps the writers had been selective in their reporting, or that the informants had been selective in their information. But when I turned to my own material collected from women, I found that in some myths intercourse is either forced on the women or illicit, sometimes both, and that again there is an absence of the nuclear family. Other myths tell of pursuit by the man and unwillingness at first on the part of the woman, but do end up with her becoming his wife. However, there is no sequel telling of their life or travels together.

The Ownership of Myths

Central Australian myths can be divided into a number of categories, in accordance with their ownership by men or women and the knowledge that each sex is permitted to have of them. The two major categories are myths belonging to men, with male heroes as the central characters, and enacted in ceremonies by men alone, contrasted with myths belonging to women, with emphasis on female characters, and enacted by women alone. In addition there are myths, belonging to men, which are dramatised with women playing minor parts under the authority of men. Women and children can see sections of these ceremonies, but for long periods they must lie face downwards with their eyes hidden (today they also cover themselves with blankets), while men patrol the rows of recumbent bodies to ensure that there is no peeping. Then there are myths, belonging primarily to men, but also shared by women, emphasising both female and male characters, whose enactment is by each sex alone (see later for an account of the Seven Sisters cycle of myths).

According to my own observations, older women know at least some of the men's secret myths, though they recite them only to mature women in a whispered voice, with no dramatisation. Two of the Yalata women, ritual leaders, once whispered to me one of the many Two Men stories (not the Two Goanna Men discussed on p. 128). They had the right to know and tell this myth because the fathers of both women were of the Two Men totem. However, so secret-sacred do the women regard some sections of the men's myths that certain ordinary words are always spoken in a whisper. For example, I was once being given a language lesson and asked the words for the various kinds of lizard. My teacher would only whisper, in the special reverential manner used for the most sacred utterances, the native words for the two kinds of goanna, *milbalhi* and *jungga*, which are the most important non-human manifestations of the Two Men. The words for the other species of lizard were spoken in a normal voice.

I have evidence that the reverse is true — older ritually important men know the women's secret myths. One day when the Yalata camp was deserted by all but the older inhabitants, the women ritual leaders displayed their secret ceremonial objects to two old men, one of them blind. It was an unforgettable experience to witness the blind old man pick up each beautiful object, turn it over reverently in his hands, determine what it was, and then recite the appropriate section of the women's myth. (At least I assume that it was the women's version, but it may have been the men's version of the same myth; or the two may be identical; as yet no comparisons have been made between men's and women's texts.)

In this question of knowing or not knowing, it is not the actual knowledge that matters, but what one is permitted to know. I suspect that many, if not most, men and women have some knowledge which their age or status forbids them to have. It is strange that small boys up to the age of six or seven years are allowed to attend secret ceremonies with their mothers, apparently in the fond belief that they are too young to understand or remember what they see.

I have discussed at some length the secret-sacred nature of the myths in order to emphasise their importance in establishing the values of Aboriginal society.

The Men's Myths

Until the diffusion into the northern Central Desert from Arnhem Land of the Gunabibi myth with the Mother as the central figure, the Desert myths told of primary creation by males only. The great ancestral heroes were capable of changing landscapes, making waterholes, and creating living phenomena, plant, animal and human. New life could come from their bodies, they could form humans out of other beings, or they could bring life out of nothingness. They could also make natural features out of their own bodies, occurrences which Munn, in a paper (1970) about the ancestors in Walbiri and Pitjantjatjara (Bidjandjara) myths, has called 'transformations'. She remarks: 'Ancestors may be wholly human or, more typically, partly human and partly non-human. Although for convenience I refer to them in general as male, they may be male or female. In this region, however, male ancestors are emphasized' (Munn 1970:143).

The Northern Aranda myth of Karora, the bandicoot ancestor, recorded by Strehlow (1947:7–13), is an example of the creative power of the male ancestors. Karora, lying in eternal sleep, at the bottom of the then dry soak at Ilbalintja, began to wake and bandicoots came out from his navel and armpits. The bandicoots came to life, the sun rose for the first time, and Karora himself arose and felt hungry. He killed two bandicoots and cooked them with the sun's rays and devoured them. As the sun set and darkness returned, he wished for a helpmate and during the night, a bull-roarer emerged from his armpit, and took human shape as his first born son. More sons were born in the same way on successive nights, and each day they hunted bandicoots and brought them back to the camp, until all the bandicoots had been killed and eaten. The sons wounded and lamed Tjenterama, a sandhill wallaby (Strehlow suggests that this may have been Karora himself in another guise), and then all the characters were swept away by a flood and returned to their eternal dreaming. Strehlow writes: 'Here we find the idea of the Great Father, who was ever from the beginning, and from whose body both the animals and the men of a certain totem have originated. It must be stressed, too, that no mention is made of women in this myth: from the original Great Father only sons have descended' (1947:10). In a footnote he suggests that, though there are some female ancestors in Western and Southern Aranda myths, 'in the great majority of Aranda myths and in practically all the Northern Aranda stories the sole parenthood of the father is elaborated and emphasized in no uncertain terms . . . It is obvious that the native story-teller himself derives an obvious delight from this very feature. It seems that this reversal of roles is partly caused by an attempt on the part of the native man to find psychological compensation for his own thwarted pride of fatherhood by picturing his totemic ancestors as men who did not need the assistance of women in order to beget their children.' More recently Hiatt (1971) and White (1970) have elaborated this view. As to Strehlow's finding that Southern and Western Aranda did recognise some female ancestors, a possible explanation for the Southern Aranda, and perhaps for the Western Aranda too, would be contact with the Flinders Ranges and Simpson Desert people, whose social organisation was based on matrilineal moieties, with consequent recognition of female ancestors. Strehlow himself suggests (1947:72) that the Southern Aranda might have had a patrilineal order imposed fairly recently on an older matrilineal order.

The contrast is shown by two Andjamathana (Flinders Ranges) myths of origin. Hercus and the present writer were told by an old Andjamathana man that in the beginning the middle strip of the rainbow represented a man and the strips on each side represented two women, one of whom gave birth to all people of the Mathari moiety, and the other to the Araru. Mountford and Harvey (1941:156–7) record an Adnjamathana belief that in the sky there are two old women, one Mathari, one Araru, with spirit children clinging to their breasts. The spirit children descend to earth and enter women of the appropriate moiety.

This difference between the myths of the Northern Aranda and those of the Western and Southern Aranda is reflected in the composition of the groups which travelled together. Strehlow remarks (1947:92): 'In Western and Southern Aranda myths we commonly find ancestors living together in small groups containing both men and women. In the Northern area, where men and women ancestors are usually kept separate, their paths are frequently said to have crossed one another.' In one instance where women appear it is not the wives of the men, but their fathers' sisters, who act as friends and helpmates (ibid:37). As we shall see later, it is the Northern Aranda pattern which is followed by the myths of the Walbiri and the Bidjandjara.

The Northern Aranda belief in males as original creators must confront the fact that for ordinary mortals it is women who bring forth children. Moreover, a child's first awareness is of a mother who has great power over him, in giving or denying food and bodily comfort. We might expect myths to reflect some realisation of the contrasting roles of women, as conquered, submissive sexual partners, and as powerful mother figures. Strehlow points out that some evidence of this contrast is shown by the Aranda myths (1947:94): '. . . the female ancestors celebrated in Aranda

127

myths are usually dignified and sometimes awe-inspiring figures, who enjoyed unlimited freedom of decision and action. Frequently they were much more powerful beings than their male associates, and the latter sometimes lived in constant terror of their mysterious supernatural strength . . . Reverently proud of the powerful feminine characters described in their ancient legends, Aranda men look down upon their own women with a certain measure of pitying contempt.'

Women therefore were not necessary for original creation throughout most of the Western and Central Desert areas, though later they made some alterations in the landscape and reproduced the species first created by the ancestral heroes. But even in the task of reproduction they needed to be entered by the life essence left in the totemic sites by the heroes. They could also be used by the male mythological beings for sexual purposes, and to provide food, water and fire, though in the last three concerns we often find the males supplying their own needs. That hunting and food-gathering roles could be reversed is shown by a Dieri myth recorded by Howitt (1904:794) in which two male heroes, one a hunter, the other a seed-gatherer, decided one day to perform each other's tasks. In this particular myth there is no mention of any women who could have been expected to supply the vegetable food.

The most revered mythical heroes of the Western Desert are the Two Men (Wadhi Gudjara),[2] pre-eminent because in their Goanna manifestation they instituted the rites of circumcision and subincision. They are also known as Milbalhi Gudjara (Two Goannas) sometimes as Wadhi Milbalhi (White Goanna Man) and Wadi Jungga (Black Goanna Man), and can have other less important non-human manifestations. They are represented by the stars Gemini, the Twins. There are many other male mythical heroes, each associated with a cult lodge (or totem), who appear usually in the myths as One Man (Wadhi Gudju). One of these is Njiru, the hero of a cycle of stories shared by men and women, in which he continually chases women. Western Desert women, when speaking English, often refer to him as the Larrikin Man.

Accounts of the Two Men, their travels, adventures, and acts of creation are given by R.M. Berndt (1941:7–12) collected from men at Ooldea, and by Tindale (1936:168–85) and Mountford (1937:5–28) from men of the Warburton Range. Berndt records that the Two Men exchange their sisters in marriage, but no further mention is made of these wives. However, other mythical women, the Seven Sisters,[3] are described by Berndt (1941:11) as 'the Kunkarankara women, who rightfully belong to the Wati Kutjara, although they were wandering round the country by themselves.' Mountford (1937:9) tells how the Two Men met the women and quarrelled over them; one man drove the other away and slept with one of the women. In Tindale's account, some of the women are wives of one of the heroes, who are brothers-in-law to each other, but the rest of the women are classed in the adjacent generations, and therefore forbidden to either man.[4] When Kulu, the Moon Man, comes looking for women, the Two Men tell the Seven Sisters to hide, but Kulu discovers them and chases them for many days. Ignoring the disappearance of the women, the Two Men continue their creative journey, though some time later they are said to be reconciled to their loss. They eventually meet up with the women, who are still being chased by Kulu and call for help. The men kill Kulu, the women rejoice and go off separately to create various natural features and finally to become the Pleiades.

These are but some of the Western Desert myths about the Seven Sisters, who may also be called Gunggaranggalba or Minjmara according to the dialect of the teller. Moreover they appear in myths recorded from other parts of Australia. In New South Wales, according to Parker (1953:105–9, 125–7), they are called the Mayi-Mayi, and are chased by a man, Wurunna, who succeeds by a stratagem in catching two of them and making them his wives, until they escape into the sky to become the Pleiades. In a story collected by Bozic (Bozic and Marshall 1972:125–7) from Eastern Arnhem Land, Pingal the moon has incestuous lust for his daughters the Seven Sisters (Yogamada). He sends his penis along the ground to enter one of them, but his wife, already a star, sends a rope down and the Seven Sisters climb up into the sky, where they continue to travel together fleeing from the moon. In the Kimberleys the Seven Sisters were chased by Eaglehawk, the Southern Cross (Kaberry 1939:12); in a Dieri myth from Lake Eyre, when an ancestral hero chased them and attempted to take one of them, he was prevented by a disastrous flood (Howitt 1904:787). In all the myths about the Seven Sisters they spend much time running away from the unwelcome and usually illicit advances of a male.

Some of the many myths about the Seven Sisters are known and enacted by women, though further research is necessary to determine whether men and women 'own' identical stories. In the women's ceremonies there is no mention of the Two Men, as these heroes are strictly in the men's domain. The Yalata women tell a portion of the Seven Sisters cycle similar to that collected by R.M. and C.H. Berndt from (presumably) male informants at Ooldea (1942–45:145 and 1964:208). It is associated with a women's ceremony which I have seen several times at Yalata and once at Indulkana (Buckley et al. 1968:113–24). I have also enjoyed a spoken version of the story with a group of women round a camp-fire. The story-teller was the Yalata 'boss' of this ceremony and also the acknowledged ritual leader of the women. She always took the part of Njiru, the man, in the performances of her ceremony because, as one of the other women explained, 'she's the only man amongst us' (she was older than the other active participants, and the only one past menopause). At a women's camp a hundred miles from Yalata, the women had spent the evening performing ceremonies (one of them the Gunggaranggalba). Before going to sleep we spent some time round the camp-fire, and the leader recited the story, with appropriate miming. In her version, Njiru (Njirana in R.M. and C.H. Berndt's version) takes the place of Kulu in chasing the women. They come from the north-west and he chases them through Meekatharra, Wiluna, Laverton, and Kalgoorlie to Cundeelee,[5] where they go into a cave to escape him, but he catches one of them and rapes her. This woman is sick, and because he calls her *gundili* (father's sister) this action is incestuous. She dies, and the other women continue in a northerly direction with Njiru still in pursuit.

At Anmanggu in the Musgrave Ranges he camps near them and is excited by the sight and smell of one of the women urinating. He sends his penis underground to rape her. The women set their dogs onto him and these bite off his penis, which then becomes a separate being Jula, 'the son' or 'the penis' of Njiru. The story-teller used the utmost dramatic effect, with particular enjoyment and sexual hostility, at the point where Njiru lost his penis. It was she who described to me the traditional procedure, which she herself had experienced, for a girl's first menstruation, and told me that the Seven Sisters ceremony was performed for her by other women during her seclusion away from the main camp.

In another version, told by the women at Indulkana, Njiru rapes a woman (not one of the Seven Sisters) who is at the time forbidden to all men because she has just given birth (Buckley *et al.* 1968:114). In one account given by R.M. and C.H. Berndt (1942–45:145; 1964:208–9), it is Minma Mingari (Mountain-Devil Woman) who sets her dogs on Njirana, after he has sent his penis underground to rape her. Julana (Njirana's penis) lives an independent existence and also chases women. All versions regard the constellation Orion or certain stars in Orion as Njiru or Njirana, and the Pleiades or Seven Sisters as the group of women he chased.

Meggitt (1966:131–8) gives the Walbiri men's equivalent of the Njiru and Seven Sisters myth under the title of 'The Travelling Women and the Incestuous Man'. The man Winggingarga, like Njiru, also rapes a woman forbidden to him by sending his penis underground, and he too loses his penis. This turns into another man who, like Jula, continues the sexual exploits of his father. He meets the Travelling Women, tries to rape one and in turn loses his penis, which becomes still another man, and the story repeats itself. In this Walbiri myth there are other male characters who rape or attempt to rape the Travelling Women; the latter do not seem to have assigned husbands.

R.M. Berndt gives other versions of incest followed by the loss of the penis in the Dingari cycle (1970:224, 231). This cycle, from the north-west corner of the Western Desert, has many elements in common with the Two Men, Seven Sisters and Njiru cycles of the Bidjandjara speakers of the Mann, Petermann, Everard and Musgrave Ranges. Though, as Berndt suggests, some elements of the fertility-mother motif from the north may have been grafted on to these myths, I perceive an older tradition, typical of the strongly patrilineally-oriented Desert society. In the Dingari cycle the Ganabuda women, who are attached to a group of men but do not seem to travel in their company, meet Gadadjilga, a mythical Spiky Lizard man, and one of them, through his love magic, is persuaded into sexual intercourse with him. The act is incestuous (in fact she is in an avoidance relationship with him), and in any case he is regarded as too old for her. The other women cut off his penis and kill him. In another section of the cycle (*ibid*: 231), and at another place, Gadadjilga again comes on the women, who run away because his penis is too large. He chases them, finally catches up with them, and has intercourse with two of them; they die from the injuries he inflicts. These are not the only instances in this cycle of rape, incest, loss of penis, and of girls being injured and dying after illicit intercourse.

Other accounts of young girls being killed by sexual intercourse are given by R.M. and C.H. Berndt, and by Spencer and Gillen. In a myth collected by the former at Ooldea (1943:257), Tilu deflowers a young Grey Kangaroo woman, in seclusion before her initiation, and causes her death. In an Aranda myth (Spencer and Gillen 1927:vol 1, 375) one of the Native Cat leaders has intercourse with a number of the Hawk women and some of them die in consequence.

In a Walbiri myth of the Two Dingoes (Meggitt 1966:142), the male Dingo tells his wife he has been performing ceremonies when he has in fact been committing adultery with other women. Later he does copulate with his wife, one of the few cases of licit intercourse recorded in Desert myths told by men. The Two Dingoes, man and wife, also appear to travel together, which is another rare occurrence. This non-typical Walbiri myth contains other acts of licit intercourse; for example, when the Spinifex Women have been disappointed by the Dingo Man, they make do with their own Spinifex Men, presumably their own husbands.

R.M. and C.H. Berndt (1942–45:204) recount a rare instance from the Western Desert of a mythical man, his wife and their children living together. An old man Tulina lives with his wife and two children. He catches a devil (*mamu*) child, which he takes home and cooks for his family. But his wife is herself a devil, she recognises the food as her own sister's child, and leaves her husband and children in order to organise a revenge expedition of her fellow devils, against her husband and children. The husband is killed but the children are saved by their mother's brothers who are also devils. This story can hardly be said to represent a normal human family.

Throughout many of the men's myths, and for long sections of all of them, no women are involved at all. R.M. and C.H. Berndt remark that 'the wanderings of the Wadi Gudjara are comparatively ascetic, as one hears little about the two women who were wives to the Two Men . . .' (1942–45:145). Women appear rarely in the myths of heroes instituting or performing the rites of circumcision or subincision, just as women have only limited and peripheral, though indispensable, functions in the actual rites as they are performed today. However, in the Western Desert there are recurring accounts of women giving the men a stone knife to save the boys from pain and possible death from circumcision by firestick. R.M. and C.H. Berndt give several mythical versions of this innovation: in each case the stone knife has first been used by the women to cut their own hymens (1942–45:90–2). Spencer and Gillen record a similar Southern Aranda myth (1927:vol. 1, 319).

Women enter some of the myths about initiation in a less favourable aspect. There are various accounts of a group of women who seduce boys during the time of their segregation, thus persuading them to commit a serious offence. For example, in the Dingari cycle (R.M. Berndt 1970:230) the Ganabuda women have intercourse with the young men, who are then burnt to death by the old men. In consequence the women are embittered against all men. In an Aranda myth recounted by Spencer and Gillen (1927: vol. 1, 385), during a Native Cat initiation ceremony, some of the segregated men have intercourse with a Wattle-Seed woman, and thus cause a disease to spread amongst the men.

The danger of women is indicated by Strehlow's report of the origin of death in Aranda mythology (1947:38). The Curlews killed one of their number who had followed women too closely. As he was rising again from the dead, the Magpie killed him once more and pushed him back underground.

The Women's Myths

Thus we see that in myths as told by Desert men, and those told by both men and women, sexual relations consist mostly of rape, incest, adultery and seduction; normal and licit sexual intercourse is rare. What of the women's myths? There is in the Western Desert a series of myths about two ancestral beings, the Two Women (Minjma Gudjara or Gungga Gudjara), an older and a younger sister. Most of these myths follow somewhat the same pattern. The Two Women travel and collect food and firewood, camp at waterholes, suffer hunger and thirst and fatigue. The younger begins her first menstruation and the older sister instructs her in the pleasures of sex. In the performance of the corresponding ceremony, which is similar to an account given by Kaberry (1939:235-6) of Kimberley ceremonies, there are unmistakable lesbian suggestions. One informant even made the remark 'we can do without men if we like'. However, they decide they want a man and go in search of one. One of the Yalata women explained to me that in the women's ceremonies, when they go in search of meat, they are in fact in search of sex, so that meat symbolises sexual intercourse or perhaps the penis itself. This might indicate that, because men traditionally do the hunting, meat can symbolise the male sex. (It would be interesting to know whether the converse is true — that when the mythological male beings search for vegetable food, this symbolises the search for a woman.) As soon as the Two Women see a man, they immediately run away from him and he chases them, having first been alerted to their proximity by smelling their urine. Their attitude at this point is ambivalent between desire and fear. (See p. 139 for the explanation given by a Yalata woman for this ambivalence.) To avoid copulating with him they push sand into their vaginas. (This, I have been told, is the way that a woman may reject any man's advances, even her husband's.) However, in the end the man catches them, they accept him as their husband and the final act of the ceremony expresses joy and triumph in a symbolic or mimed representation of sexual intercourse.

A small group of Yalata women, middle-aged mothers of families and the acknowledged ritual leaders, have twice performed for me the extremely secret ceremony of Minjma Baba and Wadhi Baba (Woman Dog and Man Dog). The ceremony begins with a group of young women dogs travelling. Their leader is white (or light-coloured) and there soon appears on the scene a black (or dark-coloured) man dog. The white woman dog urinates, he smells the urine and starts a long chase of the group of women, continuing for several scenes, in one of which all the participants dance hopping on one leg, a rather inexact representation of urinating, since most of them are supposed to be women dogs. The chase ends in the black dog catching the white dog, she submits willingly and there is an exuberent miming of sexual intercourse. The next scene, without the man, shows the woman giving birth to a number of puppies, and the ceremony ends with their joyful dancing. (This would seem to refute any lingering idea that the women of the Western Desert did not connect sexual intercourse with pregnancy.) I was told that this ceremony is a very powerful one, and some of the clothes and objects used were burnt afterwards.

The women are very open as to the love magic effect of many of their ceremonies, but when they perform them for their own enjoyment or to display them to an interested white woman, they use various devices to make sure that the effects are nullified. One device is to throw handfuls of sand into the air at important parts of the ceremony, and another is to smooth away all footsteps of the dancers before leaving the ceremonial ground. I was unable to gain a full explanation for the women's extraordinary fear of the consequences of the Dog ceremony, except for a hint that they were afraid of becoming pregnant. I have evidence that special ceremonies were performed by a group of women in traditional times for one of their number who was barren, but in trying to discover which ceremonies are supposed to be effective, I have encountered reticence quite unexpected in the light of other information which has been readily forthcoming.[6] Perhaps the Dog ceremony was one of those used to cure barrenness, since it had the birth scene immediately following the usual finale, copulation. It could be that even talking about the matter might bring about the effect and certainly none of the women participating would have welcomed another pregnancy.

One of the favourite ceremonies at Yalata is Amiwara or Yamiwara (the name for one of the tidal lakes just south of Port Augusta, and the name now used by Western Desert Aborigines for Port Augusta itself). In this the Two Women are travelling away from Yamiwara, and they grieve at leaving their home. One of them dreams of a man, she meets him and has intercourse. She returns to Yamiwara and drowns in the lake. The usual happy ending is missing in this myth, suggesting that with the women as with the man, sex can bring disaster.

The women believe, without the slightest shadow of doubt, that their ceremonies are an actual re-enactment of the heroic events, and that the dancers are temporarily transformed into ancestral beings. I had a revelation of this attitude on one occasion when, in the middle of a ceremony, three small snakes appeared in the sand between the feet of the dancers. Simultaneously a cry went up that some men were in sight. The scene became one of general panic and confusion, the snakes were quickly killed, great clouds of sand were thrown in the air, and the ceremony came to an abrupt halt. I was then told exactly what had happened: the ancestral Two Women had passed the snakes in their urine to give warning that men were approaching the ceremonial ground and might see the secret ceremony.

In the women's myths, as in the men's, there is a lack of the family situation, and sexual intercourse, though less violent than in the men's versions, is represented in single, isolated encounters. The main theme is that the woman must always flee from the man and only submit after considerable resistance.

Myths from Other Parts of Australia

A brief review of recorded myths from other parts of Australia reveals similar violence in sexual relations but contrasts with Central Australia in yielding many accounts of the family, either as man and wife, or man and wives, with or without children. Brough Smyth (1878) for Victoria, Parker (1951) for New South Wales, R.M. and C.H. Berndt (1951) for Western Arnhem Land, McConnel (1957) for Cape York Peninsula, Mountford (1958) for Bathurst and Melville Islands, and Bozic and Marshall (1972) for north-western Northern Territory all recount myths which describe husbands and wives as camping together and going about their daily tasks of obtaining food, but with no mention of sexual intercourse between husband and wife except when it assumes abnormal aspects. Another aspect of family life is revealed in some of these myths, when one partner uses extreme cruelty or inflicts death on the other, for no apparent reason (Parker 1951:165–7), for infidelity (R.M. and C.H. Berndt 1951:151–9; Mountford 1958:29–30; McConnel 1957:55–6 and 75–7), for teasing (Parker 1951:89) or for not fulfilling unreasonable demands (Bozic and and Marshall 1972:137–9).

The Family in the Western Desert

I want to put forward a further suggestion to explain why Central Australian myths, particularly those which depict in detail the day to day life of the ancestors, could have mirrored actual existence when they show men and women living separately. Throughout Australia Aboriginal men and women have defined and separate roles. Perhaps the unique desert ecology led to even further separation of the sexes than in the more fertile areas, causing less co-operation in the food quest, and thus increasing separation in other aspects of living. The desert Aboriginal concept of the family may differ from ours, coming as we do from a family-oriented society.

How then might the Aborigines perceive the family? Let us examine first the joint residence. Those who have seen a family dwelling (*wildja*) in the desert may agree with my description. A newly married couple (where there is only one wife) builds a small dwelling, shares one fire, and in this there is perhaps the equivalent of the English euphemism 'sleeping together'. But from the moment the first child is born, the arrangement begins to change. The mother now sleeps on one side of the fire with the child, the husband on the other. The break becomes more evident as more children are born and for a couple with several children the camp may come to look like two separate units, the main part with several fires, occupied by the mother and young children, the other, with a separate fire, by the husband. The youngest child may sleep through the night in his mother's arms, but an older child if upset or restless will also be soothed to sleep in the same way. If the youngest child is a boy, he is likely to sleep in his mother's embrace until he leaves for the bachelor's camp at the age of twelve or thirteen. A youngest girl, though she also will be petted or comforted by the mother, does not seem to have the same need for constant close contact as the boy; she too will leave the family camp in her early teens, traditionally at marriage, but today, when marriage is delayed until the late teens, to live in the widows' and single women's camp. The term 'sleeping together' then applies literally to the mother and her children but cannot be applied to husband and wife.

The close mother-son relationship leads to positive action by the man. In analysing the significance of male secret rites, Hiatt (1971:74-80) suggests that a point of insecurity for the men is 'the fond relationship between women and their male offspring . . . So men . . . envious of the carnal bond between mother and son, force them apart in the name of a spiritual imperative'. Initiation undoubtedly breaks the carnal bond, but not the strong affectionate tie, which is evident in the behaviour of adult sons towards their mothers.

While adults of both sexes caress and cuddle babies and young children with much greater frequency than in white society, I have never witnessed any public display of affection, not even holding hands, between sexually mature persons of opposite sex, whether married or not. This habit of restraint could well have arisen to minimise the conflicts and jealousies inevitable in a polygynous society. A demonstration of affection between a husband and one wife might be expected to hurt the feelings and dignity of his other wives. And since every woman and young girl was the wife, in residence or promised, of some man, it would certainly have aroused his anger if she were publicly caressed by a rival.

A married couple usually leave the camp for sexual intercourse (cf. Meggitt 1962:109-10), which is more likely to occur during day than night, because of the fear of evil spirits that roam during darkness. According to my observations of the modern situation, assignations between unmarried boys and girls take place about sunset, some distance from the camp, and adulterous relations are arranged during the day, since the absence of a spouse is likely to be noticed when groups form round the evening campfires.

And what about normal daytime activities? Today it is quite rare to see a married couple walking together, the more typical groupings being several women with young children, or several men. The older children walk around in gangs, divided according to sex, though today's mixed schools are tending to break down this division. At the joint ceremonies the division is always into women and children in one area, adult men in another (with the further division into generation levels, strictly observed still in the Western Desert). The sex division has perpetuated itself at the modern activities run in conjunction with the settlement or mission. At church services, film shows and meetings, men sit on one side, women and children on the other side of the hall. Even in ordinary daily occupations it is more common to see a group of women or a group of men sitting down together than it is to see a mixed group. To pass the time, women play card games for money, men play two-up (though recently there has been a tendency for some of the bolder young women to join the two-up schools). This separation would of course reflect the traditional division of labour. The only constant companions of opposite sex are some of the old couples, particularly where a devoted spouse may wait on an infirm partner. Otherwise the sole time when one may sometimes see a genuine nuclear family group around one camp

135

fire is at the evening meal, and later in the evening. Even this is not the universal arrangement, for one is just as likely to find the woman with her children in one group, joined perhaps by other women and children, the husband with friends nearby. Avoidance relationships — for example brother-sister avoidance in contrast to the close friendship ties of brothers-in-law and of sisters-in-law — are sometimes the reason for this separation. And there is the further rule that a young man may not sit down in a group with older women, whether or not potential mothers-in-law are present.

In traditional times when a group was travelling between camp sites it is likely that the sexes did walk more or less separately, each going about its own tasks in the food quest. Certainly the sexes spent most of their days apart. This is well documented by Gould (1969:Ch. 1) and Meggitt (1962: 52–3) and illustrated by sequences in Ian Dunlop's film *Desert People*. At night round the camp-fires, after the woman had shared her day's collection with her immediate family, and the men's hunting gains had been cooked and shared with a wider circle, then, as today, the nuclear family might sometimes sit together round one camp-fire, but because of avoidance relationships, conversation with others might take the husband away from the family fire.

Perhaps then the Aborigines did not share our concept of the nuclear family as a residential and operational unit. This would explain the myths in which groups of men or groups of women are described as travelling independently. Groups consisting of sisters, or mothers and children, brothers, brothers-in-law, fathers and sons, or mothers' brothers and sisters' sons, are seen as more logical units than man, wife and children. Though I would still agree that anthropologists should regard the nuclear family as the basic unit of social structure, with important social, political and economic functions, marriage seems to have been viewed by the people themselves as for sex and procreation rather than for companionship and emotional support, except perhaps for old couples where companionship might arise when sex and procreation had lost their importance.

In most descriptions of Aboriginal family life I find an underlying assumption that a husband and wife spend much time together and have a close affective relationship. I have described in some detail the separate lives led by most Western Desert husbands and wives to show that the separate and defined roles, well-documented for economic life, extend to social life too.

Where then does this leave the relationship between the sexes? A man would perceive his wife as a sexual object, the bearer and rearer of children, the provider of food, fire, and water, and to some extent as a status symbol. This is in fact the attitude of most men as I see it today in the settlements and missions. And what of the women? Husbands, who are expected to take the initiative (as in Arnhem Land, R.M. and C.H. Berndt 1951:53), are seen as somewhat bothersome in their sexual advances, particularly by those women who have already borne a number of children and want no more, though certainly the younger women see them as sexually desirable. And of course being married and having children is seen as an inevitable part of the life cycle, and absolutely necessary for adult status. Men are regarded with some fear and women are usually careful not to arouse their anger. They complain rather freely among themselves of the work they are expected to do compared with what they see as idleness on the part of the men. Rarely will a woman be bold enough to express these complaints directly to her husband and risk a beating. However, this can happen even when a wife appears to be well adjusted to her role. In January 1972 at Yalata, a mother of ten children, considered a model wife, was hospitalised after a severe beating by her husband of twenty-five years. She explained that she was going about her work and her husband, himself idle, began to criticise her every action. She finally lost her temper, told him in no un-certain terms that she did all the work of caring for the large family while he did nothing, and that if he thought she was doing things the wrong way he'd better get off his bottom and do the work himself.

The old habit of marrying young girls to much older men may lead to a part-reversal of the dominance-subservience roles in later life. One middle-aged woman, with the support of her two grown-up daughters, often makes her now aging husband fetch water and firewood. This woman told me that many years ago when it came time for her to go to her promised husband she clung to her mother weeping and begging not to be given to 'that old man', though she now admits to being fond of him, and treats him with tolerant affection. But like all other wives she speaks of him with the utmost respect when his ritual importance is mentioned. A generation after her own marriage, when her oldest daughter should have gone to her promised husband, the mother supported the girl in rebellion against the system which would have made her the second wife of a much older man. The mother was speared by the disappointed claimant, and the camp was in uproar at the challenge to male authority, but the mother and daughter won, and the daughter was married to a young man of her own choosing. It is difficult to know whether this challenge could have been won — or even been made — in traditional times, or whether it is a new development, with women taking advantage of changing conditions to win some power.

I do not want to give the impression that married couples in Western Desert society are conspicuously ill-matched or in a constant state of hostility. Joint parenthood is an important tie, and as in the other societies, different couples run the gamut from life-long affection to separation and divorce. Like human beings everywhere, most of them accept life as it is and make the best of it. One contrast to our own society is evident: that an Aboriginal husband and wife are seldom alone together and if incom-patible can more easily find emotional support in other members of the kinship group.

Discussion

The sexual fantasies and evil-doings depicted in Central Australian myths cannot be explained as a 'guide for action' (R.M. Berndt 1970:243) or as a 'pattern for living' (*ibid*:244). Nor can they be read as cautionary tales, since many of the crimes go unpunished. To me the myths read much more like *dreaming* (to return to an Aboriginal concept) where passages of ordinary prosaic existence suddenly become absurd or horrible, but may nevertheless symbolise the desires or fears of the dreamer. I am in disagreement here with Rivers (1912:314) when he suggests that 'it is not the especially familiar and uniform which becomes the subject of myth; that which is ever with us in the same form does not excite the mythic fancy . . .' A characteristic of Central Australian myth is the mixture of familiar with fantastic. Where the men's myths describe violent and illicit sexual encounters they represent male desires; when they describe mutilation they represent fears. The women's myths show women as more ambivalent, with desire for the gratification of sex accompanying fear of its consequences.

Myths therefore should be seen as giving a charter for the *values* of a society, as represented in desires and fears, rather than giving a charter for *behaviour*.

I suggest that we can view the violence of sexual relations in Central Australian myths as a reflection of the sexual values of a male-dominated society. In one of the most important men's myths, already cited, the Two Men exchange their sisters in marriage, thus validating one of the strongest social (rather than sexual) aspects of male dominance, the power to arrange marriages. Since infant bestowal is the normal rule, a man in his twenties, often older, receives a bride, little more than a child, over whom he has complete authority. There is nothing particularly heroic or virile in copulating with a child-bride, whether she is willing or not. Her consequent pregnancy would enhance his prestige but more as a religious than a sexual performer, since the belief system emphasises spirit-entry rather than intercourse as the cause of pregnancy (Hiatt 1971; White 1970). Only in pre-marital and extra-marital affairs could he prove his sexual prowess beyond doubt, the more so if the affair is dangerous, illicit, or fiercely resisted by a strong mature woman. Therefore none of the sexual encounters described in the myths are between husband and wife. And since in ordinary life men and women lived mainly separate lives, the nuclear family does not even enter into the more prosaic passages of the myths.

At the time I first wrote this paper, T.G.H. Strehlow's outstanding work, *Songs of Central Australia*, was not yet available to me. His detailed treatment of sexual relations in real life and their violent character in myth is of paramount importance because of his translations and discussions of the relevant song texts. In particular he gives the texts of love charms used by men and describes the practice of using these charms to win the women desired. The purpose might be 'to attract women whom they could not court or win lawfully', but 'their normal purpose was to enable a man to win the love of a girl who had been promised to him' (p.505). Under the influence of the love charm the women would come willingly, and there would be no necessity for the violent ravishment portrayed in the texts. In Strehlow's words 'I doubt whether the normal aboriginal male has ever been guilty of rape in the sense of forcing a female who was not prepared for the sexual act' (p.537). This reinforces the suggestion I made previously that in real life violent rape was infrequent and unnecessary.

Strehlow (p.495) reaches a somewhat similar conclusion to mine about mythical sexual violence. After transcribing a song text (a powerful love charm), which describes the violent wooing of a young girl by a Southern

Aranda ancestor, he concludes that 'we can see, if we like, a wish fulfilment of the repressed sexual urges of the younger men in a Central Australian community. . . ., however, the native youth would not have treated with such violence a girl who was coming to him aflame with passion. There is a certain element of sadism in much male love-making; and in all parts of the world the supernatural beings, who, unlike mankind, never repress any of their cruel inborn drives, rarely seem to be given to excessive tenderness towards the women who have become the objects of their passion.' He quotes a number of stories about the ancient gods of Europe to substantiate this last statement.

The many recent analyses of sexual politics in modern industrial society apply also to Australian Aboriginal society. Millett (1971:44) states that 'patriarchal force . . . relies on a form of violence particularly sexual in character and realised most completely in the act of rape'. De Beauvoir (1960:116) describes the ambivalence with which modern woman views sex and marriage, her desires competing with her fears.

Just as Millett and Greer (1970) see modern literature as a charter for male dominance, so too can we see Aboriginal mythology. Such novelists as Norman Mailer and Henry Miller, with their emphasis on male sexual aggression can be equated with the men's mythology, and the romantic novels written for the feminised women of our culture can be equated to the women's mythology. Barbara Cartland and her genre of story-writers sometimes represent their heroines as beautiful and proud, sometimes as pretty and modest, but in either case they are expected to play 'hard-to-get', with ambivalent feelings towards the handsome male who woos them, finally subsiding into sensuous subservience. Like the Aboriginal women's myths, the story usually finishes with the marriage — we are left to imagine the rest.

After I had written a first draft of this paper, I paid a short visit to Yalata and took the opportunity to ask my most sympathetic informant why the mythical women first want a man and then run away from him. The answer was a quite unexpected verification of the hypothesis I have put forward above. She gave two explanations as follow: 'They are frightened because the man's penis is too big' and after some thought went on: 'But that's just the way we women are supposed to behave. We say to a man "Come here" and when he comes, we say "Oh, no, no, no" and pretend we don't want him at all. Then we run away and he catches us'. This explanation was accompanied by all the gestures of coquetry.

Neither the myths of Aboriginal society nor the novels of western society can resolve the conflicts which engendered them. In Aboriginal society as in ours there is both overt and covert hostility between the sexes. Physical attacks by men on women and by women on men are not uncommon. Because of the man's normally superior strength it is usually the woman who suffers the more severe injury. Both sexes tend to relate with evident relish any accidents or indignities which happen to the other sex, whether in myth or reality. The most striking example I have witnessed was the occasion described above of the woman telling the story of Njiru round the camp-fire. I find in general an undercurrent of hostility in the women's attitudes particularly in those of middle-aged women. However, women do speak of their husbands, and of their brothers, fathers, mothers' brothers and so on, with extreme reverence and respect when talking about their ritual life. Similarly men respect and, as I have suggested (White 1970), envy their wives, and all women's, life-giving powers. Moreover women's own myths and rituals reflect and reinforce the female subservient role. Male dominance therefore is validated by both the men's and women's religious life.

In this deeply religious society, the mythical charter for traditional values presents a dilemma for those who would like to see an uplifting of the status of Aboriginal women, for this could only be achieved as part of a further disruption of Aboriginal culture, a further loss of Aboriginal identity. Barwick (1970) describes how, in Victoria between 1860 and 1886, resettlement policy profoundly changed Aboriginal women's life and led to an uplifting of their status not only *vis-à-vis* Aboriginal men but also in the total community. However, this was accompanied by further, and almost complete, loss of the traditional culture. Traditionally Aboriginal woman had certain advantages over her counterpart in industrial society, since her various roles were more clearly separated and defined, and these roles were valued highly by her society. C.H. Berndt (1970:45) remarks that 'there is no evidence that women in general *wanted* to change the system' (italics as in original text), an opinion which I can endorse from my own research experience.

Notes

1. My field research was financed by the Australian Institute of Aboriginal Studies, with some contributions from Monash University. From 1966–68 I was a member of a group of women research workers led by Dr C.J. Ellis; during our field trips we recorded women's ceremonies at Port Augusta, Coober Pedy, Oodnadatta and Indulkana. Since 1969 I have paid a number of visits to Yalata Lutheran Mission, and have also made expeditions with Luise Hercus to the area between Port Augusta and Marree.
2. I have found it impossible to make the spelling of native words uniform. When citing other writers I have used their spelling, but otherwise I have used the spelling suggested by the Australian Institute of Aboriginal Studies.
3. In the report of our group research, after seeing the Seven Sisters ceremony performed at Indulkana, we wrote:
   We have chosen to use this name for the Ceremony of the Many Sisters only because it has become widely known, and is referred to in the literature under this title. It has been called so by Europeans, who normally see in the Pleiades Constellation, to which it refers, only seven stars. Keen-eyed Europeans see more than seven stars, as also do many Aboriginals. The actual translation of the title does not indicate a specific number of stars (Buckley *et al.* 1968:113).
4. In the Western Desert kinship system the whole society is grouped into named endogamous generation level moieties, which are important not only in ordering marriage but also in organisation of ritual and in determining behaviour between individuals. An individual is in the same generational moiety as his grandparents and grandchildren, while his parents and his children are in the opposite moiety. It was, and still is, regarded as one of the most serious forms of incest to marry or have sexual relations with persons in the other moiety.

5. I was told that the place Cundeelee in Western Australia takes its name from this myth, because it was here that Njiru raped his classificatory father's sister, his *gundili*.

6. I have noted earlier in this paper that the Seven Sisters ceremony was performed at menarche (see p. 130). From the same informant I learned that Minggiri (Native Mouse ceremony, which I have seen several times) was the appropriate ceremony to celebrate a birth, during the seclusion of the mother and baby. This informant, one of the most lively and influential characters in the Yalata camp, is my 'close sister' in the kinship structure in which I have been allocated a place: she is old enough to have been brought up and married in completely traditional conditions. Her parallel cousin, my 'real sister', whose camp I share, is my chief informant: however, she is a few years younger, and came to Ooldea and thus under white influence as a little girl and has therefore not experienced as much of the traditional life. Most of the women older than these two are now reaching an age of sickness with declining mental and physical powers and no longer take an active part in the ceremonies. Unfortunately, my last two visits to Yalata have coincided with gaol terms for my older 'sister', on charges of drunken and disorderly behaviour and resisting arrest — she would think it improper *not* to bite and kick the policeman arresting her, even though this inevitably lengthens her sentence.

References

BARWICK, D.E. 1970 'And the lubras are ladies now'. In *Woman's role in Aboriginal society*, (ed.) F. Gale, pp. 31–38. Canberra, Australian Institute of Aboriginal Studies.

BEAUVOIR, S. DE. 1949–60 *Le deuxieme sexe*. English translation, *The second sex*, New English Library, Paperback edition, 1960.

BERNDT, C.H. 1970 Digging sticks and spears, or, the two-sex model. In *Woman's role in Aboriginal society*, (ed.) F. Gale, pp. 39–48. Canberra, Australian Institute of Aboriginal Studies.

BERNDT, R.M. 1941 Tribal migrations and myths centring on Ooldea, South Australia. *Oceania*, 12(1):1–20.

——— 1965 Law and order in Aboriginal Australia. In *Aboriginal man in Australia: essays in honour of Emeritus Professor A.P. Elkin*, (eds) R.M. and C.H. Berndt, pp. 167–206. Sydney, Angus and Robertson.

——— 1970 Traditional morality as expressed through the medium of an Australian Aboriginal religion. In *Australian Aboriginal anthropology: modern studies in the social anthropology of the Australian Aborigines*, (ed.) R.M. Berndt, pp. 216–47. Nedlands, University of Western Australia Press.

BERNDT, R.M. *and* C.H. BERNDT 1942–45 A preliminary report of fieldwork in the Ooldea region, western South Australia. Sydney, University of Sydney. Reprinted from *Oceania*, 12–15:343pp.

——— *and* ——— 1951 *Sexual behaviour in western Arnhem Land*. New York, Viking Fund.

——— *and* ——— 1964 *The world of the first Australians; an introduction to the traditional life of the Australian Aborigines*. Sydney, Ure Smith.

BOZIC, S. *and* A. MARSHALL 1972 *Aboriginal myths*. Melbourne, Gold Star Publications.

BUCKLEY, R. *and others* 1968 *Group project on Andagarinja women*, v.2 (group leader Catherine J. Ellis). Adelaide, University of Adelaide.

GOULD, R.A. 1969 *Yiwara: foragers of the Australian desert*. London, Collins.

GREER, G. 1970 *The female eunuch*. London, MacGibbon & Kee.

HIATT, L.R. 1971 Secret pseudo-procreation rites among the Australian Aborigines. In *Anthropology in Oceania: essays presented to Ian Hogbin*, (eds) L.R. Hiatt and C. Jayawardena, pp. 77–88. Sydney, Angus and Robertson.

HOWITT, A.W. 1904 *The native tribes of south-east Australia.* London, Macmillan.

KABERRY, P.M. 1939 *Aboriginal woman: sacred and profane.* London, Routledge.

MCCONNEL, U.H. 1957 *Myths of the Mungkan.* Melbourne, Melbourne University Press.

MEGGITT, M.J. 1962 *Desert people: a study of the Walbiri Aborigines of central Australia.* Sydney, Angus and Robertson.

——— 1964 Indigenous forms of government among the Australian Aborigines. *Bijdragen tot de Taal-, Land- en Volkenkunde,* deel 120:163–80.

——— 1967 *Gadjari among the Walbiri Aborigines of Central Australia.* Sydney (Oceania monograph no. 14), University of Sydney.

MILLETT, K. 1971 *Sexual politics.* London, Hart-Davis.

MOUNTFORD, C.P. 1937 Aboriginal crayon drawings from the Warburton Ranges in Western Australia relating to the wanderings of two ancestral beings, the Wati Kutjara. In *South Australian Museum, Records,* (6):5–28.

——— 1958 *The Tiwi: their art, myth and ceremony.* London, Phoenix House.

——— *and* A. HARVEY 1941 Women of the Adnjamatana tribe of the northern Flinders Ranges, South Australia. *Oceania,* 12(2):155–62.

MUNN, N.D. 1970 The transformation of subjects into objects in Walbiri and Pitjantjatjara myth. In *Australian Aboriginal anthropology: modern studies in the social anthropology of the Australian Aborigines,* (ed.) R.M. Berndt, pp. 141–63. Nedlands, University of Western Australia Press.

PARKER, LANGLOH K. 1953 *Australian legendary tales* . . . selected and edited by H. Drake-Brockman. Sydney, Angus and Robertson.

RIVERS, W.H.R. 1912 The sociological significance of myth. *Folk-Lore,* 23(3):307–31.

SMYTH, R.B. 1878 *The Aborigines of Victoria: with notes relating to the habits of the natives of other parts of Australia and Tasmania, compiled from various sources for the government of Victoria.* Melbourne, Government Printer.

SPENCER, *Sir* W.B. *and* F.J. GILLEN 1927 *The Arunta: a study of a stone age people.* London, Macmillan.

STREHLOW, T.G.H 1947 *Aranda traditions.* Melbourne, Melbourne University Press.

——— 1971 *Songs of central Australia.* Sydney, Angus and Robertson.

TINDALE, N.B. 1936 Legend of the Wati Kutjara, Warburton Range, Western Australia. *Oceania,* 7(2):169–85.

——— 1959 Totemic beliefs in the Western Desert of Australia. Part I. Women who became the Pleiades. In *South Australian Museum, Records,* 13(3):305–32.

WHITE, I.M. 1970 Aboriginal women's status: a paradox resolved. In *Woman's role in Aboriginal society,* (ed.) F. Gale, pp. 21–29. Canberra, Australian Institute of Aboriginal Studies.

Swallowing and Regurgitation in Australian Myth and Rite

L.R. Hiatt

Nicodemus said, 'How can a grown man be born? Can he go back into his mother's womb and be born again?

John, 3:4

In *The Savage Mind* (1966:91–6) Lévi-Strauss discusses Warner's analysis of a Murngin myth in which a huge snake swallows and regurgitates two sisters. Following Warner, he interprets the myth as a symbolic statement about local climatic conditions. Further, he maintains that the symbolism generates a paradox. He goes on to argue that the latter is mitigated by certain social arrangements basic to Murngin ritual life.

I begin by examining this argument. Then I go back to Warner's account and show that the mythical snake is in fact the rainbow-serpent, a creature of the imagination found throughout Australia. The climatic conditions symbolised in the Murngin myth are peculiar to the monsoonal belt of northern Australia.

I next examine some other Aboriginal myths that highlight the motif of swallowing and regurgitation, and I show that these are widely connected with the induction of young men into secret religious cults. I discuss two interpretations of this connection: Eliade's view that initiation rites recapitulate cosmogony and that swallowing means a return to chaos while regurgitation stands for regeneration; and Róheim's psychoanalytically-based view that swallowing symbolises reunion with the mother while regurgitation signifies rebirth by males. Finally, after indicating some weaknesses in these interpretations, I propose a compromise.[1]

Lévi-Strauss and 'Structures of Contradiction'

Lévi-Strauss summarises the Murngin myth (Warner 1937:250–9) as follows:

> M1. At the beginning of time the Wawilak Sisters set off on foot towards the sea, naming places, animals and plants as they went. One of them was pregnant and the other had a child. Before their departure they had both indeed had incestuous relations with men of their own moiety. After the birth of the younger sister's child, they continued their journey and one day stopped near a water hole where the great Snake Yurlunggur lived. . . . The older sister polluted the water with menstrual blood. The outraged python came out, caused a deluge of rain and a general flood and then swallowed the women and their children. When the Snake raised himself the waters covered the entire earth and its vegetation. When he lay down again the flood receded.

The Murngin live in north-eastern Arnhem Land where the year is divided into a wet season (October to April) and a dry (May to September). During the wet months, the Murngin disperse into small groups and take refuge on high ground. There they live precariously, threatened by famine and inundation. The dry season, by contrast, is a period of abundance, physical comfort, and sociality.

Warner says that the Murngin associate Yurlunggur with the wet season and the Wawilak Sisters with the dry. Furthermore, Yurlunggur, the Snake, represents the fertilising principle in nature whereas the Wawilak Sisters symbolise the reproductive and food-giving parts. Finally, the Snake stands for the secret male religious cults of Murngin society, whereas the Wawilak Sisters symbolise the profane and impure sections, that is, the women and children. The overall effect, in Lévi-Strauss's terms, is to achieve the unification of heterogeneous semantic fields: the rainy season literally engulfs the dry season as men 'possess' women, the initiated 'swallow up' the uninitiated as famine destroys plenty, and so on. Or, to use a slightly different formulation, the myth establishes homologies between significant contrasts on different planes, as shown in Diagram 1.

DIAGRAM 1

From *The Savage Mind* (1966:93)

Pure, sacred	male	superior	fertilising	bad season
Impure, profane	female	inferior	fertilised (land)	good season

Warner remarks that, as the men conceive themselves to represent higher social values than women and as the dry season is a time of higher social value than the wet season, one might expect a correlation between men and dry season on the one hand, women and wet season on the other. But an overriding consideration in native logic is that the serpent symbolises the fertilising principle in nature. Because men fertilise women, they must be identified with the serpent and hence with the wet season.

Whereas Warner makes the point in passing, Lévi-Strauss is concerned first to state the precise nature of the contradiction and then to see what native thought does about it. The dilemma is as follows. The wet season represents power (rain overcomes land), sterility (scarcity of food), and unhappiness (discomfort, decreased sociality); conversely, the dry season represents subordination (land overcome by rain), fertility (abundance of food), and happiness (comfort, increased sociality). To regard the dry season as male on the grounds of a higher value common to both would be to associate men with the female attributes of fertility and subordination. The alternative is to associate a social elite (namely, adult males) with poorly-rated weather conditions.[2]

Forced to accept the latter association as the lesser of two evils, Murngin men have attempted to disguise the inconsistency by adding a ritual distinction between initiated and uninitiated to the natural distinction between male and female (see Diagram 2). As females are ineligible for initiation, the new division creates an intermediate category of uninitiated males, who share the sex of initiated men but the ritual status of women. In so far as they are thus classified with females, uninitiated males can be conceived as participating in the latter's identification with the good season. By incorporating them into their religious cult, initiated men, even though committed to an association with the bad season, nevertheless gain something of the happy side of life through an intermediary.

DIAGRAM 2

Double Division

Now the division of society into initiated and uninitiated, the incorporation of young men into secret cults, and the ineligibility of women for membership are by no means confined to the Murngin. To anticipate the objection that he is attributing general features of Australian religious life to local climatic conditions, Lévi-Strauss maintains that it is not the weather as such that is significant but the fact that the Murngin conception of it has become incorporated into a structure of contradiction. The same principles of division for ritual purposes found elsewhere in Australia will likewise turn out to be attempts to deal with contradictions, though the content of the latter may differ from place to place and have nothing at all to do with conceptualisations of the seasonal cycle. The poverty of religious thought is such that the same solution (in this case, a double division of society as shown in Diagram 2) is used again and again for problems whose only common feature is that they are paradoxes.

Let me recapitulate the formal steps in Lévi-Strauss's argument. First, he accepts Warner's interpretation of a Murngin myth. Second, he notes that the symbolic system contains a contradiction. Third, he explains a feature of Murngin social organisation as an attempt to disguise this contradiction. Fourth, he recognises that the feature in question occurs generally throughout Australia, whereas the contradiction is in part the product of local circumstances. Fifth, he asserts that the general feature is always a response to contradiction, though the content of the contradiction varies from place to place.

In the present paper I am mainly concerned with step 1, the interpretation of the myth. But, in passing, let us note that the only evidence supporting the final generalisation (step 5) is the analysis of a single instance, that is, the Murngin. Lévi-Strauss's position seems precarious — comparable, say, with ascribing a local illness to mosquitoes and then, on discovering that the same illness occurs in areas free of mosquitoes, asserting that all instances

145

will turn out on investigation to be caused by insects. Even supposing the hypothesis were sound, the further and more important question would be, what is common to all the various insects that uniformly causes this specific reaction in humans? A similar question would need to be raised about structures of contradiction and double division: what is common to all the various contradictions that uniformly produces the same result? My own opinion is that the double division has nothing to do with structures of contradiction.

Warner and 'Weather Symbolism'

So far we have been dealing with Lévi-Strauss's summary and development of Warner's interpretation. Let us now go back to *A Black Civilization* and examine the original in more detail.

A preliminary point is that Warner actually interprets the myth at two levels: first, as a charter for ritual, and only later as a symbolic statement about the climate. He introduces the first stage of the analysis by stating (1937:245) that the Wawilak myth is fundamental to a certain group of Murngin ceremonies concerned with the induction of youths into secret male cults. I shall outline one of them, the Gunabibi [Kunapipi] (*ibid*: 290:311).[3]

Gunabibi is an alternative name for Yurlunggur, the Snake. The ceremony begins when a bullroarer representing the Snake is swung near the general camp. The men tell the women that 'the Great Father' (that is, Yurlunggur) is calling for the novices. The lads are then taken to the secret ground, where they must stay for the duration of the ceremony. For several months, the daily ritual consists of songs and dances about the animals named by the Wawilak Sisters on their journey to the coast. On two occasions the men leave the ceremonial ground, form a line to represent the Snake and then surround the women, who offer gifts of appeasement.

The ceremony comes to a climax when long poles representing Yurlunggur are brought into conjunction with a trench symbolising the generative organs of the Wawilak Sisters. The next day, at a location between the secret ground and the general camp, the women watch while the novices emerge from a framework hung with bushes and crawl under the out-stretched left arms of the men standing in a single file. The latter represents the Snake, and the novices its young.

Warner describes three other ceremonies connected with the Wawilak myth (the Djungguan, pp. 259–90; Ulmark, pp. 311–29; Marndiella, pp. 329–34). He says that, in the course of demonstrating the intimate relationship between the myth and the rites, he became aware of a 'more fundamental and unconscious level of native thought than could be discovered by a mere analysis of myth or of ritual by itself' (p. 247). The key to this deeper meaning is the symbol of the 'snake-swallowing-the-women', which dominates all others in the Wawilak ritual complex (pp.371–7). Warner's interpretation, as we have seen, is that it signifies the 'swallowing of the earth by the rainy season' (p.386).

The evidence for this equation comes partly from the myth itself, partly from native exegeses. When the Wawilak Sisters polluted the well, the

Snake spat into the sky and called for rain by hissing, acts which produced a huge black cloud and a torrential downpour. The Aborigines nowadays believe that the Snake sends the north-west monsoon. Thunder is his voice, lightning his forked tongue, rain his saliva and the rainbow a manifestation of his presence. One of Warner's informants said: 'Those two women tried to stop that rain because the water came like a flood and tried to cover them all up. That is all the same as that snake swallowing them. The women tried to stop the snake because he was the flood and the wet season covering the earth' (p.383).

Radcliffe-Brown and the Rainbow-Serpent

In 1926 Radcliffe-Brown published a paper in the *Journal of the Royal Anthropological Institute* on the rainbow-serpent myth of Australia. It begins: 'There is found in widely separated parts of Australia a belief in a huge serpent which lives in certain pools or water-holes. This serpent is associated, and sometimes identified, with the rainbow' (p.19). In the course of presenting information from various sources, Radcliffe-Brown mentions that the rainbow-serpent is often supposed to have some control over rain, and he also reproduces two cave-paintings from north-west Australia showing the rainbow-serpent in the process of swallowing humans. He concludes that 'the rainbow-serpent is not confined in Australia to any particular ethnological province . . . it is characteristic of Australian culture as a whole' (p.24).

If we regard the rainbow-serpent in Australia as a configuration of beliefs containing recurrent though not necessarily universal elements, then the mythical Murngin snake is clearly a rainbow-serpent.[4] Yet Warner never refers to it as such. This is interesting because he carried out his field investigations under Radcliffe-Brown's guidance, dedicated *A Black Civilization* to him, and twice mentioned his 1926 paper in bibliographical footnotes (pp.258, 382). Furthermore, in 1930 (just after Warner finished his field research) Radcliffe-Brown published a second paper on the rainbow-serpent. It appeared in the first volume of *Oceania*, of which Radcliffe-Brown was editor, and was accompanied by contributions on the same topic by investigators who had recently done fieldwork in widely separated parts of the continent. Warner neither participated in this symposium nor subsequently made reference to it.[5]

Once it is acknowledged that the Murngin snake is merely a particular instance of a cultural phenomenon found throughout Australia, some consideration needs to be given to the fact that the seasonal cycle symbolised by the serpent's actions is confined to the coastal parts of north Australia. One would not wish to deny, of course, that the myth analysed by Warner, and later by Lévi-Strauss, is an adaptation of a widespread substratum of mythical elements for peculiarly local purposes. But an examination of homologous features in other ecological zones may help to establish a 'wider', if not necessarily a 'deeper', significance (see Maddock's discussion of 'depth' in the present volume, p. 120).[6]

Radcliffe-Brown wrote his *Oceania* paper on the rainbow-serpent after a short period of fieldwork in New South Wales during 1929. The main point of interest is his discovery of an association between the rainbow-serpent and Bora ceremonies for the initiation of young men. By this time such ceremonies were defunct and Radcliffe-Brown was unable to obtain much information about them. In fact, over 30 years had elapsed since R.H. Mathews describe in the *Journal of the Anthropological Institute* (1895-6, 1896) two Bora rites that must have been among the last ever performed.[7] The following myth was given to Mathews (1896:297-8) in connection with the Bora ceremony of the Wiradjeri [Wiradthuri] people of central New South Wales.

> M2.   A long time ago Baiame[8] used to hand over the youths to a gigantic and powerful being called Dhuramoolan, for instruction in tribal traditions. Dhuramoolan led Baiame to believe that he always killed the boys, cut them up and burnt them, then formed the ashes into human shape, except for a missing incisor, and restored them to life. Alternatively, some tribes say that Dhuramoolan swallowed the boys and vomited them up, full of tribal knowledge but minus a tooth. In any case, Baiame noticed that on each occasion some of the youths failed to return, and, on inquiring among the survivors, he learnt that Dhuramoolan was killing and eating them. The true story about the missing teeth was that Dhuramoolan inserted his own lower incisors under the tooth to be extracted and wrenched it out. Sometimes at this point he would bite off the boy's entire face and devour it. His statement to Baiame that he burnt and then revived the youths was a lie.
>
> On hearing all this, Baiame destroyed Dhuramoolan and told the men that they must henceforth initiate the youths themselves. It was better, he thought, not to enlighten the women but to let them believe as before that Dhuramoolan takes away their sons, kills, and resurrects them.

The myth mentions that Dhuramoolan's voice resembled the 'rumbling of distant thunder' and that, after his death, men reproduced it by swinging bullroarers. The Bora ceremony (Mathews 1896:307-12) begins when the neophytes are dramatically separated from the women, who think Dhuramoolan has snatched them away. At the secret ground, where they have a tooth removed, bullroarers are swung to make the boys think Dhuramoolan is near. On the last night, they are told that Dhuramoolan is coming to burn them (presumably, in other areas, to swallow them; see Mathews 1896:297, fn.2). Their heads are covered, and they hear and feel fire approaching. Then the covers are removed and they are shown the secret of the bullroarers.

At the Bora ground Mathews observed a representation some 60 feet long of the *wahwee*, a fabulous snake-like monster which lives in a waterhole and eats people (see also Mathews 1900, 1901). According to Radcliffe-Brown (1930), the *wawi* among the Wiradjeri is the rainbow-serpent; further east, among the Kamilaroi, it is known as *karia*. Radcliffe-Brown says (1930:343): 'The most interesting point . . . is that a cult of the *wawi* or *karia* was often an element of the Bora or initiation ceremonies of the New South Wales tribes. Many of the sacred Bora grounds had a representation of the serpent in the form of a sinuous mound of earth up to 40 feet or more in length. In preparation for the ceremony the serpent was painted. A ceremony took place at the spot and the beliefs about the rainbow-serpent were explained to the younger men who were attending the initiation.'

Let us briefly compare the role of the rainbow-serpent in initiation rites in the two areas considered so far, one in monsoonal Arnhem Land, the other in central New South Wales. Whereas among the Murngin the rainbow-serpent swallows humans and has a voice of thunder produced ritually by bullroarers, among the Wiradjeri these features are associated in initiation ideology with an ogre called Dhuramoolan. The Wiradjeri rainbow-serpent is also believed to swallow humans, and it apparently plays an important role in initiation ritual. Precisely what this role is, and how Dhuramoolan and the rainbow-serpent are related in native thought, are questions for which we have no answers.[9]

Swallowing and Regurgitation

A detail omitted in Lévi-Strauss's summary of the Wawilak myth is that, after the deluge, the serpent regurgitates the two sisters and their sons onto an ants' nest[10]. Seeing them stir, the serpent swallows them again. Finally, he spews up the women, who turn to stone, but retains the two boys (Warner 1937:257–8). We have two instances, therefore, in which the initiation of young men into secret male cults is connected with a myth containing the motif of 'swallowing and regurgitation'. I shall now give four further examples recorded among the Wulamba (Yirrkala, north-eastern Arnhem Land),[11] Mara (Roper River, N.T.), Murinbata (Port Keats, N.T.), and Walbiri (Central Desert, N.T.). The ethnographers respectively are R.M. Berndt 1951 (first two cases), Stanner 1959–63 and Meggitt 1966.

The Wawilak myth, with which we began, and the related Gunabibi ceremony are also found at Yirrkala, but they differ to some extent from their Milingimbi counterparts as described by Warner. I shall begin with the myth (adapted from R.M. Berndt 1951:20–4, 35–6).

M3.   The Wawilak Sisters set off from their home territory, naming natural species encountered on the way. The younger was childless, but the elder was pregnant through incest and eventually gave birth to a daughter. Lochia polluted the waterhole of a female snake called Julunggul, who rose to the surface and sent a violent thunderstorm. The rain washed even more blood into her waterhole, and she moved threateningly towards the sisters and child. The younger sister temporarily hindered the snake's progress by dancing but the effort caused her to menstruate. Julunggul then came straight on and swallowed the three of them. Returning to her waterhole, she regurgitated them onto an ants' nest and they revived. Julunggul swallowed them all again.
    Julunggul's actions were observed by a young unmarried male snake named Liningu. After she had regurgitated the two sisters and female child, he went around the country swallowing all

the youths. But when he vomited them up, they were dead.
Indeed, only bones emerged.

The men held a meeting to discuss this outrage. They compared
Liningu with Julunggul, who vomited up her victims alive, and
resolved to kill him. After spearing him to death, they constructed
an image in his memory. They also made an image of Julunggul,
and a bullroarer to fabricate her sound. Finally, they decided to
incise their arm veins in order to produce the blood (both lochial
and menstrual) of the Wawilak Sisters.

The Gunabibi ceremony (R.M. Berndt 1951:39–56) gets under way when
a bullroarer is swung outside the general camp, signifying that Julunggul
is approaching. The novices are taken to the secret ground, and the women
are supposed to believe that they have been swallowed there by the snake
— indeed, that they have been offered to her to avert total destruction.
The youths remain secluded for several months until the ceremony ends.
The climax takes place in a trench, representing the womb of the elder
Wawilak Sister, in which the neophytes are placed, covered with bark and
told to go to sleep. Then the men place two large cylindrical representations
of Julunggul on the edge of the trench and, suddenly stripping away the
bark away from the novices, tell them to behold the objects towering over
them. The representations are allowed to fall across the trench and the
lads are lifted out.

The ceremony ends when the men come out from the secret ground and
show the 'new born' youths to the women. The action centres on a structure
consisting of two vertical forked posts connected by a horizontal pole
hung with branches. The women and children lie on the ground nearby,
covered with mats, while two men perched in the forks cry like new-born
babes. The main body of men dance around the structure and, at a given
signal, the women sit up and see the novices emerge from beneath the
bushes (where they have been concealed). They are covered with red ochre
symbolising blood from the Wawilak Sister's uterus. That night the men
dance around the lads and then lead them back to the secret ground. Later,
they all return to the general camp where the initiates go to live in the
bachelors' section.

The Mara (south-eastern Arnhem Land) likewise enact a version of the
Gunabibi ceremony. But the associated myth (adapted here from R.M.
Berndt 1951:148–52) is no longer about the rainbow-serpent.[12]

M4.   A long time ago an old woman called Mumuna lived alone
with her two daughters. By making a smoky fire, she attracted
men to her camp, then welcomed them with food and invited
them to spend the night with the daughters. Later, while they
slept deeply from sexual exhaustion, she dropped boulders on them.
The next morning she cooked and ate them, then regurgitated
them onto an ant-bed. They did not revive when bitten.
Instead, they remained as skeletons, and their bones can be seen
today in the form of stones.

The attitude of the daughters was equivocal. On the one hand
they relished the sexual role that their mother encouraged them
to play. On the other, they deplored the old woman's cannibalism

and feared its consequences. In particular, they were disturbed by her habit of hanging up the genital organs of the dead men on a tree and proposing to the girls that they eat them — an invitation they steadfastly refused.

Mumuna's grisly practices were finally put to an end by a man named Eaglehawk, a light sleeper who woke up in time to kill her before she killed him. The daughters ran away. As the old woman died, she called out *brr*, and her blood splashed onto every tree. Afterwards, in her memory, Eaglehawk cut down a tree and made a bullroarer, which contained the old woman's dying cry.

The Mara Gunabibi (R.M. Berndt 1951:144–84) begins with the swinging of the bullroarer near the general camp and the seizure of the novices who are hurried away into the bush. Officially, the women believe that Mumuna has swallowed them. At the end of the ritual, several months later, the men at the secret ground offer food symbolically to Mumuna and eat it on her behalf. In return she is said to regurgitate the novices. The latter are then smeared from head to foot with red paste and displayed to the women and children back at the general camp. The men say: 'Look at the colouring they have on their bodies: they are smeared with the inside liquids of Mumuna's womb' (p.160).

Among the Murinbata, induction of young men into the cult of the Old Woman is the highest rite in the ritual repertoire. Called Punj, it is sanctioned by the following myth (adapted from Stanner 1959–63:40–2).[13]

M5.   The people said to Mutjingga, the Old Woman: 'We shall leave the children with you while we find honey; you look after them'. She agreed, and the people went off to hunt. After the children had bathed, they settled down to sleep near her. Bringing one close on the pretext of looking for lice, she swallowed it. Then she swallowed the others, ten altogether, and left.

A man and his wife returned to the camp for water and realised what must have happened. They gave the alarm, and the others came back. Ten men set off in pursuit and eventually overtook Mutjingga crawling along a river bed. A left-handed man speared her through the legs and a right-handed man broke her neck with a club. Then they cut her belly open and found the children, still alive, in her womb. They had not gone where the excrement is. The men cleaned and adorned the children and took them back to the camp. Their mothers cried with joy on seeing them and hit themselves until the blood flowed.

The rite of Punj (Stanner 1959–63:6–9) begins when the postulants are taken to the secret ground and told that they will be swallowed alive by Mutjingga and then vomited up. On the third day men begin swinging bullroarers near the ceremonial ground and slowly converge on the assembled novices, who are told that the Old Woman is coming. Suddenly the men leap into view, and the secret of the bullroarers is revealed. Each novice is given a bullroarer which is thrust between his thighs in the position of an erect penis.

The ceremony ends away from the secret ground when the novices crawl towards their mothers through a tunnel of legs formed by the initiated men. As each youth emerges he sits momentarily in front of his mother, with his back to her, while all the women wail and lacerate their heads. The youths then return through the tunnel, and all the men rush with loud shouts back to the secret ground. After about a week the young men resume ordinary life in the community, though now with full adult status. They must not go near their mother's camp.

When Walbiri men separate youths from their mothers in order to induct them into the Gadjari cult (Meggitt 1966), the women believe that the lads will be swallowed alive by two old women. They also believe that, because the men know how to force the Gadjari women to disgorge the lads, the latter will eventually return home unscathed. The following myth (adapted from Meggitt 1966:55–60) characterises the two Gadjari women and provides a rationale for the notion of swallowing and regurgitating the novices.

M6.   A long time ago there were two Mulga-tree brothers, each with a wife and several sons. Because the area they inhabited was suffering from drought, the two men decided to take leave of their families and explore other regions for food. Before departing, they secretly circumcised their sons and inducted them into the clan totemic cult. Their wives heard about the ceremonies and became angry at their exclusion; and when the men refused to allow them to accompany them on their travels, saying they must stay behind and look after the boys, their anger increased. The husbands responded to their demands by soundly thrashing them with boomerangs. They then jumped into the air and began their journey.

After various adventures, they returned home. As they alighted from the sky, they called out happily to their wives, but there was no answer. Puzzled and apprehensive, they searched the vicinity of the camp site and to their alarm discovered evidence of a violent struggle. Leading away from the spot were two sets of footprints, which they identified as their wives'. Then they guessed what must have happened: the two women, furious at being excluded and left behind, had killed and eaten their sons.

The two men followed the tracks to a cave, around the mouth of which flies were swarming. Quickly fashioning torches they entered a large chamber where, among the boulders on the floor, they saw the putrescent remains of their sons. The flies, however, were streaming past the corpses and going further into the cave. The men raised their torches and cautiously advanced. At the end of the cave, they saw the two women, crouching like hideous demons, with flies swarming into their gaping, bloodstained mouths. The men realised that they had vomited up the lads and were ready to swallow them again. So terrifying was the scene of carnage that the men ran in terror from the stinking cavern. Outside, their courage returned. They rushed back in with armfuls of dry grass, threw it over the women and set fire to it. The women were completely destroyed.

DIAGRAM 3

The Myth Sample

Myth	Main Characters	Associated Rite	Area	Tribe	Ethnographer
M1	Yurlunggur (male serpent) Wawilak Sisters	Gunabibi	Milingimbi, N.E. Arnhem Land	Murngin	Warner 1937
M2	Dhuramoolan (ogre) Baiame (protector)	Bora	Central New South Wales	Wiradjeri	Mathews 1896
M3	Julunggul (female serpent) Wawilak Sisters Liningu (male serpent)	Gunabibi	Yirrkala, N.E. Arnhem Land	Wulamba	Berndt 1951
M4	Mumuna (ogress)	Gunabibi	Roper River, Northern Territory	Mara	Berndt 1951
M5	Mutjingga (ogress)	Punj	Port Keats, Northern Territory	Murinbata	Stanner 1959
M6	Mulga-tree brothers Their wives (ogresses)	Gadjari	Central Desert, Northern Territory	Walbiri	Meggitt 1966

153

Badly shaken by these events, the two brothers returned to their original camp where they mourned the passing of their sons. Then they pondered the question of how to replace the lads now that they were without wives and without prospects of acquiring more. That night the older brother dreamt of a magical formula that enabled the two men not only to resurrect their sons but to produce an unlimited supply of children without the aid of women.

The foregoing data (see Diagram 3) suggest a widespread association in Australia between the myth motif of 'swallowing and regurgitation' and the induction of young men into secret religious cults. I shall now consider two theories that have been advanced to account for the connection.

Eliade: Chaos and Cosmogony

In his writings on initiation rites, Eliade attempts to add a metaphysical dimension to the formal analysis of van Gennep's *The Rites of Passage*. In dealing with the Australian material in *Birth and Rebirth* (1958), he details the separation of neophytes from their mothers; their liminal, death-like state during the period of induction; and their ultimate incorporation into the category of initiated males. But his emphasis throughout is on the mystical, as distinct from the social, significance of the procedures. Thus he represents the ritual theme of death and rebirth not as a simple metaphor signifying merely the end of one status and the beginning of another, but as a complex notion symbolising, first, the simultaneous retrogression of individual and cosmos to a state of chaos and, second, their simultaneous regeneration to a state of sanctity. He says (1958:19): 'The mystical death of the boys and their awakening in the community of initiated men thus form part of a grandiose reiteration of the cosmogony . . . Initiation recapitulates the sacred history of the world. And through this recapitulation, the whole world is sanctified.'

In *Myths, Dreams and Mysteries* (1960), Eliade devotes a section to 'swallowing by a monster' (pp.218–23), which makes it clear that the motif is peculiar neither to Australia nor to initiation rites. In the context of initiation, the general meaning is as follows. To be swallowed by a monster is equivalent, in the first instance, to dying; but descent into its belly also signifies return to the embryonic state. So, on the plane of the individual, we have the symbolism of death and rebirth. At the cosmological level, the darkness of the monster's interior corresponds to the Chaos before the Creation. Hence, we are dealing with a double symbolism: 'that of death, namely the conclusion of a temporal existence, and consequently of the end of time, and the symbolism of return to the germinal mode of being, which precedes all forms and every temporal existence. Upon the cosmological plane, this double symbolism refers to the *Urzeit* and the *Endzeit*' (1960:223; see also Eliade 1958:35–7).

Although the Australian data provide firm support for the first half of the hypothesis (swallowing and regurgitation = death and rebirth of the individual), the second half (swallowing and regurgitation = Chaos and Creation) is more speculative and the evidence perhaps less substantial.

There is the added difficulty of accounting for the radical sex difference in ritual role that prevails throughout the continent. Why should responsibility for regeneration of the cosmos be a secret affair of men? Why, to put it another way, should men prevent women on pain of death from witnessing the recapitulation of cosmogony?[14] Their exclusion is a matter I shall return to shortly.

Róheim: Separation Anxiety and Ontogeny

In *The Eternal Ones of the Dream* (1945), Róheim argues that the main function of Australian myth and rite is to satisfy in fantasy the wish for reunion with the mother, while actually achieving a deflection of libido away from the mother onto the father (see Introduction to the present volume, p. 9). After reviewing the data on the rainbow-serpent (pp. 178–99), he concludes that: '. . . the snake owes its role in Australian belief mainly to two qualities. On the one hand snakes stand erect, and thus represent the phallos in erection; but they also swallow beings, and thus typify fantasies and anxieties connected with vagina and uterus' (p.196). He goes on to adduce evidence indicating that the rainbow-serpent is widely conceived as bisexual. Then, with special reference to the Murngin case, he argues that swallowing in the myth stands for reunion with the mother, while regurgitation as expressed in both myth and rite signifies 'rebirth from a male being' (p.198).

We may note that Róheim's general position accommodates the fact of male secrecy better than that of Eliade. If a purpose of initiation ritual is to deflect the libido of youths from their mothers to their fathers (a process without which, according to Róheim, 'no society consisting of several males could continue to exist', p. 198), then it is obvious that the mothers must be excluded. But there is no need to make the further assumption that the myth motif of swallowing expresses a desire for maternal reunion. Such a view encounters the difficulty that in all cases the swallowing is represented as fearsome. Moreover, in at least one case in our sample the swallower (Dhuramoolan) seems unequivocally male. Bisexuality is admittedly a recurrent feature of the rainbow-serpent but, as I hope my concluding remarks will show, it can be more parsimoniously explained simply in terms of 'rebirth by males', without the additional assumption of a 'fantasy of reunion'.

Conclusion: from Ontogeny to Cosmogony

Two common features of the myths under consideration are that they (i) act as charters for initiation ceremonies and (ii) contain the motif of swallowing and regurgitation.[15] A simple point perhaps worth considering is that the latter constitutes an apt metaphor for a 'rite of passage'. Given that the aim of such rites is to transform the postulant without obliterating his previous identity, one might even say that it is the best 'physiological' metaphor available. The respiratory system does not serve the purpose because, to ordinary observation, there is no substantial difference between what goes in and what comes out. The female reproductive system is inappropriate because here there is too much difference. That is also true of the digestive system when the process is carried to completion; but if it is reversed by vomiting (or interrupted by surgery), then changes will have occurred but the ingested object is still recognisable.

Such considerations (supposing they ever occurred to the Aborigines) would draw upon fairly elementary physiological observations. Yet two of the cases under discussion falsely presuppose a direct connection between the alimentary system and the female reproductive system. Thus Mara men say that after Mumuna swallows the novices, they reside in her uterus (Berndt 1951:147). And, as we have seen, the children swallowed by Mutjingga were found in her womb and not 'where the excrement was' (Stanner 1959–63:42). This suggests that the differences in transformational effect between 'swallowing and regurgitation' and other systems (as considered above) may be less important for symbolic purposes than a perceived similarity between the upper alimentary tract and the female generative organs, that is, a common ability to admit and expel (cf. Berndt 1951:153). Bearing this association in mind, let us now turn to the rites.

A typical feature is that, at the beginning, the uninitiated should and may believe that the novices are about to be destroyed at the secret ceremonial ground by a supernatural being.[16] They may also expect that, through the good offices of the men, the boys will be returned safely, though with altered status. In four of the six cases, the return of the novices is in some degree modelled on female reproduction. This is clearest in the Wulamba Gunabibi which features a symbolic uterus and ends with a simulated birth scene. A parallel, though less explicit, symbolism occurs in the Murngin Gunabibi. In the Mara Gunabibi the novices are brought back smeared with red paste, which the women are supposed to believe comes from Mumuna's womb. And, in the Murinbata Mutjingga cult, blood-covered novices return to their mothers from between the legs of the initiated men. On this and other evidence from outside the sample, we can say that in Australia the metaphorical re-birth of boys as initiated men is frequently, though not invariably, carried out on a model of natural parturition.[17]

Thus, given the formal separation of sons from mothers that regularly precedes the ceremonies, the basic message from the men seems to be something like: 'This boy is your offspring; we must take him now and destroy his attachment to you; then we will reproduce him as one of us.' I shall now indicate how four of the myths rationalise and reinforce this message either by imputing malevolence to women, by emphasising the protective aspects of men, or both.

In the three stories about ogresses (M4, M5, M6), initial trust is reposed in women; the trust is betrayed when the women wantonly attack those living under their auspices; and the victims are avenged or saved by men. In the Wiradjeri myth (M2), the lads are saved from Dhuramoolan's violence by the benevolent might of Baiame. In so far as Dhuramoolan and Baiame may be understood to represent respectively the threatening and protective aspects of adult males, the mythical charter implies that admission to the secret cult constitutes an escape from male threat (which recedes once the lads are separated from their female kin) to male protection.

Female malevolence is absent from the Murngin Wawilak myth (M1), and male protectiveness is less in evidence than male aggression. A modified line of analysis is therefore required. The myth reaches a climax when the 'Great Father' snake, provoked by menstrual blood, swallows two women and their sons. This we might interpret as an attack on female sexuality and maternity. The episode ends when the snake regurgitates the women but retains the boys,[18] thus signifying the separation of mother and son, and the irresistible incorporation of the latter into the male cult.[19] One could say that, whereas the ogress myths set out to justify the separation of youths from their female kin by discrediting women, and the Dhuramoolan-Baiame myth tries to temper its harshness by offering a benign alternative under veiled threat, the Murngin Wawilak myth merely proclaims it as a function of male ascendancy.[20]

A different interpretation is required for the Wulamba Wawilak myth (M3), in as much as the snake Julunggul and its victims are all female.[21] It will be recalled, however, that a young bachelor snake named Liningu unsuccessfully tried to emulate the female snake's performance, choosing youths as his victims and vomiting them up dead. In this myth, it seems to me, the central concern has shifted away from the separation of youths from women towards the means of their 'reproduction' as men. The failure of the bachelor snake signifies that the natural male model is unsuitable for the purposes of symbolic re-birth (Linigu's victims are 'still-born'). The female model is appropriate and, in conjunction with male ritual operations, effective.

We may now return to the association noted earlier between the upper alimentary tract and the female reproductive organs.[22] In the context of initiation, it is apparent that 'swallowing and regurgitation' is, or may be, a dual-purpose symbol, on the one hand communicating threat, on the other serving as a substitute for the natural model of female generation. It is thus ideally suited to serve the twin purpose of 'separation' and 're-birth by males'. We may note that activation of the symbol in its reproductive capacity entails an ability to control its destructive propensity. Sometimes this is explicit, as in the case of the Mara Gunabibi. Although in the myth Mumuna (M4) regurgitated her victims dead (as did Liningu, M3), men now have a technique for persuading her to return the novices alive.[23] Similarly, the Gadjari ogresses destroyed their sons in the myth (M6), but Walbiri men know how to make them disgorge novices unscathed.[24]

In the preceding analysis I have concentrated on features of the myths that make them appropriate charters for rituals whose purpose is to weaken the relationship of youths to their close female kin and to induct them into a solidary group of men. One may properly ask at this point what the cults do, apart from initiating new members. Here Eliade's formulation would express the native ideology well enough: an important part of the dramatic and liturgical content of the rituals represents a recapitulation of cosmogony and anthropogony. It should be noted that the ceremonies we have been discussing extend over fairly lengthy periods, often up to three or four months and longer, and that only a portion of that time, mainly at the beginning and the end, is devoted to what we may strictly regard as the formal induction and incorporation of neophytes. Other parts are concerned with mythical acts of creation, in some cases contained in the main charter myths but in other cases described in independent traditions.

In effect, then, the rituals and their supporting myths remove the sexually-maturing male from the family of orientation (which, of course, may include other females besides his mother)[25] and, through the symbolism of parturition, place him in a situation of dependence upon men, who for the next five or ten years will guide and govern the sublimation of his raw energies.[26] The relationship between the inductional and cosmological components of the ritual complex merits a closer investigation than I am able to undertake in the present paper. But it is apparent that in some instances both components are manifested through a single mythical being, which accordingly performs a double function.[27] Thus Yurlunggur, the Snake, and Mutjingga, the Old Woman, are not only swallowers and regurgitators of neophytes, but also cosmic creators. It is possible that the imagery on both levels stems from certain notions that develop in the course of ontogeny, notions in particular that develop in the mind of the child about himself in relation to his parents. An enormous snake, known as the Great Father, constitutes an appropriate symbol for intimidating neophytes and for representing cosmic power because real fathers, especially in their phallic aspects, may seem intimidating and powerful to their small sons. A similar, though rather more complex point, might be worked out for the cannibal woman known as Mother-of-All. The figurative use of natural motherhood as a model for cosmic creation requires no special explanation. But projection of infantile hostility (including cannibalistic impulses) onto real mothers might need to be assumed in order to account for the attribution of malevolence to the All-Mother.[28]

Notes

1. This essay grew out of a brief comment on Lévi-Strauss's analysis of the Wawilak myth that I made at the 1972 A.I.A.S. symposium. The main ideas were developed during my tenure of an Overseas Fellowship (1972–73) at Churchill College, Cambridge, and I thank the Master and Fellows for the privileged circumstances in which I worked. I also thank my colleagues, too numerous to mention by name, who heard the paper and offered their comments. I am, however, indebted especially to A.P. Elkin, Meyer Fortes, and Roy Rappaport for their interest and help. Following my discussions with Stephen Hugh-Jones in Cambridge, Terence Turner's brilliant paper on the Kayapo fire myth (A.S.A. Conference, Oxford 1973) convinced me that comparisons between Australian and South American myths will prove to be a fruitful area for future research.

2. For a critical comment on Warner's view that the Murngin prefer the dry season to the wet, see C.H. Berndt 1970:1321. I share her scepticism and have been unable to validate Warner's view among the Burera, whom he lists as a Murngin tribe (see Hiatt 1969:5;1965:2–3).

3. In this summary of the Gunabibi ceremony, as in my subsequent descriptions of other rituals, I omit for reasons of space what might well be regarded as significant details. The same applies to the presentation of myths. A proper evaluation of my analysis would thus entail a reading of the originals.

4. It is enormous, lives in a waterhole, is identified with the rainbow, controls the rain and swallows humans. For confirmation of my assertion that Warner's snake is the rainbow-serpent, see Berndt 1951:16.

5. It may be noted, however, that in *The Andaman Islanders* Radcliffe-Brown interpreted an important myth as 'an expression of the social value of the phenomena of the weather and the seasons' (1922:375).

6. I would make a similar remark (substituting 'cultural' for 'ecological') about Munn's recent analysis of the Wawilak myth (Munn 1969), which relates it to images of body destruction (sorcery) and regeneration (ritual).

7. Professor Elkin (personal communication, 10/4/73) was assured in the early 1930s that initiation rites were still being performed near Kempsey (north coast, New South Wales).

8. For a recent review of the literature on Baiame, a so-called 'High God' or 'Supreme Being' of south-eastern Australia, see Eliade 1973:ch.1.

9. *Cf.* Meggitt 1966:90–1. At the end of a comparative analysis of male cults in widely-dispersed parts of Australia, Meggitt (*ibid*:78–91) concludes that 'the evidence supports fairly well the hypothesis that all these major ceremonial complexes are best viewed as particular local developments or manifestations of a more general configuration of Australian Aboriginal initiation ritual'. The argument of the present paper may be seen as an attempt to corroborate and develop this proposition.

10. *Cf.* Lévi-Strauss's remarks on vomiting in *The Raw and the Cooked*, p. 135.

11. 'Wulamba' is a term used at Yirrkala for the people of north-eastern Arnhem Land (Berndt 1951:2); 'Murngin' is a term of narrower reference used by Warner for the same purpose (1937:15, fn. 2). I use the designation 'Wulamba' merely as a convenient way of distinguishing Berndt's version of the Wawilak myth from Warner's.

12. Though, in a variant form of the myth, Lightning plays a subsidiary role (Berndt 1951:152–3).

13. I have already summarised the myth and the associated rite for a different purpose in the Introduction to this volume (pp. 11–12).

14. Eliade in several places (1958:78–80, 1960:202) inflates the transcendental content of women's secret ceremonies in order to maintain that, in principle, they are on a par with those of the men (see also his argument that in earlier times there was greater religious collaboration between the sexes, 1973:121–7). My own impression is that, in Australia, women's ceremonies are emphatically carnal and probably in some degree subversive (see, for example, C.H. Berndt 1950, 1965:243; Reay 1970; also Ardener 1972, who raises a general issue about the relationship between male and female models within the same culture).

15. This is not strictly true of M5, in which the children are extracted from Mutjingga's belly. But, for the purposes of the associated ritual, she is supposed to swallow and regurgitate the novices.

16. Though at the beginning of the Murngin Gunabibi rite, the serpent is said merely to be calling for the novices.

17. See Hiatt 1971. In that place I argued that the purpose of secret pseudo-procreation among the Australian Aborigines is to extend male mastery into areas where women have natural advantages. With reference to induction into male cults, I think now that this formulation gives undue weight to a particular temperamental proclivity of the male animal, at the expense of the adaptive functions of symbolic separation and re-birth, as emphasised by Róheim.

18. Warner (1937:257, fn. 9) says that: 'In some accounts a boy and girl are swallowed, and usually also regurgitated; but in many of the stories told by the older Liaalaomir men the children are male, and not spewed up by the

snake.' Warner's informants say that the snake retained the boys because he was Dua moiety and they Yiritja (1937:258). But in a version of the myth recorded by C.H. Berndt (1970:1308), the same reason is given to explain why, in this case, the children were not retained (see also fn. 19 below).

19. In versions of the Wawilak myth recorded by C.H. Berndt (1970:1308) the serpent, who is male, swallows the two sisters and their child(ren), regurgitates them, then re-swallows and retains the women but leaves the child(ren). In one version, the child has been vomited up dead. This reversal of the situation described in M1, where the serpent finally regurgitates the sisters but retains the boys, poses some difficulties for my analysis. But it should be stressed that we are dealing here with female versions of the myth. Berndt makes the astute observation that, with regard to ritual, the symbolism of swallowing and regurgitating novices applies only to males and that hence, 'we could say that, once swallowed, the Wawalag did not *need* to be vomited whereas their male child(ren) did' (*ibid:*1323). I would go further and suggest that these female modifications of the myth elements highlight what, to a woman, are the significant aspects of male cult life: the subordination of female interests and the 'death' of her son (who, as far as she is concerned, stays 'dead' — his 're-birth' is men's business).

20. See Layton 1968:122. Although Layton touches on some of the themes I have discussed, he is primarily concerned to explain myth variation.

21. Bettelheim (1955:199–200) interprets swallowing in the Wawilak myth in terms of an alleged male desire to acquire female sex characteristics; and regurgitation in terms of an alleged ambivalence (fear as well as desire) towards these characteristics. This hardly squares with the facts (a) that in the Wulamba Wawilak myth the snake and her victims are all female and (b) that in the Murngin Wawilak myth the snake, who is male, swallows two boys as well as two women. A more general criticism is that Bettelheim's interpretations, unlike Róheim's, lack an adaptive or sociological dimension.

22. I am grateful to Professor Meyer Fortes for a comment that prompted me to work out this point more thoroughly than I would have otherwise.

23. In M3 and M4, the regurgitated victims are not only dead, but reduced to bones. Following Maddock (1969), we might keep open the possibility of a secondary reverberation from the sphere of mortuary procedures, where in certain areas or circumstances the bereaved eat the deceased's flesh and keep his bones (see also Hiatt 1966).

24. Professor R. Rappaport has made the observation (personal communication) that 'swallowing' in Australian religion might be seen as a sacrament in reverse, i.e. the 'deity' ingests the 'worshipper', rather than vice versa. Here I would also draw attention to elements of sacrifice in the rituals reviewed: Murngin women make gifts of appeasement to the Snake; Wulamba women are told that the youths have been offered to the Snake in order to avert general disaster; and Mara men offer food to the Old Woman to induce her to return the novices. I am aware that Stanner (1959–63:2–21) has interpreted 'swallowing and regurgitation' in Murinbata religion on the model of sacrifice, but I would not necessarily regard his hypothesis and my own as being incompatible.

25. Sisters, half-sisters, and other wives of his father (who may be close to his own age).

26. There is an important connection here with polygyny, which in Australia entails that men marry later than women (the former at about 25–30 years, the latter at about 15 years). Adultery is an offence, and young bachelors are therefore expected to be celibate. By inducting them into transcendental mysteries, and also by encouraging their simultaneous development as warriors (see, for example, Warner 1937:ch. VI), married men divert youthful energy upwards (so to speak) and outwards, and thus away from the women over whom they wish to retain a sexual monopoly. With reference to the

relative emphases on transcendentalism and militarism as solutions to the problem of celibacy, a comparison between Australia and other places (for example, New Guinea) might be of some interest.

27. See Campbell 1959:ch. 2; *cf.* also Turner 1964:30, and various later works.

28. See Klein 1954; also Freeman 1968. One should not however, rule out the possibility that real mothers harbour hostile feelings towards their children.

References

ARDENER, E. 1972 Belief and the problem of women. In *The interpretation of ritual: essays in honour of A.I. Richards*, (ed.) J.S. la Fontaine, pp. 135–58. London, Tavistock Publications.

BERNDT, C.H. 1950 Women's changing ceremonies in northern Australia. *L'Homme*, 1:1–87.

—— 1965 Women and the 'secret life'. In *Aboriginal man in Australia: essays in honour of Emeritus Professor A.P. Elkin*, (eds) R.M. and C.H. Berndt, pp. 238–82. Sydney, Angus and Robertson.

—— 1970 Monsoon and honey-wind. In *Échanges et communications: mélanges offerts à Claude Lévi-Strauss à son 60ème anniversaire*, (eds) J. Pouillon and P. Maranda, 2:1306–26. The Hague/Paris, Mouton.

BERNDT, R.M. 1951 *Kunapipi: a study of an Australian Aboriginal religious cult*. Melbourne, Cheshire.

BETTELHEIM, B. 1955 *Symbolic wounds: puberty rites and the envious male*. London, Thames and Hudson.

CAMPBELL, J. 1960 *The masks of God: primitive mythology*. London, Secker and Warburg.

ELIADE, M. 1958 *Birth and rebirth: the religious meanings of initiation in human culture*. New York, Harper.

—— 1960 *Myths, dreams and mysteries. The encounter between contemporary faith and archaic realities*. New York, Harper.

—— 1973 *Australian religions: an introduction*. Ithaca, Cornell University Press.

FREEMAN, D. 1968 Thunder, blood, and the nicknaming of God's creatures. *Psychoanalytic Quarterly*, 37:353–99.

HIATT, L.R. 1965 *Kinship and conflict: a study of an Aboriginal community in northern Arnhem Land*. Canberra, A.N.U. Press.

—— 1966 Mystery at Port Hacking. *Mankind*, 6:313–17.

—— 1969 Fieldwork carried out from May to July, 1967, among the Gidjingali of northern Arnhem Land, under the auspices of the University of Sydney and the Australian Institute of Aboriginal Studies.

—— 1971 Secret pseudo-procreation rites among the Australian Aborigines. In *Anthropology in Oceania: essays presented to Ian Hogbin*, (eds) L.R. Hiatt and C. Jayawardena, pp. 77–88. Sydney, Angus and Robertson.

KLEIN, M. 1954 *The psycho-analysis of children*. London, Hogarth.

LAYTON, R. 1968 Myth and society in Aboriginal Arnhem Land. Unpublished M.Phil. thesis, University of London.

LÉVI-STRAUSS, C. 1966 *The savage mind*. London, Weidenfeld and Nicolson.

—— 1970 *The raw and the cooked*. London, Jonathan Cape.

MADDOCK, K.J. 1969 Necrophagy and the circulation of mothers: a problem in Mara ritual and social structure. *Mankind*, 7(2):94–103.

MATHEWS, R.H. 1895–96 The Bora, or initiation ceremonies of the Kamilaroi tribe, parts I and II. In *Royal Anthropological Institute, Journal*, 24:411–27; 25:318–39.

—— 1896 The Burbung of the Wiradthuri tribes. In *Royal Anthropological Institute, Journal*, 25:295–318.

—— 1900 The Burbung of the Wiradthuri tribes. In *Royal Society of Queensland, Proceedings*, 16:35–38.

—— 1901 Initiation ceremonies of the Wiradjuri tribes. *American Anthropologist*, 3:337–41.

MEGGITT, M.J. 1967 *Gadjari among the Walbiri Aborigines of central Australia*. Sydney (Oceania monograph no. 14), University of Sydney.

MUNN, N.D. 1969 The effectiveness of symbols in Murngin rite and myth. In *Forms of symbolic action*, (ed.) F. Spencer, pp. 178–207. Seattle and London, University of Washington Press.

RADCLIFFE-BROWN, A.R. 1922 *The Andaman Islanders*. Cambridge, Cambridge University Press.

—— 1926 The rainbow-serpent myth of Australia. In *Royal Anthropological Institute, Journal*, 56:19–25.

—— 1930 The rainbow-serpent myth in south-east Australia. *Oceania*, 1(3):342–47.

REAY, M.O. 1970 A decision as narrative. In *Australian Aboriginal anthropology: modern studies in the social anthropology of the Australian Aborigines*, (ed.) R.M. Berndt, pp. 164–73. Nedlands, University of Western Australia Press.

RÓHEIM, G. 1945 *The eternal ones of the dream: a psychoanalytic interpretation of Australian myth and ritual*. New York, International Universities Press.

STANNER, W.E.H. 1959–63 *On Aboriginal religion*. Sydney, (Oceania monograph no. 11), University of Sydney.

TURNER, V. 1964 Symbols in Ndembu ritual. In *Closed systems and open mind*, (ed.) M. Gluckman. Edinburgh, Oliver and Boyd.

WARNER, W.L. 1937 *A black civilization*. New York, Harper.

A Death in the Family:

Some Torres Strait Ghost Stories

Jeremy Beckett

The story of Aukam and Tiai was the point of departure for this study, and I shall take it as my key myth. It consists of two episodes, the second of which develops and resolves events occurring in the first. The first episode describes the circumstances giving rise to a killing; the second, the transformation of the spirit of the victim into a ghost, and its departure for the land of the dead. This second episode has as its theme the establishment of death as an irreversible event, and the consequent separation of the worlds of ghosts and mortals, through an individual's act of choice. I see as the narrative's 'dynamic principle' (Turner 1969:62) the intersection of two pairs of familial relations: mother-son and brother-sister. A survey of Western Torres Strait mythology,[1] which has been exhaustively collected (Haddon 1904; Lawrie 1970; Laade 1971), supports my view, for it reveals the kind of redundancy that Leach has said we should expect (1967:2). The two pairs occur more frequently than others within the family, together in several instances (as in the key myth), and in association with killing and ghosts.

I shall begin the study by outlining the story then draw out the more obvious social and cultural implications. I shall then move on to other myths, not only to show repetitions but to discover elements which seem to be implicit though not brought out in the key myth. In a final section I look cursorily at the mythologies of Eastern Torres Strait, south-western Papua and finally Cape York, to see whether the same motifs and elements recur. First, however, I shall provide a brief ethnography of the region. (For a more extended summary of the sources, see Beckett 1972, and Moore 1972.)

The Western Islanders

For our knowledge of the Torres Strait Islanders we are almost wholly dependent on the work of the Cambridge Anthropological Expedition of 1898. As the six volumes of the *Reports* attest, Haddon and his six colleagues worked diligently to record what they could of the indigenous culture. But even then they had to rely on the memories of old men rather than direct observation. Early in the second half of the nineteenth century, pearlers, trepangers, missionaries and government officials had established themselves in the Strait. And within less than a generation they had transformed its traditional way of life. Thus there were many questions that Haddon and his colleagues could not find an answer to; and not a few that they

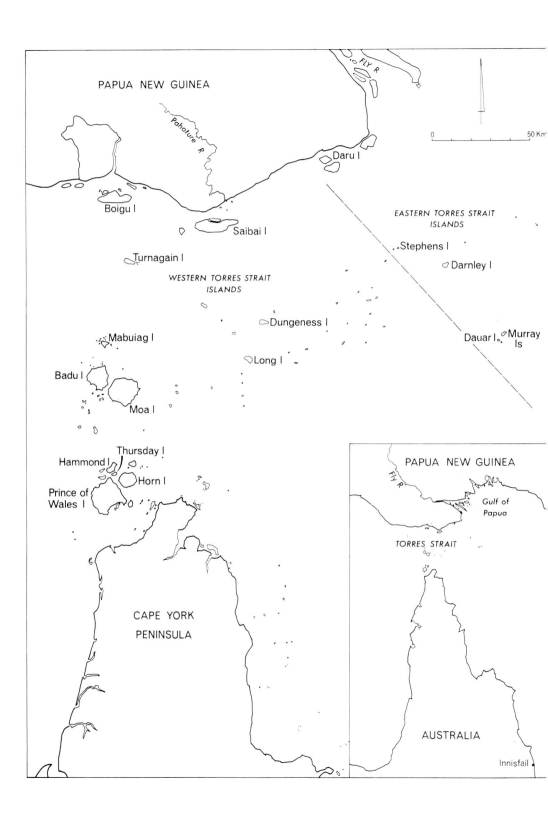

PAPUA NEW GUINEA

FLY R

Pahoture R

Daru I

EASTERN TORRES STRAIT
ISLANDS

Stephens I

Darnley I

Boigu I

Saibai I

Turnagain I

WESTERN TORRES STRAIT
ISLANDS

Dungeness I

Dauar I   Murray
Is

Mabuiag I

Long I

Badu I

Moa I

Thursday I

Hammond I

Horn I

Prince of
Wales I

CAPE YORK

PENINSULA

0   50 Km

PAPUA NEW GUINEA

FLY R

Gulf of
Papua

TORRES STRAIT

AUSTRALIA

Innisfail

failed to ask. Those who have worked in the Strait over the last decade, including Mrs Lawrie, Dr Laade and myself, have found a rich store of tradition and folklore. But many problems relating to ecology, religion and social organisation, will probably always remain unanswered, unless some archival source comes to light. The general picture is, nevertheless, reasonably clear.

For those interested in drawing cultural boundaries, the Torres Strait Islands (particularly the western group) present a fascinating problem as the place where Melanesia meets Australia. The Western Torres Strait language (unlike the Eastern) is of Australian Aboriginal type, though not represented on the mainland. But the people would be taken for Melanesians, and their culture had a decidedly Papuan flavour. They knew about cultivation, but its importance relative to hunting and gathering varied. In the islands near Papua, as in the eastern group, gardening was regularly practised. Further south its importance dwindled, until, in the islands off Cape York, it was a marginal source of food. The islands and the seas surrounding them were rich, while the populations seem to have been relatively small. Although I have surveyed myths from all the islands in the western group, almost all those relevant to the present discussion come from three islands, Mabuiag, Badu and Moa, which occupy a midway point, geographically and in terms of this ecological spectrum. The people probably lived in fairly small residential groups, shifting up and down extensive stretches of foreshore and exploiting the hinterland as they went.

Foreshores were associated with patrilineal totemic clans, a social form that stretched from Cape York to Papua. Residence was commonly, but not necessarily, patri-virilocal (Haddon 1904:229–30). Unlike their Australian neighbours, islanders did not assign a kinship role to every member of the society. Rather they distinguished non-kin, with whom they married, from kin, with whom they did not. Kin included all members of the totemic clan,[2] but also matrilateral kin and, less certainly, the kin of father's mother.

Ideally, men exchanged their sisters in marriage. However, exchanges of real sisters seem, in fact, to have been rare (Haddon 1904:241–2), but the inclusion of classificatory sisters may have brought reality closer to the ideal. Marriage also involved exchange of goods, though its economic importance was small, as well as certain ritual obligations, particularly in death. Then in the next generation, a sister's son brought his uncle further payments and, when the boy grew up, he also brought him protection in a possibly hostile community. In return, the uncle led the boy through initiation, and acted as his spokesman in marriage negotiations.

There was a rich diversity of ritual activities, some concerned with economic affairs, others concerned with death and warfare. There were elaborate funerary rites, ending with the disposal of the body and the preservation of the skull which could be used for divination. However, the dead were remembered in ghost dances. Warfare also ended with the retention of skulls, as trophies, for divination, or for the canoe trade with Papua. Associated with these practices there was a rather loosely integrated corpus of beliefs about the condition of the dead, the possibility of communication with them, and the benefits to be derived therefrom.

165

Aukam and Tiai

Here is an outline of the myth, omitting certain details which are not required for the analysis or an understanding of the narrative sequence. For full versions I refer the reader to the sources from which the outline has been taken (Haddon 1904:56–62; Lawrie 1970:24–6). I have numbered the main steps in the narrative for convenience.

Myth I

1.   Aukam, a woman, lives alone on the western side of Moa Island.

2.   Her two old brothers live nearby, but separately. They are also unmarried and without children.

3.   Brother A goes fishing, but by a deception persuades Aukam to give him part of her catch.

4.   Brother B does not go fishing, but remains inside a log, complaining that his sister never brings him fish.

5.   Aukam bears a son, Tiai, unbeknown to her brothers.

6.   She leaves the child unguarded, to go fishing.

7.   Brother B discovers the child and kills him.

8.   Aukam returns to find Tiai dead. She discovers brother B's tracks, and, following him back to his log, burns him to death.

9.   Aukam hangs Tiai's bones around her neck.

10. Tiai's spirit takes the form of a youth.

11. He leaves for Boigu Island where he marries and has 'plenty sweetheart'.

12. Aukam goes in search of Tiai, proceeding through every island lying west of Moa, until she reaches Boigu.

13. She discovers Tiai among his friends and shows him his bones around her neck.

14. Tiai realises for the first time that he is a spirit and is 'ashamed'.

15. Aukam asks him to return to Moa. But instead he instructs his affines to erect a funerary platform. By so doing he denies himself the possibility of becoming a man again.

16. Tiai mounts the platform, descends, mounts and desecnds again, performs a funeral dance and then, stepping backwards, enters a hole in the ground.

17. He tells his mother that having followed him, she must join him, and together they descend.

Ghosts and Mortals

Although we are not specifically told so, it seems as though Tiai made death an irreversible event and set up the domain of ghosts (*mari*),[4] separate from that of mortals. Ghosts are in many ways the opposite of mortals: they are white and soft; they are cold; they smell 'stale' and dislike the smell of a pregnant woman (Haddon 1904:359); they eat their food raw (*ibid*:357); they communicate by whistling; they travel underground and through the air. They have their own place, variously located under the ground and where the sun sets. Aukam and Tiai travel from Moa in a westerly direction, until they reach Boigu, the westernmost island of the group. Islanders said that the dead set out from the westernmost point of Boigu to reach the place of ghosts. The same direction is followed in other myths about death; conversely, bearers of fertility travel eastward.

The worlds of ghosts and mortals are demarcated, but there can be transactions between them. Ghosts are not confined to their own place. They visit the place of mortals, though they are shy of encounters and likely to cover their faces. Mortals with 'strong hearts' can approach them, for example through skull divination, and gain benefits; but they must be careful to control these contacts and keep the ghosts at arm's length for fear of being lured away.

Myths and folktales instance mortals living among ghosts, and ghosts among mortals, but the anomaly is always resolved sooner or later. I have heard accounts of mortals who, in severe illness, find themselves in ghostland. But after a while they are sent back with the advice: 'Your time is not yet.' There are two myths in which a mortal marries a ghost (Haddon 1904:83–8). Curiously, in both the boy is called Tabepa and the girl Uga, but in one Tabepa is mortal and Uga the ghost (Myth II, below), while in the other their states are reversed. Both end with the mortal partner becoming a ghost. In the second myth, the mortal Uga returns from ghostland to bear her baby by her ghost husband. The baby is born, but in the ensuing battle between ghosts and mortals, the two become ghosts.

There is one exceptional instance of a mortal living permanently among ghosts — German (nowadays John) Wislin, the hero of the 1913 Cargo cult (Haddon 1935:46–7; Beckett n.d.). His mother died and was buried while he was yet in her womb. But he lived and was born in due course. He emerged from the grave and returned to his kin.[5] They drove him away and he departed for ghostland. There he took command of the ship that would one day drive out the whites and bring cargo. This event would herald the merging of the two worlds of ghosts and mortals, that is, an upsetting of the cosmic order.

The critical line, it must be noted, is not between the living and the dead, but between mortals and ghosts. And while mortals are made by natural means, ghosts are made by ritual — that is, cultural — means, namely funeral rites. These, in the pidgin of Haddon's day, were called '*mekim debil*' (Haddon 1904:90). Their importance is brought out in the story of Mutuk (*ibid*:89–92; Lawrie 1970:68–9), which tells how a man, presumed dead, is killed when he reappears because the rites have already been performed. Correspondingly, spirits for whom funerary rites have not yet been completed are a danger to their kin. The mortal who has been made a ghost, and the spirit who has not, both present dangerous anomalies requiring resolution.

Haddon has transmitted to us his informants' accounts of the Western Islanders' funerary rites (1904:248–62). The affines of the deceased undertook the work while the kinsfolk gave themselves over to mourning. They exposed the corpse on a roofed platform, standing guard over it during the first few days. During this period the body was dangerous and the spirit never far away. After decomposition had set in they pulled the head away from the body. In order that it should come off easily, the kinsfolk must first drive the spirit away. The body was then covered and left until only bones remained, when the female kin took them and deposited them in a cave. Evidently no further interest was taken in them. Meanwhile the affinal guardians had placed the skull in a termite hill for cleaning. After this they decorated it, placed it in a basket and ceremonially returned it to the bereaved. Often a mother's brother or sister's son took charge of it. The bereaved then rewarded the officiants for their trouble. The heads of victims in war were cooked, and after certain portions had been eaten, were cleaned, decorated and deposited with others in a shrine on the men's ceremonial ground (*ibid*:305).

The general ideas underlying the funerary rites are familiar enough. Hertz (1909) long ago pointed out the parallel between the transformation of the deceased's physical remains and that of his spirit. However, it is not simply that the desiccated bones represent the spirit in its settled and innocuous state, though this idea may be present. The ghost leaves the body when the head is detached. And once the head is cleaned it is decorated, though the face is not remodelled like that of the victim. It is kept by the bereaved. Haddon's informants explained that this was a remembrance, 'all same photograph' (Haddon 1904:364; *cf.* Hiatt 1966). But it is also a means of divination, of re-establishing contact with the ghost under controlled conditions (*ibid*:361–2). Thus the dead can maintain a presence in the land of the living in a form that is acceptable, as the ghost and corpse are not. Interestingly, my island informants sometimes spoke of ghosts as 'soft' and 'boneless'. And in the myth it is the sight of his bones that sends Tiai off to ghostland. In fact it is the skull in particular that attracts most of the attention. But the significance of skulls and heads is one of the unsolved puzzles of Papuan ethnography.

Terence Turner has observed that:

> Traditional narrative genres such as myth, tale and legend, typically begin with an action or event that violates or mediates the structure of the prevailing order, giving rise to a situation in which actors and elements stand in ambiguous or contradictory relationships to each other. The 'plot' or narrative sequence proceeds from this point through a series of permutations of the relations between these actors and elements toward a final state of equilibrium in which all elements again stand in unambiguous (synchronic) relations to each other. The beginning-middle-end phase structure of such traditional narrative genres thus manifests itself at the level of content as a dialectical alternation between synchronic order and diachronic disorder. (1969:33)

Turner's generalisation is applicable to a wide range of myths, but not strictly to those describing the institutionalisation of some element in the cosmic order. In such cases, the initial situation is represented as an absence of order, a primeval chaos, anomalous only in terms of the order subsequently established. Thus Tiai's entry into the Boiguan community and his marriage in the second episode (MI:9–17) violates the separation of the living and the dead which he had yet to set up. And he was not bound to set it up. According to the story (MI:15) he had the possibility of becoming a man again, that is, of making or keeping death a reversible event. To understand his choice, we must go back to the first episode, which also begins with a violation of the prevailing order.

Sisters and Brothers

The situation described in the initial stages of the myth is abnormal on two counts. Aukam's brothers are already old, but they have neither wives nor children, and so are without the domestic, procreative and economic benefits of marriage. Similarly, Aukam is husbandless. The two conditions are connected because the bestowal of a sister entitled the brother to receive a wife.

The birth of Tiai aggravates the situation. We are not told the circumstances of his birth, whether by parthenogenesis[6] or illicit sexual intercourse. If the latter, then Aukam has been 'stolen' from her people, and the boy is *puru kaz*, a child of theft. But the precise circumstances are unimportant. The point is that the brothers are without the means of acquiring wives *and* brothers-in-law, and stand in an anomalous relationship to their sister's son because they are his only relatives.

When a girl was bestowed in marriage, her family received certain payments, which were repeated when a child was born. Husbands performed various other services for their wives' brothers, for example, sailing a canoe. Brothers were said to be jealous of their sisters, showing hostility towards suitors (Haddon 1904:223). Relations between brothers-in-law were reserved and, in keeping with this distancing, they performed one another's funerary rites on behalf of the bereaved kin. Between mother's brother and sister's son the relation was, as I have indicated, cordial. They made free with one another's property, and they gave one another protection in times of danger. The latter could be of crucial importance when the two belonged to different and potentially hostile communities.

For a man, then, his sister's marriage was figuratively, and in fact, a matter of life and death. Tiai's birth represents a negation of the ties established through exogamous marriage, and a distortion of the uncle-nephew relationship. The resentment normally vented on the sister's husband is displaced on to the child. Thus we have a 'motive' for Brother B's killing of Tiai, beyond the stated motive of Aukam's failure in another wife-like duty, the provision of food.

The anomaly which is Tiai's birth is cancelled out by his death. But the killing is itself a violation of the normative relation between mother's brother and sister's son. As I have already indicated, the relationship stands for peace and is in every respect free and benevolent. Brother B's inversion of this relationship is cancelled out when Aukam kills him, but Brother A survives. He plays no further part in the narrative, but his survival remains significant through to the end. Had Tiai returned with his mother, as she wished, he would have recreated the old disordered situation. In effect,

169

Brother A bars the way. By becoming a ghost, Tiai removes himself from the situation altogether. Aukam similarly removes herself. Brother A thus loses her wife-like services, of which he previously took advantage. He also loses a means of gaining brothers-in-law. Both brothers are left without anyone to make them into ghosts.

Of fourteen myths in which the characters are linked by familial ties, five (six, if we accept a variant version) include the brother-sister pair. In only one, the story of Mutuk (p.167) above are relations between them positive: both are married. The mortal Uga marries the ghostly Tabepa (p.167) in order to avoid the incestuous demands of her brother, but this is an anomalous marriage which offers the brother no possibliity of getting a wife in exchange. He kills Tabepa, an action which ends with Uga and her child also becoming ghosts. In the Saibai story of Karbai (Lawrie 1970:172–3; Laade 1971:29) the sister approaches the brother, who takes flight in the form of a bird: both are unmarried. In one version of the story, Waiat persuades his sister Kuda to place her two sons in his charge, and subsequently kills them. Kuda has no husband. Waiat has a wife and daughter, but they have been killed before he kills the boys (Lawrie 1970:115–7).[7] In a Boiguan myth, the boy Bukia is killed by his uncles. His mother is widowed (Lawrie 1970:224–5).

What emerges from all these stories is the danger inherent in the brother-sister relationship, if the sister does not have a husband. When she has a son, but no husband, we have another anomalous situation which receives even more frequent mention in the mythology.

Sons and Mothers

The son-mother pair occurs more frequently than any other in Torres Strait mythology. Of the fourteen myths in which the characters are linked by familial ties, eight include a mother and son. Only two include a father-son pair, and one of these is eliminated in an alternative version. Only one includes a father-daughter pair, and only one a mother-daughter pair. In only one of the eight, the story of the mortal Tabepa, is the father an actor and his role is negated (see Myth II). In two the father is said to be dead (Bukia) or to have gone away (Kwoiam). In the remainder he is not mentioned at all.

The lack of a father is the irregularity that triggers off the sequence of events in several myths. The impropriety is the greater if the son is approaching manhood, as the story of Waiat states specifically (see Myth IV). The son is wholly dependent on his mother for physical safety, and without a sponsor in the adult male world — unless it be her brother. The mother is without a sexual partner, and thus the possibility of incest is posed. It is also posed in the stories with unmarried brothers and sisters. When brother, sister and sister's son are unmarried, uncle and nephew become incestuous rivals. The mothers in these stories are never actively malevolent, but, except for the story of Bukia, they are all in some sense responsible for the separation which occurs, and the changes in state which their sons undergo. The sons reciprocally are responsible for their mothers' change of state.

The possibility of mother-son incest is never stated in the myths, nor is it among modern islanders. However, the mother is said to be jealous of her son's sexuality, even when she is married. This is expressed through her hostility to his lovers. The theme comes out most clearly in the story of the mortal Tabepa.

Myth II

1.   Tabepa is a youth still living with his mother and father.

2.   Tabepa has many lovers, but while his father encourages them, his mother drives them away.

3.   The mother mentions the name of Uga, a ghost girl, as a suitable wife for her son.

4.   Uga hears her name spoken and comes to Tabepa. They have sexual intercourse and she promises to come for him the following month.

5.   Tabepa sadly takes leave of his mortal sweethearts and departs with Uga.

6.   A jealous ghost lover of Uga kills Tabepa.

7.   Tabepa's father and the people discover what has happened and upbraid but do not kill the mother.

This myth provides some interesting variations and inversions on Myth I.

(i)   Aukam is unmarried; Tabepa's mother is married, but she overrules her husband.

(ii)   Aukam antagonises her brother and leaves the infant Tiai defenceless against his spite; Tabepa's mother exposes him to the spite of Uga's rejected lover.

(iii)   Aukam stops the dead Tiai from marrying a mortal; Tabepa's mother encourages him to marry a ghost.

(iv)   Aukam finally becomes a ghost and departs with Tiai; Tabepa's mother does not rejoin her son and does not become a ghost.

In both stories, the mother's jealousy leads to the son becoming a ghost. But in Myth I Aukam is unmarried, prevents Tiai's anomalous marriage and changes her state to depart with him. In Myth II, the mother is married, establishes Tabepa in an anomalous marriage, and stays alive (with her husband) when he becomes a ghost.

When Aukam puts a stop to Tiai's amorous adventures, she effectively 'un-mans' him. When she shows him his bones he is 'ashamed'. Similar confrontations occur in a number of stories. Kwoiam (Haddon 1904:71–9; Lawrie 1970:88–101) is shamed when his mother swears at him (though mistaking him for someone else), kills her, embarks on an orgy of head-hunting to 'pay back' for her, and is finally killed. Kwoiam's sexuality does not directly figure in the action, but Haddon makes it clear that success in war enhanced a man's sexual attraction more than anything else (1904:298).

Gelam and his mother live alone. When shooting birds, he eats the best ones himself. His mother finds out and dresses up as a monster to frighten

171

him. He discovers the ruse and deserts her, going to Murray Island in the form of a dugong. There he becomes a hill and a source of the island's fertility. His mother turns into a rock (Haddon 1904:38–40; Lawrie 1970: 279–9). Here, of course, the change of state is not death, but transformation into a topographical feature — a common denouement in Torres Strait myths. Of the six myths involving mother and grown-up son, Myth II is the only one in which the son changes his state but the mother does not. This is the only one in which the mother has a husband.

Aukam turns the grown up Tiai into a ghost. She is also responsible for his death (MI:6–7). Similarly, Kuda gives her two boys into the keeping of Waiat who will kill them (Myth IV). And the mother of Upi leaves her child alone so that he falls into the hands of others (Haddon 1904:46–8). This last myth also provides some interesting inversions of Myth I.

Myth III

1. Upi,* a baby boy, lives alone with his mother.

2. The mother leaves him hanging in a basket and goes to the gardens.

3. The boy is found by a childless couple who adopt him.

4. Men of the village seize the boy, tie him up and use him for target practice. The foster parents are unable to stop them, but persuade them to aim only at his arms and legs.

5. Upi suddenly becomes a youth.

6. He persuades his foster parents to free him and runs away.

7. He finds two skulls and obtains their advice to hide in some bamboo.

8. His tormentors pursue him, but are cut to pieces by the bamboo.

9. He returns to his foster parents.

10. He divides the widows of his victims between himself and his foster father.

11. He finds his mother and persuades her to live in the village.

The divergence from Myth I begins with event 3, when Upi acquires foster parents. These save him from death, though not from injury. Thus he grows up as a mortal, whereas Tiai grows up as a ghost. He defeats his enemies, whereas Aukam takes revenge on Tiai's behalf (MI:8). He marries successfully, whereas Tiai cannot. He goes in search of his mother, whereas Aukam pursues Tiai, and is reunited with her in life. But the two are no longer isolated, as Aukam and Tiai are at the end of Myth I.

To sum up this section. The transformation from mortal to ghost is represented in Torres Strait myths as a product of the mother-child relationship. The mother who is the agent of birth is likewise the agent of death, though the killer is always male. If we accept the story of Aukam and Tiai as an origin myth, then the mother is responsible for her son's murder

---

* Upi is the name of a sharp variety of bamboo. Knives, including the knives used for severing heads in headhunting, were made from it.

at the hand of her brother, and precipitates his decision to make death irreversible, thus establishing the domain of ghosts. Thereafter mothers send their sons to death simply by bearing them. But in five other myths the mother is responsible for the son's death in a more direct sense. This is because she controls his relations with outsiders, either through being his sole parent or through overruling the other parent (Myth II). Underlying these stories, then, is the theme of sexual antagonism.

Women, Boys and Men

In Myth I:10–11, Tiai miraculously grows from a baby to a youth after he has been murdered. Thus he is able to marry when he reaches Boigu. Under normal circumstances, a youth who had reached puberty underwent initiation, not merely to bring him into adult status but to enhance his sexual attractions. Haddon's informants, otherwise not very forthcoming on the topic of initiation, made much of this point (Haddon 1904:211, 213). The mother's brother acted as the guardian during the ordeals and instruction which were part of the rite (*ibid*:211, 213). Tiai's death at his uncle's hand, then, is analogous to initiation. We do not know whether the islanders actually represented the rite as a symbolic death, though the idea is common enough in other Oceanic cultures. The same motif occurs in other myths. In Myth III Upi also grows miraculously after his ordeal at the hands of certain men, and soon becomes a fighter and the husband of many wives. The story of Waiat, to which I have already referred, deals with the matter more specifically. In discussing it I am faced with some difficulty because the versions of Lawrie (1970:115–7) and Haddon (1904:49–55) diverge on a number of important points. In Lawrie's version the murderous Waiat is brother to the boys' mother Kuda. In Haddon's version she is not. The older version deals much more specifically with ritual matters, on which modern islanders are ill-informed, and I shall therefore rely mainly on Haddon.

Myth IV

1. Kuda lives with her two sons. Their age is not entirely clear. They are referred to as 'little fellows' at one point, but they are already skilled dancers. Waiat's assertion that it is improper for them to go on living with their mother suggests that they are pubescent.

2. Waiat lives with his wife and daughter in the bush.

3. He hears the sound of drumming and is drawn to Kuda's place, where he sees the boys dancing while their mother plays.

4. He tells her to place the boys in his care. She agrees, provided that he feeds them properly.

5. Kuda has a beard, but no breasts; Waiat has breasts, but no beard. They exchange.

6. Waiat sends Kuda some distance off and tells her not to look while the boys dance.

7. Waiat sets out on a journey, collecting masks and other ceremonial paraphernalia. He returns.

8. Waiat sends the women away, and tells the other men to kill any women liable to see the ceremonies.* This results in their killing his wife and daughter.

9. Kuda's sons, after dancing, eat a turtle which Waiat has kept for his own use. Waiat kills them as they sleep.

10. Kuda and her people, discovering the killing, tear Waiat to pieces and roll his body on the ground till his skin comes off and he 'looks like a white man' (or a ghost, presumably).

11. Waiat turns into a rock fish and the other people turn into different kinds of ants (including the kind used to clean skulls).

The theme of the separation of the sexes is manifest when Waiat and Kuda exchange breasts for beard, in other words, strengthening their differences; when Waiat takes over the boys; and when he orders that women are not to see ceremonies, and are to be killed if they do. The boys, however, are the focus of conflict between Kuda and Waiat, and his betrayal of trust leads to his death. In this story, unlike the others I have discussed, Kuda has 'people', though apparently no husband, to avenge the killing.

It seems arguable that Waiat's attack on the boys (and, though not mentioned above, also on a companion) is to 'pay back' for the killing of his wife and daughter, somewhat as Kwoiam paid back for his killing of his mother. As I mentioned earlier, while in Lawrie's version, Waiat is Kuda's brother, in Haddon's version he is previously unknown to her. However, his position is analogous to a brother. He takes charge of the boys on the ceremonial ground. Moreover, with the death of his wife, he is in a similar position to Aukam's brother and the other 'wicked uncles' we have mentioned.

One can also see that the uncle stands for adult men in general. Mothers may be loth to give their sons over to the rough handling the men will give them at initiation, but they can refuse only by denying the boys manhood. The separation theme that occurs in every myth having the mother-son pair, then, has its real life counterpart in the shift from the parental hearth to the men's ceremonial ground.

In still more general terms one can see a conflict between the sexes, not only over the control of sons, but of the produce that the women collect. It is this economic conflict that leads to the killing of Tiai.

The Missing Father

I have already suggested that the father is not merely absent in these myths, but is conspicuous by his absence. Unfortunately, we do not have a clear notion of what is missing, because the father is also absent from the ethnography. Haddon and Rivers were so fascinated by the mother's brother — sister's son relationship that they tended to ignore fathers and

---

* For reasons that are not clear, the people of Mabuiag 'thought of Waiat' during the death ceremonies (Haddon 1904:54). In a story from Tutu (central Torres Strait), he with Naga, brought them mortuary ceremonies. In some accounts, the two are fused in the one person (cf. Haddon 1904:54; Lawrie 1970:115).

sons, beyond saying that a boy cared for his uncle more than for his father (Haddon 1904:147). However, it seems that the father was the author of his son's existence, not just in the sense of procreation, but because fathers killed unwanted infants (*ibid*:198). Through him the boy derived his social placement in ritual affairs, and it was he who ordered that the boy should be initiated. The uncle acted as guardian, but this was a service for which the father paid him. According to a tradition, some fathers killed their sons for breaking out of seclusion (*ibid*:210). It was only by the father making the appropriate payments, and allowing his property to be plundered, that the son could establish a proper relationship with his mother's brother. Thus it can also be said of the father-son relationship that it is a matter of life and death, both literally and figuratively. A boy without a father, then, exists without authorisation, without placement and without the human or material resources to be a social being.

Isolation and Community

One final theme needs to be drawn out of the myths I have discussed. Aukam and Tiai, Upi and his mother, Karbai and his sister, Waiat and his family, Gelam and his mother, and many other characters not mentioned here, are all specified as living by themselves. The traditional residential system in Western Torres Strait is unclear, since it had been changed by the missionaries long before Haddon's arrival. The islands close to New Guinea seem to have had settled villages, but those further south did not, probably because they gardened less and relied more on fishing and gathering. The few accounts we have, speak of flimsy shelters set up on the foreshore and moved at frequent intervals. Probably only a small number of families camped together regularly, though the men assembled on the local ceremonial ground from time to time. However, living in isolation would seem to invite attack at a time when raiding was endemic. Solitariness was a mode peculiar to sorcerers and men of uncertain temper. Waiat seems to belong to this class, but the isolated women with their infant sons obviously do not. Is this situation yet another of the irregularities with which the stories begin? The story of Upi (Myth III) which ends with son and mother going to live in the village, suggests that it is. My guess is — and it can be no more than a guess — that given the abundance of wild foods and the wide bays and beaches, there was some tendency for communities to disperse into family units, which, however, rendered them vulnerable to attack and made difficult the organisation of a full programme of magico-religious activities.

In the light of the other myths, Aukam and Tiai may be restated as follows: Tiai is born 'out of society' and without the means of social placement, so that he cannot become a man or marry. Lacking a father and patrilateral kin, his birth disorders relations among his matrilateral kin. In particular, his mother's brother cannot take him through initiation because there is no one to pay him for the service. However, because of these disordered relations, the uncle kills his nephew instead. This enables the boy to grow up, leave his mother, enter society and marry. His membership of society is anomalous because he is dead, but by acquiring affines he has the means of leaving it to become a ghost.

175

The collection of myths considered thus far deals with three kinds of real life separation: sons from mothers at initiation; sisters from brothers at marriage; and ghosts from mortals at the funeral. Each separation is necessary, making possible the one that follows.

Some Related Myths from Torres Strait

Certain themes and motifs in the Aukam and Tiai myth are quite widely distributed, as I shall show in a moment. But first I shall consider two myths from neighbouring peoples which are related in the sense of one being derived from the other, or both deriving from common forms. The Eastern Island myth of Aukem and Terer is a simpler, perhaps impoverished version of our key myth. The Kiwai saga of Sido, by contrast, is more extended and elaborate.

The Eastern Torres Strait Islanders spoke a Papuan type language. Living in higher density than their western neighbours, on islands of greater fertility, they concentrated more on gardening. But their formal social organisation was like that of the Western Islanders, and their ritual life similar. Their mortuary ceremonies were likewise comparable, though extending to a form of mummification (Haddon 1908).

The Eastern Islanders were in contact with the Western Islanders and according to their traditions acquired their major cults from the west. It is not, therefore, surprising to find the myth of Aukem and Terer, and to find the characters impersonated in the death dances. Both Haddon (1908:31–3) and Lawrie (1970:322–3) have published versions of the myth.

Myth V

1.   Aukem lives with her son Terer, who is about 18, on Murray Island. He has no father.

2.   Terer, playing his drum, disturbs some cultists in the bush.

3.   They seize him and scrape off the outer layer of his skin, so that he appears white. (This was also the first stage in the preparation of corpses.)

4.   They release him and he returns to his mother. She is shocked by his appearance, declaring that he must be a ghost.

5.   Ashamed he sets off around Murray Island in a westerly direction, dancing as he goes. He crosses to the neighbouring island of Dauar and continues to dance, even on the canoe.

6.   His mother follows him. (In one version she now feels sorry for him and puts on mourning. In the other she carries two human bones in her hands.)

7.   When Aukem finds Terer she rebukes him for not having gone to ghostland as she had bidden him. Finally, they reach the westernmost point of Dauar. Terer dives in and calls his mother to join him. (In Haddon's second version, he reproaches his mother for having 'spoiled' — ridiculed — him, and tells her that they are both dead now.) She dives in after him and together they leave.

Aukem, like Aukam, has no husband. Terer is of marriageable age, but still living with her. Aukem has no brother; instead the boy is killed by cultists. The conflict appears to be between his unbridled youth and the secret rituals of mature men. What Haddon calls the 'passion for dancing' that seizes him after the encounter with his mother may stand for his sexuality, but unlike Tiai he does not marry. Even more than the western story, Aukem and Terer turns on the mother's shaming of her son and his consequent bitterness.

Apart from the eastern version of the Gelam myth, which scarcely differs from the western there are three stories in which mother and son — or sons — live alone: Kos and Abob (Haddon 1908:25–8; Lawrie 1970:342–3), Nageg and Geigi (Haddon 1908:5–9; Lawrie 1970:306–10) and Meidu (Haddon 1908:13–15; Lawrie 1970:314–5). Geigi is the only one to die at the hands of an old cannibal, and his mother revives him. In this and the other stories, the denouement is the transformation of mothers and sons into natural or topographical features. Otherwise, the most common familial relations are siblings of the same sex, and this seems simply to be a means of establishing a set of characters.

The Kiwai-speaking peoples occupied the islands in the mouth of Fly River and the coast from the right bank to the Pahoture River. Gunnar Landtman studied the Kiwai soon after the Cambridge Expedition. He has left a rich account of their beliefs and ceremonies (1927), and a large collection of 'folktales' (1917) — but little regarding their social organisation.

Briefly, they were cultivators, fishermen and hunters. They lived in nucleated settlements, children and married adults in a long house; the unmarried men lived in a separate house that was also used for cult activities. There were patrilineal totemic clans, but their functions are not clear. In funerary practices and headhunting, the Kiwai were like the Western Islanders.

The Kiwai were in regular contact with the islanders so that it is not surprising to find that they knew a number of the islanders' stories. However, Aukam and Tiai are, so to speak, absorbed by the saga of Sido. The story is long and there are numerous variations which cannot be considered here (but see Landtman 1917:95–119). My own summary is even briefer than Landtman's (*ibid*:18–20).

Myth VI

1. Sido's father copulates with the ground. A boy is born and quickly growing up, joins his father in the village.

2. Sido falls in love with Sagaru and marries her.

3. They quarrel over food. She leaves him and he follows.

4. She goes to live with another man, Meuri.

5. Sido finds her, fights with Meuri and is killed. This was the first such fight and Meuri had evidently not intended to kill him.

6. Sido's spirit turns homeward (eastward) and the body follows in a canoe. He tells the people to throw away his body so that others shall not die, but they do not do so.

7. Sido's spirit takes several forms and as a shell fish impregnates a woman, who is one of a pair of women linked together. He is born, they raise him and he separates them.

8. Sido lay at the bottom of a grave, hoping to pass out of his own body and acquire a new one, but the people disturbed him. Had they not done so, death would not have become irreversible.

9. Sido's spirit sets off westward, telling his mothers not to follow.

10. His mothers nevertheless do follow, overtaking him in Boigu where he is dancing.

11. He asks for water. His mothers give him water to drink in his own skull, which they have carried with them. This means that he can no longer return to life, and, after him, all men must die.

12. He spears his mothers who are transformed into turtle and dugong.

13. He continues his journey westward to the place where the ghosts are to live. It has three inhabitants who live underground and are, in effect, cultureless. He introduces fire, cultivation and transforms himself into the long house where ghosts will live.

The saga of Sido incorporates almost all the key elements found in myths about death throughout Oceania: the primeval killing; reincarnation through rebirth and through the shedding of the old body, followed by the acquisition of a new one; death becoming irreversible; the separation of ghosts and mortals; and the establishment of a ghostly land. The theme of reincarnation is lacking in the story of Aukam and Tiai, otherwise the ensemble is the same.

In other respects the two myths (VI and I) differ. In his first incarnation, Sido has a father but no mother. He marries and through this meets his death. In his second incarnation he has a mother — two in fact — but there is no further reference to his sexuality, unless the dancing in Boigu be taken to imply this. The mothers are not involved in the original killing, even indirectly, but only in the separation of ghosts from mortals. They do not go with Sido to the land of the ghosts, though they are transformed. There is no 'wicked uncle' — the brother-sister relationship scarcely features in Kiwai folklore — and no initiation theme, though men's secret ceremonies were no less important than in the islands. What the saga of Sido finally shares with Aukam and Tiai, and its Eastern Islands counterpart, is the focus on the mother(without husband)-son pair at the point where ghosts are separated from mortals. The separation is effected by the mother confronting her son with the physical evidence of his death: his bones in Western Torres Strait; his skull among the Kiwai; and his scraped skin in Eastern Torres Strait. On the eastern side of the Papuan Gulf, the spirit of Iko is finally persuaded to go to the land of the dead by being shown a piece of his own flesh (Williams 1940:119–20). But it is his mother's brother who confronts him. To the west, among the Marind Anim, Zoo's attempts to return from the dead are frustrated by his wife, repelled by the stench of his decomposing flesh (van Baal 1966:199). These are the only cases of confrontation I can find in the rather meagre sources of Papuan mythology.

Nor can I find myths in which the mother-son pair figures in the separation of ghosts and mortals, though it is present in two about death (Williams 1936:312–14; Burridge 1960:155).

Except for McConnel's collection (1957), the mythology of Cape York is little known, least of all that of the tribes who were directly in contact with the islanders. R.M.W. Dixon has collected the myth most like Aukam and Tiai from the Mamu of the Innisfail district. It is not yet published but he has allowed me to reproduce it here.

Myth VII

1. Two brothers live with their mother. The elder one is married: the younger is not.

2. The younger brother has intercourse with the elder's wives.

3. The elder brother discovers the adultery and kills the younger.

4. The mother takes charge of the body, keeping the head in a sack, where it putrifies.

5. The spirit of the younger brother tries to return to the camp. The mother repeatedly warns him off, but he persists until shown his own head.

McConnel records two myths in which the ghost is separated from the living (1957:151–5), but in the original myth the dead man himself declares that he will go away, while in the other it is the brother who adjures him to go.

There are, of course, numerous myths concerned with death from other parts of Australia. Here I can discuss them only in the most general terms. Some start with a situation in which there was no death, and go on to tell how it came about. Others start with a situation in which men died, but came alive again until someone made the event irreversible. There is no reason why the themes should not occur together, as they do in Sido myth, but I have found no examples. Either poses the same problem of whether the dead should be separated from the living, which is the central concern of our key myth, but not often taken up in Australia.

Death and the Dialectic

Burridge in a recent article writes: 'Lévi-Strauss ignores Hegel's insistence that a contrary should also be a contradiction, and he leaves out of account whether what is a contrary, or a contradiction, in one culture is necessarily so in another.' (1967:112). These remarks are of particular interest here, for he goes on to consider 'Life' and 'Death' in these terms:

> 'Life' and 'Death' are certainly 'contraries'. But in what sense are they necessarily 'contradictions'? By 'contradictions' we normally refer, surely, to goal directed activities, or on-going processes, which effectively and simultaneously negate each other. 'Life' and 'Death' are alternatives: either 'alive' or 'dead'. A real contradiction would involve, at any level, the experience of 'life' and the experiences of 'death' at one and the same time. Which is unusual without shading in the meanings of 'life' and 'death'. (*ibid*:112).

179

Murphy takes up Burridge's critique, but meets his final — and, to me obscure — point with a direct quotation from Hegel. 'To Hegel', Murphy comments, 'the opposed elements do not negate each other in a simple mutual cancellation process but as an essential part of their existence'. (1972:205).

Part of the difficulty here stems from the confusion of 'real life' and mythical or 'mentalistic' representations of it — the confusion being itself part of 'real life'. Burridge's suggestion that what is a contrary or a contradiction in one culture, may not be in another, is well taken. The Western Islanders and their neighbours evidently see mortals and spirits not yet made ghosts as being in contradiction. Mortals and ghosts, on the other hand, are simply contraries.

The dialectic goes as follows. The contradiction between life and death is mediated by the survival of the spirit. This, however, sets up a contradiction between the living and the dead. The representation of the dead as vindictive, or as wanting to take their kinsfolk with them is well nigh universal (*cf.* Goody 1962:21). Thus in the Torres Strait myths both Tiai and Terer reproach their mothers and lure them away. The contradiction also appears at another level, between the spirit and its physical remains: its bones among the Kiwai and the islanders, its cut up flesh in Orokolo, its decomposing flesh among the Marind Anim, its rotting head among the Mamu. Both kinds of contradiction are resolved by 'making ghosts'. Indeed, in the myths it is the confrontation of the spirit with its remains that precipitates the separation. The domains of ghosts and mortals are contraries, not only in general terms but, as we have seen (p.167) in particulars. They are not, however, in contradiction. Rather they are stable and complementary, with mortals remembering the dead, and ghosts bringing them various benefits, but each side keeping to their own domain. The skull is now the means of bringing the ghost back into relations with mortals. These relations are controlled and stable, just as the ghost's physical remains have been controlled and stabilised.

Here we are back with the Lévi-Straussian opposition of 'nature' and 'culture'. The natural fact of death is transcended in myth through representation as a consequence of deliberate human action, just as the corpse becomes an artefact through human intervention in the natural processes of decomposition. Finally, by a *tour de force*, this artefact becomes a means of extending man's control over the environment.

Notes

The author worked for two years in the Torres Strait Islands as a research scholar of the Australian National University. Little now remains of the traditional culture, and this study relies mainly upon the findings of the Cambridge Expedition of 1898. Nevertheless discussions with islanders have provided certain insights. I am indebted to Michael Allen, Ron Brunton and Dick Davis for their comments on earlier drafts of this article.

1. I use the word myth in the broadest sense and would be equally content to use an alternative such as folktale.

2. Lévi-Strauss has suggested that Western Torres Strait clans may have taken on a stronger sense of physical and psychological affinity with their totems

as exogamy broke down (1966:115–6). However, he gained this impression from a secondary source. Had he consulted Rivers' genealogical work, he would have found that 'although the structure was in an advanced state of decay, the rules of exogamy were still observed' (Haddon 1904:233–47). In the case of Saibai they still are.

3. According to Lawrie's informant, he was Aukam's mother's brother.

4. The root seems to be *mar*, which also means shadow or reflection. *Mari* is the term most often used. *Markai* seems to be a ghost that appears before mortals, an apparition; the term was also applied to white people. When the spirit of one near to death wanders abroad it is called *kudumar*, literally end-spirit. The spirit of one lately dead is *kainmar*, literally new-spirit. The Eastern Island word *lamar* is clearly related.

5. Landtman lists two Kiwai stories in which boys are born after their mothers' death, but neither woman had been through the funerary rites and the boys were accepted by their people (1917:518–9).

6. The islanders believed that conception occurred when semen congealed with menstrual blood. There seemed to be no notion of male and female contributing different elements in the child's body, or of spirit conception.

7. Lawrie's version differs somewhat from Haddon's, see p. 173.

References

BAAL, J. VAN 1966–67 *Dema: description and analysis of Marind-Anim culture (south New Guinea)*. The Hague, Nijhoff.

BECKETT, J.R. 1972 The Torres Strait Islanders. In *Bridge and barrier: the natural and cultural history of Torres Strait*, (ed.) D. Walker, pp. 307–26. Canberra, A.N.U. Press.

—— n.d. Whatever happened to German Wislin?: the last flickers of a cargo cult. Unpublished ms.

BURRIDGE, K.O.L. 1960 *Mambu: a Melanesian millennium*. London, Methuen.

—— 1967 Lévi-Strauss and myth. In *The structural study of myth and totemism*, (ed.) E.R. Leach, pp. 91–115. London, Tavistock Publications.

GOODY, J.R. 1962 *Death, property and the ancestors: a study of the mortuary customs of the LoDagaa of West Africa*. Stanford, Calif., Stanford University Press.

HADDON, A.C. 1904 *Reports of the Cambridge Anthropological Expedition to Torres Straits, v.V: Sociology, magic and religion of the western Islanders*. Cambridge, Cambridge University Press.

—— 1908 *Reports of the Cambridge Anthropological Expedition to Torres Straits, v.VI: Sociology, magic and religion of the eastern Islanders*. Cambridge, Cambridge University Press.

—— 1935 *Reports of the Cambridge Anthropological Expedition to Torres Straits, v.I: General ethnography*. Cambridge, Cambridge University Press.

HERTZ, R. 1960 A contribution to the study of the collective representation of death. In his *Death and the right hand*, 27–86. Glencoe, Ill., Free Press.

HIATT, L.R. 1966 Mystery at Port Hacking. *Mankind*, 6(7):313–17.

KIRK, G.S. 1970 *Myth: its meaning and functions in ancient and other cultures*. Cambridge, Cambridge University Press.

LAADE, W. ed. 1971 *Oral traditions and written documents on the history and ethnography of the northern Torres Strait Islands, Saibai-Dauan-Boigu, v.1. Adi-myths, legends, fairy tales*. Wiesbaden, Franz Steiner.

LANDTMAN, G. 1917 *The folk-tales of the Kiwai Papuans*. Helsingfors (Helsinki), Finnish Society of Literature.

—— 1927 *The Kiwai Papuans of British New Guinea*. London, Macmillan.

LAWRIE, M.E. 1970 *Myths and legends of Torres Strait*. Brisbane, University of Queensland Press.

LEACH, E.R. 1967 Genesis as myth. In *Myth and cosmos: readings in mythology and symbolism*, (ed.) J. Middleton, pp. 1–13. New York, Natural History Press.

LÉVI-STRAUSS, C. 1966 *The savage mind*. London, Weidenfeld and Nicolson.

McCONNEL, U.H. 1957 *Myths of the Mungkan*. Melbourne, Melbourne University Press.

MOORE, D.R. 1972 Cape York Aborigines and Islanders of western Torres Strait. In *Bridge and Barrier: the natural and cultural history of Torres Strait*, (ed.) D. Walker, pp. 327–43. Canberra, A.N.U. Press.

MURPHY, R.F. 1971 *The dialectics of social life: alarms and excursions in anthropological theory*. New York, Basic Books.

TURNER, T.S. 1969 Oedipus: time and structure in narrative form. In *Forms of symbolic action*, (ed.) R.F. Spencer, pp. 26–68. Proceedings of the 1969 Annual Spring Meeting of the American Ethnological Society. Seattle and London, University of Washington Press.

WILLIAMS, F.E. 1936 *Papuans of the Trans-Fly*. Oxford, Clarendon Press.

——— 1940 *Drama of Orokolo. The social and ceremonial life of the Elema*. Oxford, Clarendon Press.

'Myth and Rite' and 'The Content of the Legends',

from *Mythes et Légendes d'Australie*

Arnold van Gennep

Translated from the French by Enid Watkin Jones

Arnold van Gennep was born in 1873 at Ludwigsburg in the kingdom of Würtemberg. His father was descended from French *émigrés*, and his mother belonged to a Dutch aristocratic family with French connections. In 1879 his parents separated, and he accompanied his mother to France where she subsequently remarried.

On leaving school, where he had shown a talent for languages, van Gennep studied at L'École des Langues Orientales in Paris. He also read ethnography, sociology, and comparative religion in L'École des Hautes Études. In 1898, he published his first ethnographic work — a translation of J.G. Frazer's *Totemism*. After a period as a teacher of French in Russian Poland, he returned to Paris, where he worked as a translator in the Ministry of Agriculture. He continued his studies at Hautes Études and in 1904 completed *Tabou et Totémisme à Madagascar*. Then, in 1906, he published *Mythes et Légendes d'Australie*.[1]

Mythes et Légendes d'Australie is divided into two main parts: Introduction (pp.I-CXVI) and Myths and Legends of Australia (pp.1–185). The latter is a translation into French of 106 Aboriginal myths, taken from works by Brough Smyth, Curr, Langloh Parker, Spencer and Gillen, Howitt, and Roth. The former, comprising 10 chapters, is intended as an ethnographic and theoretical background. Chapters I–VIII deal with such matters as the physical characteristics and racial affiliations of the Aborigines, systems of filiation, the role of the individual in social innovation, ideas on conception and reincarnation, and magic and religion. Chapter IX, on the relationship between Aboriginal myths and rites, and Chapter X, on the content of the myths, are translated below.

The book draws heavily on the writings of Spencer and Gillen (1899, 1904). In the chapter on 'Myth and Rite', one of van Gennep's chief concerns is to stress the importance of the individual in Aranda religion and to play down the corporate role of the totemic group. Thus he points out that totemic ceremonies are individually owned by men who have either invented the ceremony (through dreaming or conscious invention) or received it from a previous owner; that transfer of ownership may take the form either of a gift from the owner to a man whose totem the ceremony celebrates or of an agnatic inheritance after the owner's death;[2] and that, although members of a totemic group have the right to attend any performance of a ceremony celebrating their totem, non-members frequently participate both as actors and spectators.

These points are no doubt directed against Durkheim's view of totemism as the collective and anonymous force of each clan concentrated upon its own totemic emblem (Durkheim 1902, 1915).[3] It is true that van Gennep makes no explicit reference to Durkheim at this juncture, but elsewhere in the book he is openly critical. For instance, at the beginning of Chapter IV he says: 'We have seen that Durkheim explains social change by "the needs of society", but without indicating why or whence these needs arise, without moreover justifying the assumption that a society, however small, may have "needs". It is through an identical process of *animation* that we are told of "the call of the Fatherland" or "the voice of the people". Durkheim anthropomorphises, though he may deny it' (1906:xxxv). No doubt this early opposition to meta-organic sociology helped to disqualify van Gennep from the *Année Sociologique* circle.[4]

On the matter of totemic rights and privileges, we can now say that widely throughout Australia totemism enables clan members both to affirm their own corporate identity and to cultivate amity and mutuality with others. Maddock has recently set out a number of cases on a continuum between obligatory interdependence and autarchy (1973:36–40). Thus, among the Dalabon, each patriclan owns religious property (totemic designs and dances associated with the clan estate) but the control of this property is vested in certain non-members, namely, the sons and sons' sons of female members. Wikmunkan clansmen, by contrast, control their own totemic property and decide whether outsiders may see it, and whether they may participate in the rituals. The Aranda (and here Maddock follows Strehlow 1947 and 1965, rather than Spencer and Gillen) are an intermediate case in that, although each Aranda patriclan controls the religious property associated with its own totemic centre, it must invite other patriclans with totemic centres of the same species to its ritual performances, where they exercise censorial authority. Generally speaking, then, the clan is neither singularly pre-eminent in religious affairs (Durkheim), nor relatively insignificant (van Gennep).

Another main concern of 'Myth and Rite' is Robertson Smith's hypothesis that rite is antecedent to myth ('. . . it may be affirmed with confidence that in almost every case the myth was derived from the ritual, and not the ritual from the myth'; Robertson Smith 1889:19). Van Gennep acknowledges that the Aranda material seems to confirm the proposition: first a ceremony is invented, then a myth is introduced or elaborated in order to account for it. But he believes that, since in this area the myth is really a description of the ceremony, the question of anteriority is trivial.

The issue whether rite precedes myth, or vice versa, attracts little attention these days, and finding new evidence to re-open the debate would be difficult. No doubt Radcliffe-Brown, following Robertson Smith, was correct in supposing that rites are more stable than doctrines (1952:157). But this would not rule out the possibility of a dialectic between rite and myth in which, for example, a rite generates myth variants as it diffuses, and the variants in their turn inspire modifications in the rite. As to van Gennep's statement that in certain Aboriginal tribes '. . . the myth actually occurs as a recounted rite, and the rite as an acted myth' (see below, p. 187), it would be wrong to regard this as exemplifying a general Australian pattern. In numerous cases, the charter myth is not at all a scenario for the related ritual (cf. my summaries of myths and accompanying rites in 'Swallowing and Regurgitation in Australian Myth and Rite' in the present volume); furthermore, myths occur in the absence of ritual counterparts, and rites in the absence of myth counterparts. But to say that the relationship between myth and rite is often not of the literal kind described by van Gennep is not to maintain that it is unimportant. It means, rather, that typically the connections are subtle, and that the task of elucidating them is of a different order from comparing a libretto with a performance (see my exposition of Stanner's approach, Introduction to the present volume pp. 11–12).

'The Content of the Legends' begins with a discussion of terminology. Van Gennep acknowledges that he uses the words myth and legend interchangeably (one of the terms in the title of the book therefore seems redundant); and he maintains that European categories are inappropriate to the Australian material. He also rejects classifications of narratives based on relational criteria, such as whether or not the story is an object of belief or is associated with ritual (see Introduction to the present volume, p. 3). He then proposes a tripartite division of Australian narratives depending on whether the heroes are animal, human, or hybrid (i.e. animal/human). In expounding the classification, he comments on such matters as Aboriginal theories about the origins of living things, the function of myths, and the view of Spencer and Gillen that Aranda legends record historical stages in the evolution of Aranda society (see Introduction to the present volume, p. 4). Finally, he conjectures that the notion of the Thunder-God may turn out to be the central element in all Australian mythologies (see present volume, pp. 147–49).

A difficulty with van Gennep's typology is that, instead of applying his stated criterion consistently, he seems to shift between two considerations: the nature of the actors, and the purpose of the stories. Because there are probably no Australian stories in which the actors are 'animals and animals only' (see below, p. 194), the first criterion will not really serve to distinguish type 1 (animal heroes) from type 3 (hybrid heroes). In stories assigned by van Gennep to the former category, the animals behave, think, or feel in distinctively human ways (for example, Bustard Hen envies Emu Hen and tricks her into clipping her wings). A better ground for division here might be the purpose of the story: type 1 narratives account for phenomena incidental to man's social life, whereas type 3 narratives account for features of human social life or natural phenomena that have been incorporated into it (totemic sites). Unfortunately, this criterion fails to distinguish type 3 from type 2 stories, as both are concerned with the ratification of institutions. Thus a valid division, using one criterion or the other but not both, would comprise only two types (if the first criterion, types 1 and 3 merge; if the second, types 2 and 3 merge).

185

A further objection is that the nature of the actors is not a good guide to the nature of the action. For instance, Langloh Parker (1896:15–8) and Stanner (1959–63:40–2) have recorded what may reasonably be regarded as variants of the same myth; yet because the protagonist in Stanner's version is human (Mutjingga the Old Woman) but hybrid in Langloh Parker's version (Gooloo the Magpie), the narratives would have to be assigned to different classes. These are criticisms of detail: the fundamental question, I suppose, is whether typology serves any useful purpose in myth analysis. The present volume suggests that limited categorisation is a necessary part of defining and pursuing a problem: myths about Eaglehawk and Crow, patrimoieties, the emu, sexual violence, swallowing and regurgitation, and death. But bearing in mind that there are innumerable ways of classifying any large collection of complex items, it is a fair assumption that global classifications formulated in the absence of perceived problems are likely to be theoretically barren.

In the translations below, editorial additions to van Gennep's notes are enclosed in square brackets. Myths indicated by Roman numerals, both in the text and the notes, are to be found in the second part of *Mythes et Légendes d'Australie*. I have shown their English sources. Quotations translated by van Gennep into French have been returned exactly to their original state.

I am deeply grateful to Enid Watkin Jones for her painstaking care over the translation, which, on my request, aims at literality. To Andrée Rosenfeld, who read the draft and made many valuable suggestions, and to Lance Ridley, Evelyne Winn, Rhys Jones, Rodney Needham and Margaret Clunies Ross, who helped on particular points, I am likewise indebted. Finally, I must thank the publishing house of Éditions G.-P. Maisonneuve et Larose (Paris) for permission to reproduce the chapters in translation.

L.R.H.

Notes

1. Further biographical details may be found in K. van Gennep 1964; see also Needham 1967.

2. I cannot find any support for van Gennep's assertion that an owner of a ceremony may give it to whomsoever he pleases (see below, p. 188).

3. *Cf.* van Gennep's remark, quoted in Lukes 1973:526, that Durkheim's well-known tendency to 'perceive the collective (social) element before all else and to give it first place' led him to neglect 'the influence, formative of institutions and beliefs, of various individuals'. Lukes adds in a footnote: 'A subject that had been investigated by van Gennep himself in his *Mythes et Légendes d'Australie* (1896) [sic], a work which Durkheim ignored' (*ibid*, note 39). Mauss (1907) reviewed it critically.

4. *Cf.* Needham (1967:xi), who believes that van Gennep's exclusion is a 'puzzle which it would be important to the history of ideas to see elucidated'; see also Lukes (1973:524, note 35): 'It is striking that van Gennep was ignored and excluded by Durkheim and his colleagues. M. Davy has confirmed that they did not take him seriously (personal communication)'.

References

DURKHEIM, E. 1902 Sur le totémisme. *L'Année Sociologique*, 8:118–47.
——— 1915 *The elementary forms of the religious life.* London, Allen & Unwin.
GENNEP, K. VAN. 1964 *Bibliographie des oevres d'Arnold van Gennep.* Paris, Picard.
LUKES, S. 1973 *Émile Durkheim.* London, Allen Lane.
MADDOCK, K. 1973 *The Australian Aborigines.* London, Allen Lane.
MAUSS, M. 1907 Review of *Mythes et légendes d'Australie.* In *L'Année Sociologique*, 10:226–29.
NEEDHAM, R. 1967 Introduction to van Gennep, A. *The semi-scholars.* London, Routledge & Kegan Paul.
PARKER, LANGLOH K. 1896 *Australian legendary tales.* London, Nutt.
RADCLIFFE-BROWN, A. 1952 *Structure and function in primitive society.* London, Cohen & West.
ROBERTSON SMITH, W. 1889 *The religion of the Semites.* Edinburgh, Black.
SPENCER, W.B. *and* F. Gillen 1899 *The native tribes of central Australia.* London, Macmillan.
——— 1904 *The northern tribes of central Australia.* London, Macmillan.
STANNER, W.E.H. 1959–63 *On Aboriginal religion.* Sydney (Oceania monograph no. 11), University of Sydney.
STREHLOW, T.G.H. 1947 *Aranda traditions.* Melbourne, Melbourne University Press.
——— 1965 Culture, social structure, and environment in Aboriginal central Australia. In *Aboriginal man in Australia*, (eds) R.M. *and* C.H. Berndt, pp. 121–45. Sydney, Angus and Robertson.

Myth and Rite

Nowhere, except perhaps in Vedic India and North American Indian societies, do we find as in certain Australian tribes rite and myth in such intimate relationship that the myth actually occurs as a recounted rite, and the rite as an acted myth.[1] This is particularly striking among the tribes of central Australia.

It has already been said that all the country occupied by the Arunta is divided up into a very large number of sacred 'places', each inhabited and owned by a 'local group' of individuals and related to a particular totem (animal, plant, etc.), which gives its name to the local human group. One such 'totemic centre' (*oknanikilla*) is related to the emu, another to the wild cat (*dasyurus*), etc. With each of these *oknanikilla* are associated specific Ancestors who lived a long time ago during the epoch called *Alcheringa*[2] and who performed brilliant deeds there, carried out certain ceremonies of which they were the owners, descended under the ground or went up to the sky, and in various places left *churinga*.[3] Associated with these same places are ceremonies which are sometimes the mimed representation of certain of their acts, sometimes the development in act of one or other of their intentions. These ceremonies, being associated with specific localities, are the property of individuals who, through reincarnation, are so to speak the 'children' of these localities.

Thus, not only each totem, but each part of a totemic group possesses its own ceremonies, which are transmitted like all other property among the Arunta, through the male line. The ownership of these ceremonies, however, is neither absolute nor exclusive, each owner of a ceremony being able to give or lend it to whomsoever he pleases without having to take into account the totem with which the ceremony is linked, nor the totem or the matrimonial class of the new owner. Furthermore, it is not necessary that the actors who perform a ceremony associated with a particular totem should bear this totem or be of the same matrimonial class as the mythical Ancestor whose acts they perform. In the same way the totem and the class of the spectators are not taken into consideration. Without doubt, all members of the totemic group to which the ceremony belongs have the right to be present at the performance, to which no individual of a different totem would dare attend without being invited; but this invitation is freely given and often the 'ceremonial headman' (*alatunja*) begs even strangers to play an active role in it. Finally the totem of the novice does not determine that of the ceremonies.

To put it another way, the totemic ceremonies are independent of the social organisation in its two forms (matrimonial and totemic), at least among the Arunta. What appears from this again is that, although the connection between the 'totemic place' and any particular totem determines the kind of ceremonies to be carried out, these are not however restricted to this totem alone. There is no fixed sequence, no rigid programme. Everything depends on the *alatunja* who, if such and such a totemic group happens to be represented by more individuals or more knowledgeable ones, invites those he wishes to carry out this or that ceremony, regardless of their totem.[4]

Here is an example: a ceremony concerned with the Wild Cat ancestors was performed in a locality of the Wild Cat totem. It belonged to the *alatunja* of the Imanda local totemic group of the Emu totem. He received it from his father, a Wild Cat, and it was carried out at the present owner's request[5] by an old man who was the *alatunja* of the totemic group of the Large White Bats.[6]

Most of these ceremonies in relation to the totems come to the current owner directly from his *Alcheringa* Ancestors. Others are communicated by a special category of Spirits called *Iruntarinia*, also supposed to date from the *Alcheringa*, to individuals with the power to see them and to enter into relations with them. This is to say that such individuals are endowed with a more inventive mind or have imagined the ceremony in a dream.[7] It is accepted that the *Iruntarinia* can communicate the idea and the scenario of such a ceremony to whomsoever they please, regardless of the totem of the individual chosen. The favoured person can reserve the ownership of it for himself or hand it over occasionally or permanently to a friend, provided that the latter be of the same totem. It is thus that a ceremony associated with the Eagle-hawk totem was imparted by the *Iruntarinia* to a celebrated magician of the Witchetty Grub totem, who in turn gave it to his father, the *alatunja* of an Eagle-hawk locality.[8] Since then it has remained the property of the Eagle-hawk men; and it was performed by two [other]⁹ sons of the present *alatunja*, whose totems were in one case Eagle-hawk and the other Emu.

When therefore an individual has invented a new scenario, either in the waking state or during sleep, he communicates it directly or indirectly to the old men gathered together for the *Engwura* ceremonies (the final phase of the initiation ceremonies, lasting several consecutive months), in which occasionally natives from places many hundreds of kilometres away take part. They rehearse the new ceremonies, perform them in public, approve them or reject them. And it is in this way that individual invention becomes common property, is 'socialised'.

Spencer and Gillen mention on several occasions ceremonies of individual invention, that is to say, according to native explanation taught by the *Iruntarinia* to such and such a man still in living memory. But it is beyond doubt that many other totemic ceremonies of the same order owe their origin to the same cause, although their point of departure must have been forgotten after five or six generations at the most. At this moment the individual inventor is, I believe, suppressed and the ceremony attributed directly to the *Alcheringa* Ancestors. Not that I find direct proofs that things have happened in this way; but we can explain the astonishing richness of the totemic myths of central Australia only by such a process of assimilation of individual invention by the community.

These individual inventions are interesting from still another point of view. Their psychopathic origin is definitely denied by Spencer and Gillen;¹⁰ they admit — after inquiry, it goes without saying — only conscious invention and invention through dreaming. It is not a new myth that the 'gifted'¹¹ individual or the individual favoured by the *Iruntarinia* creates but rather a new ceremony, or a new phase to be intercalated into an old ceremony; that is to say, a scenario which, once executed and adopted, becomes a rite. As the circumstances of time, actors, accessories, and presentation are imposed on the individual by his education, and by the entire social and mental *milieu* in which up to now his life has been spent, he invents in the same direction as his predecessors and contemporaries. That is to say, he will activate the *Alcheringa* Ancestors, the fundamental idea of the scenario will be totemic, the objects used will be of the same kind as the *nurtunja* or the *waninga*,¹² the decorations will be paintings in ochre or in blood edged or overlaid with bird-down,¹³ and so on. The degree of invention, so it seems, is thus quite weak, at least today.

As it is not stated anywhere that individuals first invent myths that they then put into action, it must be admitted that, in the case at least of revelation by the *Iruntarinia*, the rite is anterior to the myth. First the individual gesture, modifying the customary gesture — then the explanatory narrative, the myth.

Again, the invention of a myth does not necessarily follow that of a rite: *Iruntarinia* of a totemic group of the Hakea plant showed a magician of the Witchetty Grub totem an immense cross formed by two decorated poles, each six feet long and stuck in the ground. They told him to erect a similar one, to show it to the people, and to warn them that no one would be able to extract this cross from a human body where the *Iruntarinia* had implanted it. He did as he was told, and the ceremony he invented consists in sticking a huge cross in the ground. Three actors approach it and then move away, making all sorts of contortions and grimaces which delight the spectators; while the old men sing about the *Iruntarinias'* adventures during the *Alcheringa* in the country of the Arunta.[14] Thus the myth associated with the *Iruntarinia* exists already and expresses itself through certain ceremonies. To these, a magician adds a new rite for which he gives a simple explanation that does not take the form of a myth. The true myth, recited by the old men, refers not to the cross of recent invention, but to the manner of life of the *Iruntarinia* during the *Alcheringa*. There has been an intercalation of a new rite into the old ritual, but not yet the creation of a corresponding myth.

It is therefore by crystallisation of both rites and myths invented by individuals in the course of centuries that the very complicated ritual of the Arunta has been formed. And as the circumstances of origin of the rites have been progressively forgotten, the myths have been juxtaposed, combined and extended backwards into the *Alcheringa*. Except for some, these myths are all combined by means of identical elements and following the same model: they are really myths made up of interchangeable parts.[15] The existence of the rite is affirmed in some of these myths: for they refer to ceremonies or ritual objects belonging to such and such an Ancestor, or group of Ancestors, which the latter carried on their journeys, communicating them sometimes to the people they met.

Whereas we know of cases where the rite is performed without being accompanied by the telling of a myth, the reverse seems impossible. Never did Spencer and Gillen hear myths recited except in explanation of various phases of totemic increase ceremonies (*Intichiuma*), initiation ceremonies (*Lartna, Engwura*), or simply totemic ceremonies. And it is not only to knowledge of the oral traditions that the wise old man (*oknirabata*) owes his high position in Arunta society, but also to his qualities as a producer, stage-manager and, according to the circumstances, actor-qualities often worthy of admiration.[16] He must very carefully superintend and direct the 'dressing-up',[17] a ceremonial phase much more important[18] than the performance in front of the public, since the latter is recruited, as we have seen, without taking into account classes or totems; whereas the dressing-up may be witnessed only by members of strictly defined totemic groups and matrimonial classes.

Without doubt Spencer and Gillen say the oral traditions are the 'sacred treasure' of the tribe; and they see the proof of this in that the novice hears mention of the Mythical Ancestors only from the sixth day of the second initiation ceremony (*lartna*, circumcision) and above all during the last of these ceremonies, the *Engwura*.[19] But from the fact alone that there is no fixed sequence, no programme for the performance of the ceremonies in which the *Alcheringa* Ancestors are represented, it follows that no real value of 'degrees' could be assigned to the various phases of the initiation ceremonies. We must be careful here not to think too much of Egyptian, Greek or Roman initiation rites, where in effect the neophyte arrived progressively at knowledge of the central mystery. And in the tribes like the

Warramunga, where the sequence of ceremonies is fixed, it is so only because the deeds of the Ancestors of the *Wingara* (equivalent to the *Alcheringa* of the Arunta) are represented in the very order in which the traditions state they were carried out.[20]

The pivot, if not the central mystery, of all the ritual and mythology of the tribes of the Arunta 'nation' seems in certain respects to be that category of sacred objects, oval-shaped and ornamented, to which with Spencer and Gillen we can leave their Arunta name of *churinga*, although they are found in many other tribes. The novice learns about them only towards the end of the initiation ceremonies. Lang has put forward a theory about them that would in his opinion account for the 'Arunta anomaly' — that is to say, a 'localised' totemic system with patrifiliation.[21] I have said already that I would rather see ideas on conception at the base even of totemism. However that may be, if we admit with Lang[22] that the invention of myths about the *Alcheringa* Ancestors is due to finding *churinga* in old burial-places, we would note once again the priority of rite over myth. It remains to be seen whether the phrase 'they descended under the earth', which returns like a *leit-motiv* in a large number of central Australian legends,[23] has the meaning which Lang gives it, 'they died and were buried', and thus is only an allusion to certain funeral rites. For we also often read, 'they continued their journey underground', which means that the Arunta conceive the interior of the earth as a region which is analogous to its surface and to which caves, dried-up wells, etc. lead.[24] Yet another *leit-motiv* in the legends is 'they climbed up to the sky, continued their journey there and only came down at . . .'[25] By what ancient rites would Lang explain these passages? In fact it is the notion formed of the subterranean, terrestrial, and aerial world that conditions these details of the story.[26]

The telling of myths, however, is not solely the accompaniment of mimed ceremonies: 'When [the young man] is thought worthy of this honour, and at the time appointed by the Alatunja of the local totemic group to which he belongs, he is taken, accompanied by the older men, to the *ertnatulunga*. There he is shown the sacred *churinga* which are examined carefully and reverently, one by one, while the old men tell him to whom they now belong or have belonged. While this is going on a low singing of chants referring to the *alcheringa* is kept up, and at its close the man is told his *churinga* name and cautioned against ever allowing anyone, except the men of his own group, to hear it uttered'.[27]

All the preceding applies principally to the tribes of the Arunta nation, and in a lesser degree to the more northerly tribes. As for the tribes of the Gulf of Carpentaria and Queensland they seem much less rich in both myths and ceremonies. In the southern and south-eastern tribes, now for the most part extinct, there must also have been a concordance of these two types of institution. This at least is established for the Murring who perform the actions of their civilising hero Daramulan while the old men recite the sacred traditions to the novices;[28] and for the Dieri about whom Howitt, reporting a legend collected by Siebert describing circumcision rites as practised by the *Muramura*, says: 'This description of the procedure at the ceremony of circumcision is part of the legend. For every custom and rite there is an equivalent in a *Muramura*[29] legend.

Thus the recitation of myths in the tribes on which we have detailed information exhibits a clearly religious character.[30] And, in a certain number of cases, especially among the Arunta and Dieri, the myth is really an oral rite.[31] For this reason, by definition, the question of the anteriority of myth over rite, or vice versa, remains in the final analysis insoluble, if it can even be posed. For that comes back to asking whether the word precedes the thought, or vice versa. These are subjects for scholastic discussion and nothing more.

Notes

1. [The text reads: '. . . le rite en relations intimes avec le mythe au point que le mythe s'y présente proprement comme un rite raconté et le mythe comme un rite agi.' This is evidently an error: in the final phrase the words 'mythe' and 'rite' should be transposed.]
2. This word would signify 'time of the dream' or 'epoch of the dream'. I believe that we should not attribute to it a mythological importance as great as Lang does (see Lang 1896, 1897, 1898*a*, 1898*b*, 1899, 1903, 1904, 1905*a*, 1905*b*), but translate it simply as 'the Past' (*cf.* Thomas 1905).
3. See, among others, legends nos. XLVIII, LXXIII, LXXXVII, LXXXVIII, XCI. [Taken respectively from Spencer and Gillen 1904:619–20, 438–40; 1899:440–2; M. Howitt 1902:407; Spencer and Gillen 1904:498–9.]
4. Spencer and Gillen 1899:277–80.
5. [The text reads: '. . . à sa requête . . .' The words 'the present owner's' have been added to remove an ambiguity; see Spencer and Gillen, *ibid:* p. 299.]
6. *Ibid*:299.
7. *Ibid*:278.
8. [The text reads: '. . . à un magicien célèbre ayant pour totem le Ver-Witchetty, fils de l'*alatunja* d'une localité Aigle-Faucon auquel il la donna.' *Cf.* Spencer and Gillen, *ibid*:294.]
9. [The text reads: '. . . elle fut executée par les deux fils de l'*alatunja* actuel . . .' I have added 'other' in order to distinguish these two sons, of the Eagle-hawk and Emu totems respectively, from the previously-mentioned son of the Witchetty Grub totem; see Spencer and Gillen, *ibid*:294.]
10. There are few societies for which the epithet 'shamanistic' (Powell 1902:103) is more inappropriate than it is for the Australian Aborigines, because in their case the magicians never control political affairs (which are reserved for the old men, singly or in council) nor religious affairs (except in some southern and south-eastern tribes in a state of profound disorganisation); and because the 'magicians', far from going into a trance (see Mauss 1904:41), let alone being recruited from among hysterics and degenerates of every kind, are healthy, sane and, most importantly, calm and reserved (see Spencer and Gillen 1899:278, note 1, 515–6).
11. *Ibid*:515.
12. *Ibid*:627–9.
13. Spencer and Gillen 1904:179.
14. Spencer and Gillen 1899:519.
15. [The text reads: '. . .ce sont proprement des mythes à tiroirs.']
16. *Ibid*:280–1.
17. [The text reads '. . . surveiller et diriger "l'habillage" . . .']
18. *Ibid*:313; Spencer and Gillen 1904:179, etc.

19. Spencer and Gillen 1899:277, 311. Spencer and Gillen themselves observe that the traditions are fixed in the novices' memories especially through ceremonies. Besides, it is not correct to say that the novice learns about the Alcheringa ancestors only from the sixth day of the second ceremony, because on the first day the Unthippa-women are represented (*ibid*:443), and on the fourth the Little Hawks, who modified the method of circumcision (*ibid*: 223–4). Actually these questions of date are hardly important, because the 'programme' for the ceremonies varies according to the 'local centre' and the totem of the people present (*ibid*:212).

20. Spencer and Gillen 1904:193.

21. [The text reads: '. . . un systéme totémique à filiation paternelle et *localisé*.']

22. Lang 1904.

23. See, among others, legends nos. XVIII, LXXVIII, LXXXI, LXXXVI. [From M. Howitt 1902:414–7; Spencer and Gillen 1899:436–7, 432–4, 389–90.]

24. An idea analogous to hell and other subterranean worlds; *cf.*, among others, Sébillot 1904:415–7 and *ff.*

25. See, among others, legends nos. LXXX and LXXXV. [From Spencer and Gillen 1899:315–6, 336–7.]

26. For other objections of principle, see Thomas 1904. On the idea of three worlds as developed in south and south-east Australia, see Howitt 1904:426–7 and the note to legend no. XVII.

27. Spencer and Gillen 1899:140.

28. Howitt 1904:538.

29. *Ibid*:647, note 2.

30. It is the same, for example, among the Cherokee of North America; *cf.* Mooney 1900:230.

31. The same again among the Cherokee (*cf.* 'The Sacred formulas of the Cherokee', 7th Ann. Rep. Bur. Ethnol.), the Hupa of California (*cf.* van Gennep 1905:279), and so on.

The Content of the Legends

It will have been noticed that, in describing the traditions of Australian tribes, I use the words myth and legend indifferently. Folklorists, however, like to distinguish one from the other, and both from a third type of literary production, the tale. Sometimes, in order to give an appearance of precision to this classification, they even say myth, saga and *märchen*; and as sub-divisions they define legends as aetiological, heroic, romantic, historic, hagiographical, etc. Such a scheme can be of value for the popular literature of Europe, though only in some cases. But as soon as we study closely the literary production of any semi-civilised group, we notice that each of the assumed classes overlaps the others. That is why Lang,[1] to whom we owe the best attempt at classifying folk narratives (civilised, as well as semi-civilised), is reduced in the final analysis to distinguishing only two major categories: the explanatory narrative (myth or legend) and the romantic narrative (tale, epic, etc.). This classification is, as we see, based on the content of the narratives.

But one may equally take a sociological viewpoint and classify narratives according to their social function. That is what Hubert and Mauss[2] have done when they distinguish narratives that are an object of belief (myth or legend) from those that are solely an aesthetic production (tale, epic). The result is, at first sight, the same. However, if there can be little dispute about the definition of the constituent elements of a narrative, it is often difficult, sometimes even impossible, to know whether a particular narrative is an object of belief or not. Strictly speaking, mathematical axioms, historical facts, astronomical laws, chemical formulae, in a word all the sciences, are an object of belief for the vast majority of people. The only domain which is not an object of belief for an individual is that very restricted one where he observes and experiments directly. Up to what point are tales, like those from Africa with Ananzi the Spider as hero, or like Puss in Boots or John the Fearless, objects of belief or not? Have they, or not, the right to be called myths in the sense that the sociological school gives this word?

It is true that Hubert and Mauss, having noted the intimate relationship that binds myth and rite,[3] appear to reserve the term myth for those traditions which express themselves through ritual acts. But in the course of social transformations a rite may disappear while the corresponding myth survives intact: how, in this case, is it to be named, supposing that it does not create 'in its turn, rites by analogy'?

That is why classification according to content seems to me preferable, at least for the moment and for Australia. And the best criterion of classification is, it seems, the notion formed by the Australians of the essential nature of animals and man.

In the numerous narratives collected by Roth[4] among the tribes of central and northern Queensland the heroes are animals and animals only: 'A galah and an opossum were fighting one day, with the result that they both got very much damaged: the parrot had his neck and breast all cut open (red plumage), while the opossum received a black mark on his snout.'[5] Again: 'A snake and a fish had a fight; the former turned out victorious and for punishment made the victim carry his skin (the scales) and bones (dorsal fin) on his back.'[6] Such is the usual run of these narratives. We find similar ones, in the south and south-east of Australia — among others, in the Euahlayi tribe studied by Langloh Parker. They are not tales in the European sense of the word, nor even animal tales in the African sense.[7] They do not describe the habits of animals in order to amuse or to draw a moral lesson; they try only to explain the characteristics of the animals, particularly their physical features. These Australian narratives are thus explanatory legends ('aetiological').

Roth, Langloh Parker and other collectors have obtained them as isolated instances.[8] We may speculate whether they are in an early or a recent form. As a matter of fact, in a certain number of cosmogonic legends of the south and south-east, we find an intercalation of narratives identical in style to the narratives of Queensland. Thus a Kurnai legend of the Flood ends with an explanation of the plumage of the pelican (see legend No. LXI).[9] But in other narratives of the same region the pelican is presented not merely as an ordinary animal but as an animal of superior nature. The same applies with other animals. The Kurnai word for present-day animals is *jiak*; animals of former times which appear in the legends are called *muk-jiak*, that is, 'remarkable animals'. Now, these animals are also called *muk-kurnai*, that is, 'remarkable men'.[10] And in fact it is impossible to know which of their two natures, human or animal, predominates in these legendary heroes.

Two Australian theories are current here. In certain tribes it is thought that the earth was originally inhabited by men who for various reasons changed into animals; in others, it is believed that animals existed first and that the various human groups descended from them.

The first theory is distributed in the south and south-east; for example among the tribes of Victoria (see legends Nos. LVIII, LXIV, LXXIV),[11] occasionally among the Euahlayi,[12] and in Queensland: '. . . when a native [of northern Queensland] wishes to speak of the earliest conceivable eras, he usually expresses himself somewhat in the form of: "When the animals and birds were all black fellows" '[13]; and, 'The large majority of the stories refer to animals with human attributes, and in this connection it is well to remember the traditional superstition throughout [the central and northern districts of Queensland] of those extremely remote times when all the birds and quadrupeds were blackfellows'.[14] However, it is the animal nature of the heroes that predominates in these narratives, except in a few (see legends Nos. XXXIII and C)[15] where beings of a hybrid nature appear.

The Australian point of view is well illustrated in the following interpretations reported by Taplin (1878:68): 'The natives told me that some 20 years before I came to Point Macleay they first saw white men on horseback, and thought the horses were their visitors' mothers, because they carried them on their backs! I have also heard that another tribe regarded the first pack-bullocks[16] they saw as the whitefellows' wives, because they carried the luggage'.

The second theory brings out the other aspect of this point of view (see legend No. LXXVII).[17] We find it formulated in part at the beginning of legend No. LXII:[18] 'Before the earth was inhabited by the existing race of black men, birds had possession of it. These birds had as much intelligence and wisdom as the blacks — nay, some say that they were altogether wiser and more skilful in all things'. But here it would no longer be a question of an individual animal which, through metamorphosis, gives birth to all men, to all humanity. For although there is a great variety of animals, there is only one human species — the Australian with black hair and coloured skin. Only the arrival of the Whites obliged the Australians to complete their theories on this point.[19] That is why the various animal species give birth to groups of a special kind, neither political nor geographical but religious — namely, the totemic groups.

Now the two theories just discussed are the result of a dissociation of concepts. The primitive notion of the identical nature of all living things, when subjected to analysis, is at this stage resolved into two different notions, those of man and animal, which however have not yet been unequivocally separated. The survival of the ancient identification expresses itself in the two theories, the human origin of animals and the animal origin of human groups. To assert that one is prior to the other seems useless. At any rate, the anteriority readily conceded to the second theory does not seem to me capable of direct proof. The most that can be done is to show that it co-exists with institutions said to be superior, that is to say, posterior from the point of view of general cultural evolution. Even so, this co-existence is neither universal nor constant.

In fact, the two theories are the two divergent aspects, both evolutionistic, of a point of view well-characterised in its leading form among the tribes of central Australia.

In all the tribes occupying the immense territory from Spencer's Gulf in the south to the Gulf of Carpentaria in the north, we find a belief in a mythical epoch for which the Dieri, Yaurorka, Wonkganguru and Kuyani (of the Dieri 'nation') have no special name; and which the Urabunna (of the Dieri 'nation') call *Ularaka*, the Arunta, Unmatjera and Kaitish *Alcheringa*,[22] the Warramunga, Tjingilli, Umbaia and Gnanji *Wingara*,[23] the Mara *Intjitja*, the Binbinga *Mungaii*, and the Anula *Raraku*.[24] During this remote period there lived Beings on whose number and mode of activity opinions differ from tribe to tribe but on whose nature there is unanimity.

These Beings were in the first place larvae; at any rate, this evolutionistic idea has been encountered so far among the Dieri, Wonkganguru, and Yaurorka of the Dieri 'nation'; among the Arunta, Unmatjera, and Kaitish of the Arunta 'nation'; and perhaps among the Yuin and Wathi-Wathi of South Australia. These larvae evolved either by themselves, through the influence of the sun, or thanks to the intervention of other beings such as the *Ungambikula*, the crow-man, or the wren,[25] and took the form of beings with arms and legs.

Only a few of the mythical Beings, however, are the result of such an evolution; the Arunta allow it for only five,[26] the Unmatjera and Kaitish for only seven, whose descendants are separated from those of the others on the north side by a little stream.[27] From this limit, the idea of primitive larvae is no longer encountered. The Warramunga, Umbaia, Gnanji and Nibinga legends only recount the great deeds of beings who were born fully formed as an emanation of a single original ancestor.[28]

Whatever their origin, these Beings bear the name of an animal or, more rarely, of a plant, and act like men. But they are neither strictly men, nor animals, nor plants. They are a combination.[29] Thus the hero of legend No. LXXXIII[30] can be called at will emu-man or man-emu; the heroes of legend No. LXXXIV[31] are men-dingoes or dingo-men; and the men-ducks of legend No. XLVI[32] 'come flying'. Spencer and Gillen say that the identity of human individuals is 'sunk in'[33] that of the animal or plant whose name they bear and from whom they are supposed to descend,[34] since it is from these various Beings that all present human groups are descended through successive reincarnations. Some, however, are represented nowadays among the Arunta only as animals, particularly lizards and birds, who are then 'mates'[35] of other groups.[36] Thus the Arunta emu people[37] have as 'mate' a little striated wren.

These hybrid Beings were much more powerful than men and animals today. They could quite naturally, without effort or magic, accomplish certain acts that at the present time are difficult and reserved for only some among the most learned and wise of men. They could at will climb into the sky or descend under the earth in order to continue their journeys in these two lands, conceived as identical with the Australian countryside.[38] While travelling, either alone or in small groups, these Beings accomplished remarkable deeds, in memory of which were formed terrestrial features (springs, wells, isolated stones, rocks, hills, chains of mountains, solitary trees, small woods, etc.). Thus the narratives of central Australia are at the same time nature myths (or legends). Those Beings who ascended into the sky became sometimes — for it is not the rule — planets or constellations.

The important fact is that these Beings, either by depositing *churinga* on earth or by emanation, gave birth to animal or plant species and to human groups, which are the divided components of the hybrid Ancestor.[39] That is to say, the hybrid nature of the mythical Ancestors explains the intimate bond that today still unites a given human group with the animal or plant species which is its totem.

Now in central Australia the word 'totem' does not have the sense usually given to it of 'protector' or 'coat of arms'. It is neither through respect nor veneration that a member of the kangaroo group, for example, does not eat kangaroos, save in exceptional cases, but because he is responsible for the continuity of the kangaroo species whose members can be eaten by grass-men or emu-men. Australian totemism is an economic rather than a religious system; at any rate, religious acts have an economic objective. Whatever the differences in detail, a single principle is valid in all the central tribes from Lake Eyre to the Gulf of Carpentaria: namely, that each totemic group is obliged to ensure the multiplication, continuity and utilisation of the being or object (sun, fire, water, etc.) whose name it bears and with which it is associated. As has been said, the totemic groups of central Australia are 'societies of cooperative magic'.[40] Each group strives to ensure not its own subsistence but that of all its neighbours; kangaroo-men provide kangaroos for emu-men, lizard-men, seed-men, water-men, etc., from whom they expect in return emus, lizards, seed, water, etc., in sufficient quantity. But these kangaroo-men do not have the right to eat kangaroos. In certain tribes they may kill them, in others it is even their function to do so, but only in order to give them immediately to the members of other totemic groups.

But in as much as each totemic group is subjected to a dietary taboo regarding its totem, it is impossible to look on the legends of central Australia as aetiological myths, except for the central idea of a consubstantial unity, since in these legends each totemic group gets its normal, perhaps even its only, sustenance from the animal or plant totem, that is to say, from itself. According to the legends, the mythical ancestors therefore would have practised a kind of endocannibalism (see legends Nos. LXXVIII, LXXXII, LXXXIII, etc.).[41]

There is therefore good ground for distinguishing, with Spencer and Gillen,[42] two categories in the corpus of central Australian legends: first,

197

legends describing present-day institutions in order to explain their origin and mechanism; for example, legends about marriage rules (see legends Nos. LXVII to LXXXIII),[43] circumcision rites, the invention of fire by drilling and sawing (see legends Nos. XLVI to XLIX),[44] and rarely the purpose of the *intichiuma*; and second, legends simply describing the journeys of the mythical Ancestors in order to explain natural features and the formation of the *oknanikilla* (local totemic centres), without mention of institutions of former times except by allusion.

It should be added that many elements in legends of the second category appear in those of the first; and both play the ritual role spoken of in the preceding chapter. The sole difference between them is that one category speaks explicitly about institutions, whereas the other makes allusion to them in passing. It is therefore not possible to deal uniformly with these aetiological legends and to conclude disdainfully, like Lang, that: 'All such fables, of course, are valueless as history; and in the savage state of the intellect, such myths were inevitable'.[45]

Now the inability to determine, for want of a criterion, what is historical fact in popular traditions is such a common experience that when by good fortune we have this criterion we should at least put it to the test and not discard it without more ado. Even the word 'hypothesis', and the repeated use we make of this method of explanation, reminds us that the gap is not so great between us, the civilised, and those who are still 'in the savage stage of intellectual development'.[46]

Thus, with regard to the legends of central Australia, the question of the historical and sociological value of traditional narratives raises itself in precise terms and with some chance of a positive answer. An analysis of all the Arunta traditions make it possible to define four periods of the *Alcheringa*: (1) The *Ungambikula* transform the primitive larvae (*inapertwa*) into zoo- and phyto-anthropomorphic beings, who are each the ancestor of a totemic group; at this time, circumcision rites are carried out with the aid of a burning stick. (2) The group of hawk-men arrives in the land, bringing the method of circumcision by stone-knife, continuing the work of the *Ungambikula* by carving *inapertwa*, and introducing the custom of class names. (3) The group of wildcat-men introduces the rite of subincision (*ariltha*) and fixes the sequential order of initiation ceremonies, namely (a) circumcision, (b) subincision, (c) *engwura*. (4) Some 'wise' emu-men come from the north and institute the marriage rules currently in force.[47]

The important fact is that, in the legends that tell of the earliest two periods, only a single system of social organisation is mentioned, the totemic system; and that not only are present-day taboos (against marrying a woman of the same totem and against eating one's own totem, except during the increase rites called *intichiuma*) not mentioned, but on the contrary it was the custom to marry within one's totemic group and to subsist on one's totem, although this was not an absolute rule.[48] The same can be said of the first mythical Ancestors as represented in the legends of tribes further north.[49] That is to say that the system of totemic taboos nowadays is exactly the opposite of that of the mythical period. It is remarkable that, with the possible exception of the Kaitish tradition cited below, we do not find a single legend whose object is to explain the most important fact of totemism, namely the sexual and food taboo, or to look for its origin and *raison d'être*.[50] Furthermore, these legends are translated into action during various ceremonies, especially initiation ceremonies. Thus worm-men, who today cannot eat their totem, ritually represent their worm-men Ancestors in the act of feeding on worms. And this contradiction neither embarrasses nor surprises them. Such concordance between Arunta, Unmatjera, Kaitish and Warramunga legends should not be regarded as trivial, and must correspond to a formerly real way of life. I cannot see, any more than Spencer and Gillen, how to explain this social transformation and absence of legends. At all events, the historicity of the legends should not be doubted on this score, an historicity also admitted by Durkheim in his remark that in the 'myths historical memories may be included, but only those that lend themselves to integration are in fact integrated; the others are eliminated and thus disappear from memory' (1902:96).

That is to say, if I understand Durkheim correctly, that traditions only preserve elements which are useful, be they explanatory, ritual, or descriptive, and thus regulative. This is certainly not valid for the traditions of which we have just spoken because it is hard to see for what reason memories of a state of affairs precisely the opposite of that of today would, in the absence of any mention of the transition (whether progressive or abrupt), 'lend themselves to integration'. On the other hand, Durkheim's formula is valid for legends which refer to the establishment of the various initiation rites, the class system and the marriage rules.

In legends dealing with the second period of the mythical age, no reference is made either directly or by allusion, to marriage rules. The moieties and classes, however, exist already,[51] and the totems are divided more or less strictly between the two moieties, whether they bear a special name or not.[52] These legends usually say[53] to what totemic group and marriage class the heroes of the narrative belong.[54]

But one fact whose importance seems to have escaped the theoreticians is that neither the totem nor the marriage class is fixed. In legend No. LXXXI,[55] we see a woman of the Panunga class pass into the Kumara class while keeping her own totem; and, later, a Kumara woman become Panunga by virtue of a rite performed on her. On the other hand, the legends do not state precisely that there is a strict link between the totemic organisation and the class organisation, as there is today, at least among tribes other than the Arunta. This seems to me to be a proof of the anteriority, not only legendary but real, of totemism over the class system. A study of the present relationships between these two institutional systems would also demonstrate this anteriority.

Besides, the class names given to legendary heroes have scarcely even the value of an epithet, for although categorised by their totem and class, these heroes are not subject to the very complicated marriage rules that this categorisation implies today. This absence of rules is affirmed by several legends (see legends Nos. LXXIII to LXXVII),[56] whose precise aim is to explain their origin. I see no reason to deny the historical value of these legends, at least basically for several of them, and even as to detail for legend No.

LXX,[57] where first of all, four wise old men each independently try out certain rules, then gather together to discuss the implications of their endeavours, and in the end acquiesce in the opinion of one of their number and later adopt it in their respective groups. It is precisely in this way that social modifications are invented, tried, discussed and adopted at the present day.[58] That is why the opinion of Spencer and Gillen, when they accord a factual significance to the legends of central Australia, should be accepted until there is effective proof to the contrary.

Howitt is of the same opinion with regard to the southern tribes. He has a deep familiarity with the social organisation and mentality of the Australians of the south and south-east, and has also compared the information he has collected in recent years about the tribes of the Dieri 'nation' with that published by Spencer and Gillen. Among the tribes living between Spencer's Gulf and Lake Eyre (approximately 25° latitude)[59] there are prevailing legends analogous to those of central and northern Australia. In them are presented mythical ancestors called *Muramura*, who are more human than animal. Here again we can recognise several cycles: the formation of the first human beings and their totems (see legends Nos. IV and V),[60] the establishment of circumcision and subincision, ceremonies with an economic end (analogous to the *intichiuma* of central Australia), and marriage rules (see legends Nos. LXVII and LXVIII).[61] After a critical analysis of these traditions, Howitt concludes (1904:482): 'It seems to me that these legends may be taken to be not merely mythical, but rather dim records of former events, such as the wanderings of the early Australians, dressed in a mythic garb, and handed down from generation to generation, from father to son, in the sacred ceremonies'. Judging from the few legends published by A.W. and M. Howitt,[62] I even believe it is possible to regard the legends of the Dieri and their neighbours as being of greater value for the history of their institutions than those of the tribes of the Arunta 'nation'.

Thus the Australian narratives discussed so far are all useful narratives. They are at one and the same time fragments of a catechism, a liturgical manual, a history of civilisation,[63] a geography textbook, and to a much smaller extent a manual of cosmography. In the legends of Victoria and New South Wales, on the other hand, identification of the constellations holds the preponderant place (see legends Nos. XXXIX to XLV),[64] the explanation of institutions and the determination of rites being only of secondary importance.

Furthermore, we encounter a genuine literary theme in legends about the discovery and appropriation of fire (see legends Nos. XLVI to LVIII).[65] Practically every tribe has its fire myth, and in almost all the idea is that fire, having been discovered usually by birds, was jealously guarded by the inventor, to the great chagrin of other living beings. But a clever thief turned up, seized the fire and made off with his precious booty. For one reason or another, usually because he did not know how to use it, the thief set fire to the grass and thus made public a knowledge hitherto held by only one. This idea is not peculiar to the Australians, as Lang has noted,[66] but indeed is universal. We find it again also in certain water myths (see legend No. LX).[67] From the number and details of the different variants of fire myths we may, I believe, justly conclude that fire has been discovered in different ways and by many tribes, in complete independence. I doubt whether we can determine an original centre for the invention of fire in Australia. In any case two methods are used, drilling[68] and sawing, the second of which may very well have been invented several times.

Finally, certain mythical characters are neither totemic ancestors nor animals in the strict sense of the word, but men conceived as civilising heroes. The notion of the individualised civilising hero is one of the most interesting in Australian mythology. It has given rise to many discussions, the difficulty being to determine the extent to which these supernatural beings have the right or not to be regarded as gods. They occur in very few myths and legends; for the most part, the information we have about them is descriptive. However, Langloh Parker has collected some legends about Bayamie; we already had some about Nuralie, Bunjil, etc. I have translated them here, and in the notes on each of them will be found a statement of facts and a discussion of theories. One of these individualised supernatural beings, called Muramura (who was also one of the best known), was quickly withdrawn following the discovery by Siebert of a whole cycle of legends about an entire category of mythical Ancestors called *muramura* (see legend No. LXVIII).[69] It seems to me that Nuralie (see legend No. XXVII)[70] must suffer the same fate. Perhaps even Bayamie is a collective term (see legend No. XLVI).[71] To the ancestors of the *Alcheringa* of the Arunta, the Dieri *Muramura*, etc. we should also add, I believe, the *Murrumbung-uttia* of the Wurunjerri (see legend No. XXXIX)[72] and perhaps the *Brambambull* of the Wotjobaluk (see legend No. XCIII),[73] as well as some other supernatural beings like the *Ulthaana* that Gillen speaks of, and the Atjira described by Kempe and Strehlow.

There is finally a category of supernatural beings who are scarcely mentioned in the legends. For that reason I have not been concerned with them here. They are Mungan-ngaua and his emulators. Their god-like character is admitted by most theorists, some regarding them as indigenous, others (for example, Tylor) believing them due, at least in part, to Christian influences. They are associated with thunder and lightning, live in the sky and have god-bullroarers as subordinates or parents. They sometimes play the role of civilising heroes, but they are, however, more than that. In the final analysis, I believe they are in this case nature gods, more precisely Thunder-Gods of the kind mentioned in legend No. IX.[74] It may even be that the notion of Thunder-God is the central element in all Australian mythologies.

Notes

1. Lang 1896, *passim.*
2. In the [first] eight volumes of *L'Année Sociologique;* see indexes under *conte, légende, mythe*; cf. among other statements, 'Myth . . . and legend . . . have an essential common characteristic, that of being objects of belief' (vol. 5, 1902:289) [from a review by Hubert of Gunkel, H., *Genesis*, Göttingen, 1901].
3. Cf. especially *L'Année Sociologique*, vol. 6, 1903:244–5.

4. Roth 1897; 1903:11–5.
5. Roth 1903:14. [The author has translated 'dorsal fin' as 'arête dorsale'; *cf.* 'nageoire dorsale'.]
6. Roth 1903:11.
7. See Lang 1896, *passim*; Basset 1903.
8. [The text reads: '. . . les ont obtenus à l'état isolé'.]
9. [From Brough Smyth 1878, vol. 1:477–8.]
10. See Brough Smyth, *loc. cit.*
11. [From Brough Smyth 1878, vol. 1:461, 449; Dawson 1881:27.]
12. Typically, in the narratives collected by Langloh Parker, we see animals characterised as such co-existing with men who are only men. Thus in legend No. LXV [from Langloh Parker 1898:90–1], the *Bungun-bungun* are frogs only; in legend No. LVI [from Langloh Parker 1897:24–9], *Butulgah* is a crow, *Gunur* is a rat, etc. If these animals seem almost human, the fault lies with Langloh Parker who leaves them with their vernacular name and misuses capital letters. With these two erroneous elements removed, Euahlayi narratives are identical in style to those of Queensland.
13. Roth 1903:15.
14. Roth 1897:125.
15. [From Roth 1903:7, 13–4.]
16. [The author has translated 'pack-bullocks' as 'buffles de bât.']
17. [From Spencer and Gillen 1899:189–9.]
18. [From Brough Smyth 1878, vol. 1:430.]
19. The various explanations invented by the Australians about the Whites are very interesting for the light they throw on the mentality of these 'savages'. See, among others, Roth 1903:16; Howitt; 1904:442–6.
20. At least, Howitt speaks only of the Epoch of the *Muramura*, which is the name of the mythical beings.
21. Spencer and Gillen 1904:145.
22. Spencer and Gillen 1899:119; 1904:152. See also, on this word, Strehlow cited by Thomas 1905.
23. Spencer and Gillen 1904:162, 191.
24. *Ibid*:223.
25. See legends Nos. I to VI, XLVI and LXXIX. [From Spencer and Gillen 1899: 388–9; 1904:153, 399–400; Howitt 1904:779–80, 780–1, 484–5; Spencer and Gillen 1899:445–6, 390.]
26. See the end of legend No. I. [From Spencer and Gillen 1899:388–9.]
27. Spencer and Gillen 1904:153, 159.
28. *Ibid*:161 (Warramunga 'nation'), p. 170 (Umbaia and Gnanji), p. 171 (Binbinga). Nothing is said on this point with regard to the coastal 'nations'.
29. This at least is what Spencer and Gillen affirm in *The Northern Tribes of Central Australia*, pp. 154 and 156. But they say the opposite, that is, that the Unmatjera believe that certain animals are descended from true men, on p. 442 of the same book and in summarising a legend which is a continuation of legend No. XIX [from *op. cit.*, pp. 400–3] where, however, the hybrid (human-animal) nature of the main hero is indicated precisely; for a discussion of the facts, see p. 6, note 3 of the present volume [i.e. *Mythes et Légendes d'Australie*.]
30. [From Spencer and Gillen 1899:551.]
31. [From *ibid*:434–6.]
32. [From *ibid*:445–6.]
33. [*Ibid*:119; van Gennep uses 'fondue'.]

34. [Van Gennep presents this statement as a quotation from Spencer and Gillen but in fact it is a selection from three separate statements: Spencer and Gillen 1899:119, 121, 231.]

35. [Spencer and Gillen, *ibid*:448; van Gennep uses 'associés.']

36. *Ibid*:447–9.

37. [The text reads: '. . . le groupe anthropo-animal arunta de l'émou . . .']

38. *Ibid*:121–2; Spencer and Gillen 1904:154, 145, 162, 170, 171; Howitt 1904: 475–82. For journeys into the sky, see legends NOS. XXIV, XXVIII, LXXX, LXXXV [from Spencer and Gillen 1899:561–2; 1904:626; 1899:315–6, 336–7] and the note to legend No. XXXII. For journeys under the earth, see legends Nos. XVIII, LXXVIII, LXXXI, LXXXVII [from M. Howitt 1902:414–7; Spencer and Gillen 1899:436–7, 432–4, 440–2], as well as the discussion on p. XCVIII of the present volume [*Mythes et Légendes d'Australie*].

39. [The text reads: '. . . qui sont le dédoublement de l'Ancêtre hybride . . .']

40. [The text reads: '. . . "sociétiés coopératives magiques" . . .']

41. [From Spencer and Gillen 1899:436–7; Curr 1886, vol. 2:55; Spencer and Gillen, *ibid*:551.

42. *Ibid*:387, 421–2.

43. [From Howitt 1904:481; Curr 1886, vol. 2:48–9; Spencer and Gillen 1904: 412–13; 1899:420–21; 1904:429, 438–9, 439–40; Dawson 1881:27; Brough Smyth 1878, vol. I:423–4; Langloh Parker 1899:491; Spencer and Gillen 1899:198–9, 436–7, 390, 315–6, 432–4; Curr 1886, vol. 2:55; Spencer and Gillen 1899:551.]

44. [From Spencer and Gillen 1899:445–6; 1904:620, 619–20, 621–2.]

45. Lang 1903:140. This sentence comes at the end of a paragraph devoted to 'Savage Speculations as to the Origin of Totemism'. On Arunta myths, see Lang, *ibid*:75–80.

46. This is in fact recognised by Lang in his recent book, *The Secret of the Totem* (1905:160): 'There is perhaps no modern theory of the origin of totemism, including my own, which has not been somewhere, and to some extent, anticipated by the mythical guesses of savages.'

47. *Cf.* Spencer and Gillen 1899:387–422, and legend No. LXX [from *ibid*:420–1]. Spencer and Gillen (*ibid*:421) presume that marriage regulations were instituted at the same time as class names. Nothing, it seems, has emerged from their second journey of exploration to confirm this hypothesis.

48. Spencer and Gillen 1899:207–9, 392–4; 1904:321–3. See also legend No. LXXXVIII [from M. Howitt 1902:407].

49. Spencer and Gillen 1904:321–6, 413–4.

50. *Ibid*:323, 327.

51. Spencer and Gillen 1899:120; 1904:147, 157, 162.

52. For detailed information on the class system in Australia, as well as attempts at interpretation, see Durkheim 1898, 1902, 1905. For criticism of Durkheim's views, see Lang 1903, 1905.

53. But not always: *cf.* legends Nos. XXVIII, XXX, XXXI, XLVI, LXXI, etc. [from Spencer and Gillen 1904:626; 1899:564–5, 564, 445–6; 1904:429].

54. See legends Nos. XIX, XXIV, XLVI, XLIX, LXXII, LXXIII, LXXVII [from Spencer and Gillen 1904:400–3; 1899:561–2, 445–6; 1904:621–2, 438–9, 439–40, 1899:198–9].

55. [From Spencer and Gillen 1899:432–4.]

56. [From Spencer and Gillen 1904:438–40; Dawson 1881:27; Brough Smyth 1878, vol. 1:423–4; Langloh Parker 1899:491; Spencer and Gillen 1899:198–9.]

57. [From Spencer and Gillen 1899:420–1.]

58. See ch. IV [*Mythes et Légendes d'Australie*]. Individual action, which is not unimportant today, is also recognised in the legends, where in the great majority of cases the mythical ancestor is designated by proper name. Even if this euhemeristic nuance were a projection of present-day point of view into the past, it would still show that in societies like those of Central Australia, where the social element seems at first sight to be sovereign master, there is a recognised and definite place for individual action. It remains to be seen whether this role of the individual, and the 'individualisation' of certain institutions like marriage property and the control of hunting, politics, religion and military affairs are, as is usually believed though without proof, the sign of an advanced evolution.

59. For the distribution of these tribes, see the map on p. 101, *Journal of the Anthropological Institute*, vol. 34, 1904.

60. [From Howitt 1904:779–80, 780–2.]

61. [From *ibid*:481, 480–1.]

62. A.W. Howitt 1904; M. Howitt 1902.

63. I do not believe, however, that these myths provide the key to the historical problem properly so-called, that is to say, of the Australian races and their migrations. Mathew (1899:14–22) has attempted an interpretation in this sense of Eagle-hawk and Crow legends, which occur frequently in the southeast (see legends Nos. LXVII, LXXV, CIII [from Howitt 1904:481; Brough Smyth 1878, vol. 1:423–4, 425–7]). His point of departure (that they concern two totems) is correct, but his conclusions (for example, that the conflict between the two animals in the legends is a memory of conflicts between two totemic groups) have little foundation.

64. [From Brough Smyth 1878, vol. 1:432–4, 427–8, 431; Taplin 1878:56–7; Langloh Parker 1897:62–4, 40–6; Taplin 1878:57–8.]

65. [From Spencer and Gillen 1899:445–6; 1904:620, 619–20, 621–2; Roth 1903:11, 25; Howitt 1904:432; Brough Smyth 1878, vol. 1:458, 459, 459–60; Langloh Parker 1897:24–9; Brough Smyth 1878, vol. 1:460:1, 461.]

66. Lang 1896:39*ff.*

67. [From Brough Smyth 1878, vol. 1:429–30.]

68. [The text reads '. . . deux procédés, par forage (ignitérébrateur) et par sciage . . .' 'Ignitérébrateur' presumably means 'fire-drill', from 'igni-' and 'térébrateur'.]

69. [From Howitt 1904:480–1.]

70. [From Brough Smyth 1878, vol. 1:430.]

71. [From Spencer and Gillen 1899:445–6.]

72. [From Brough Smyth 1878, vol. 1:432–4.]

73. [From *ibid*, vol. 2:53–4.]

74. [From Roth 1903:15.]

References

BASSET, R. 1904 *Contes popularies d'Afrique*. Paris, Guilmoto.

CURR, E.M. 1886–1887 *The Australian race*. Melbourne, Ferres.

DAWSON, J. 1881 *The Australian Aborigines*. Melbourne, Robertson.

DURKHEIM, E. 1897 La prohibition de l'inceste et ses origines. *Année Sociologique*, 1:1–70.

────── 1902 Sur le totémisme. *Année Sociologique*, 5:82–121.

────── 1905 Sur l'organisation matrimoniale des sociétes australiennes. *Année Sociologique*, 8:118–47.

GENNEP, A. VAN 1905 Publications de l'Université de California. *Revue de l'Historie des Religions*, 52.

HOWITT, A.W. 1904 *The native tribes of south-east Australia*. London, Macmillan.
HOWITT, M.E.B. 1902 Some native legends from central Australia. *Folk-Lore*, 13:403–17.
LANG, A. 1896 *Mythes, cultes et religions*. Paris, Alcan.
——— 1896 Introduction to K. Langloh Parker: *Australian legendary tales: folk-lore of the Noongahburrahs as told to the piccaninnies*. London, Nutt.
——— 1898*a* *The making of religion*. London, Longmans, Green.
——— 1898*b* Introduction to K. Langloh Parker: *More Australian legendary tales*. London, Nutt.
——— 1899 Australian gods: a reply. *Folk-lore*, 10:1–46.
——— 1903 *Social origins*. London, Longmans.
——— 1904 A theory of Arunta totemism. *Man*, 4:67–9.
——— 1905*a* *The secret of the totem*. London, Longmans, Green.
——— 1905*b* Introduction to K. Langloh Parker: *The Euahlayi tribe: a study of Aboriginal life in Australia*. London, Constable.
MATHEW, J. 1899 *Eaglehawk and crow*. Melbourne, Melville, Mullen and Slade.
MAUSS, M. 1904 L'origine des pouvoirs magiques dans les sociétés australiennes. In *École pratique des hautes études*. Rapport annuel: 1–55.
MOONEY, —. 1900 *The Myths of the Cherokee*. Washington, Bureau of American Ethnology.
PARKER, LANGLOH K. 1896 *Australian legendary tales*. London, Nutt.
——— 1899 Letter to Andrew Lang. *Folk-Lore*, 10:489–94.
POWELL, J.W. 1902 An American view of totemism. *Man*, 2:101–6.
ROTH, W.E. 1897 *Ethnological studies among the north-west-central Queensland Aborigines*. Brisbane, Government Printer.
——— 1903 *Superstition, magic, and medicine*. Brisbane, Government Printer.
SEBILLOT, P. 1904–1906 *Le folk-lore de France*. Paris, Guilmoto.
SMYTH, R.B. 1878 *The Aborigines of Victoria*. Melbourne, Government Printer.
SPENCER, *Sir* W.B. *and* F.J. GILLEN 1899 *The native tribes of central Australia*. London, Macmillan.
——— 1904 *The northern tribes of central Australia*. London, Macmillan.
TAPLIN, G. 1878 *The Narrinyeri*. 2d. rev. ed. Adelaide, Wigg.
THOMAS, N.W. 1904 Arunta totemism: a note on Mr Lang's theory. *Man*, 4:99–101.
——— 1905 The religious ideas of the Arunta. *Folk-Lore*, 16:428–33.

Index

207

Tribes and Peoples

Myth Characters

General